International business marketing in emerging
country markets

International Business Marketing in Emerging Country Markets

The Third Wave of Internationalization of Firms

Hans Jansson

Professor
Baltic Business School at the University of Kalmar, Sweden

Edward Elgar
Cheltenham, UK • Northampton, MA

Published by
Edward Elgar Publishing Limited
Glensanda House
Montpellier Parade
Cheltenham
Glos GL50 1UA
UK

Edward Elgar Publishing, Inc.
William Pratt House
9 Dewey Court
Northampton
Massachusetts 01060
USA

A catalogue record for this book
is available from the British Library

Library of Congress Cataloguing in Publication Data

Jansson, Hans.
  International business marketing in emerging country markets : the third wave of internationalization of firms / Hans Jansson.
     p. cm.
  Includes bibliographical references and index.
1. International business enterprises–Developing countries. 2. Corporations, developing country. 3. Business networks. I. Title.
  HD2932.J35 2007
  658.8'4091724–dc22

                   2007011683

ISBN 978 1 84720 251 2

Printed and bound in Great Britain by MPG Books Ltd, Bodmin, Cornwall

Contents

Figures   vii
Tables   ix
Abbreviations   xi
Acknowledgements   xiii
Forewords
    Peter J Buckley   xv
    Häkan Häkansson   xvii
Preface   xxi

1. Business marketing networks, institutions and MNC organization   1
2. The international business marketing model   29
3. Network, linkage and competitive strategies   55
4. Project marketing cycles and action networks   83
5. European, Chinese and Russian business networks   111
6. Business marketing strategy in the internationalization process   135
7. Internal network organization of the internationalized firm   163
8. Local and regional network organization for dyads and triads   189

Bibliography   213
Name index   229
Subject index   233

Figures

1.1	The outline of the book	25
2.1	The main concepts of the inter-organizational approach	36
2.2	The international business marketing model	42
2.3	Major factors of international business marketing	47
3.1	International business marketing strategy	57
3.2	Network map	59
3.3	Network capability profiles	73
4.1	The international business marketing process	86
4.2	Project marketing cycles	88
4.3	Map of project network	89
4.4	An intelligence network	91
5.1	Impact of basic rules on international business networks	120
6.1	Major factors of the internationalization process	141
6.2	Stages of internationalization	142
6.3	Relationship stages	144
6.4	The five/five stages model	148
6.5	Entry strategy	152
6.6	Entry roles related to entry nodes and entry modes	158
7.1	Types of international firms	168
7.2	Relocation of the Geocentric MNC	172
7.3	Authority, social and lateral nets	177
7.4	The clustered group network	183
8.1	Network linking grid at the local hub	197
8.2	Organization of the regional hub	205
8.3	Types of regional network organization	207

Tables

1.1	Major income classes in India	9
2.1	Transactional selling versus relationship marketing	38
5.1	Comparison of the international business networks according to the basic rules	122
6.1	The relationship process	146
7.1	Major dimensions of the hierarchical network	176
8.1	Pros and cons of different options of regional organization development	195

Abbreviations

ADB	Asian Development Bank
AFTA	Asean Free Trade Area
ASEAN	Association of Southeast Asian Nations
MNC	Multinational Corporation
BA	Business area
BRIC	Brazil, Russia, India and China
BU	Business unit
CBN	Chinese business network
CEE	Central and Eastern Europe
Chindia	China and India
CNH	Case-New Holland
EBN	European business network
EU	European Union
FAO	Food and Agriculture Organization
FDI	Foreign Direct Investment
GM	Group management
IBM	International business marketing
IBRD	International Bank of Reconstruction and Development
IDA	International Development Authority
IFC	International Finance Corporation
IM Group	Industrial marketing group
IMP	Industrial marketing and purchasing
IMP1	European research programme on industrial marketing and purchasing
JV	Joint ventures
MENA	Middle East and North Africa
MGN	MNC-government network
MSO	Multi-sets organization
OEM	Original equipment manufacturer
OSO	One-set organization
POS	Prescribed organization sets
PRUs	Product responsible units
RBN	Russian business network
RHQ	Regional headquarters
R&D	Research and development
SEA	Southeast Asia
SMEs	Small and medium-sized enterprises

SIDA   Swedish International Development Authority
UNDP   United Nations Development Programme
VCE   Volvo Construction Equipment

Acknowledgements

I want to express my deep gratitude to all the students at two master programmes in international marketing and international business, who have contributed to this book as well as the 'twin-book' 'International Business Strategy in Emerging Country Markets – The Institutional Network Approach' also published in 2007 by Edward Elgar. The students have helped me with it in many ways even contributed directly to the book through some of their master theses. Originally, I started to write these two books for the International Business programme at the Graduate Business School, Göteborg School of Economics and Management, Göteborg University. I saw a need for more advanced textbooks for master courses on international marketing and international business in emerging country markets. I have finalized the present book by continuously testing it in the masters programme 'Growth Through Innovation and International Marketing' at the Baltic Business School, University of Kalmar. Some ideas for the book originate from my previous positions at the School of Management, Lund University and Department of Business Studies, Uppsala University.

I also want to thank my present colleagues at the Baltic Business School and former colleagues at the Center for International Business Studies at the Graduate Business School, Göteborg University. As previously, I am especially indebted to my old friend, Professor Hans-Fredrik Samuelsson, who encouraged me to start this book project for our joint master course on emerging markets at Göteborg University. I also want to thank my 'senior' colleague professor Sten Söderman, now at the School of Business, Stockholm University, and Université du Luxembourg. I am indebted to assistant professor Joachim Ramström at Yrkeshögskolan Sydväst, Åbo, Finland and associate professor Martin Johanson at Uppsala University for our joint research that lies behind Chapter 5.

In particular, I want to thank my associates at the Baltic Business Research Center and the Baltic Business School for their continuous assistance in reading and discussing various versions of the book, namely Mikael Hilmersson, Bertil Hultén, Susanne Sandberg and Joachim Timlon. Special thanks and appreciation go to Carina Bärtfors for her highly professional editing of the book.

A great deal of thanks goes to my wife Carina, and to Erik and Emma for their constant support and encouragement in writing the book. To all of you I give my thanks and my love.

Foreword
Peter J Buckley

The rise of China and India has made emerging countries far more salient in the global economy. Attention to the 'bottom of the pyramid' of the income distribution of poorer countries has drawn attention to the importance of marketing in emerging countries. It is, therefore, opportune that Hans Jansson's new book examines international business marketing in emerging countries.

The importance of business-to-business marketing in emerging countries has until now been largely neglected due to the overwhelming attention paid to consumer marketing in larger emerging countries. Hans Jansson's book addresses this omission whilst paying a great deal of attention to the institutional network in the host countries and the embeddedness of marketing practice in these institutions. A further virtue of this book is the attention to both strategy and process within the marketing function.

This is a careful analysis of networks, linkages and competitive strategies from which the links to internationalisation strategies are drawn thus creating a pioneering effort and an original contribution to marketing and international business.

Peter J Buckley
Professor
Leeds University Business School
July, 2007

Foreword
Håkan Håkansson

MARKETS ARE NOT ENOUGH

This book is focused on two major issues that many companies are facing. The first can be seen as a combined strategic and organizational problem and has to do with how to organize the company's own network within the existing network of business companies. This includes what the company should specialize on in relation to important customers and suppliers and complementary producers. It also includes the development of well functioning business relationships with the counterparts including a constant pressure for development and efficiency. The second issue has to deal with and approach some new fast growing and thereby highly interesting economic regions. It includes finding efficient methods to approach them and to find ways to integrate these new activities with the existing internal structure. These two issues are problematic in themselves but there are also obvious links between them as the book demonstrates. Its main contribution is that it gives an interesting frame for analysing and formulating the issues and thereby also gives support for finding suitable ways to deal with them.

The two issues in combination certainly create some challenging problems but are at the same time full of positive possibilities. This was nicely described by a manager of a UK company involved in the fish industry: 'We buy white fish in Norway, freeze it and transport it to China where it is defrosted and cut into fillet, frozen again and transported to the UK. When we started with this operation it was just in order to utilize cheap labour in China, but after a while we also realized that we could get more out of the round fish as the work was done by hand and that increased the yield by almost 20 percent.' This is just a small and mundane example of new and unexpected outcomes when restructuring and rearranging activities within an established network through involving new actors from a developing economic region.

It also demonstrates another theme underlying the book which is also a major managerial issue. Companies should not just treat these new regions as 'markets' from which they can freely buy or to which they can sell. The big opportunities do not lie in these markets in themselves but in the organizing of a much more elaborate interface with these regions – to find a way to identify how the company's own features can be matched with features of specific counterparts in these regions. Each company involved has to organize the interface in terms of developing a set of business relationships, that is an own network. The existence of 'free markets' is in this way not enough from an organizational point of view. There is a need for a more substantial type of organizing and networks seem to be such an organizational form. The substance is formed through interaction processes that are much deeper than pure market exchanges. One aim in these interaction processes is to create linkages between involved companies, which in turn require that the involved companies have a substantial knowledge about each other. The book gives a number of such examples.

To develop a more substantial organization gives every company a whole set of managerial issues. A first one is to find a systematic way to combine what it will be doing in the new region with what it is doing in all others, that is the company needs an elaborate internationalization strategy. This includes the need to find a way to organize its activities in different countries and regions in such a way that the different units together create an efficient whole. This is dealt with in the book in connection with the development of MNCs, which to an increasing rate is managed in terms of an internal network. Each business unit has to have the freedom to develop in relation to suppliers and customers but in this development there must be linkages to other business units or their customers/suppliers within the MNC.

A second issue has to do with how the company establishes itself within each country or region. Here we get a whole set of questions regarding entry, as the book demonstrates. These are questions around the entry mode, entry node, entry process and entry role. It is a difficult task, which requires both endurance and local competence. The basic issue is to create a place within the network of already established companies. The company needs to adapt and to challenge, and to become involved in the continuous networking that is already taking place.

A third issue has to do with creating specific linkages with technical, administrative or political content between a company's own units and the different actors within the country/region in question. In the case of the new regions there are often a number of special governmental and consultancy units playing an important role. One important goal is to find a structure in these linkages giving the company a unique role within the network. However, that is not enough because linkages also have to be created between these locally involved companies and customers/suppliers or own business units in other countries/regions.

A fourth issue has to do with the differences in traditions, culture and ways of doing business in different regions. Again there are adaptations needed and also innovations in terms of finding new ways of combining different cultures and traditions. Both China and Russia in this respect are not homogeneous countries but regions with large variations within them.

The book gives an account of a wonderful and challenging economic world that modern management is facing. A world that is full of new problems and opportunities, especially if the company manages to become involved in the right way. The book analyses some of the key problems and suggests different ways of dealing with them. It gives a basic frame that can be used both by managers and students, and also by researchers. However, it might provide to be most important for those trying to enhance this development – all those involved in developing international trade or regional economic development. The book can be used as an important argument for much more involvement from governmental bodies or agents in building business networks. Again the opening up of 'markets' is not enough. The systematic matching of local and international companies demands mobilization of local as well as international actors. This is not to go back to some 'hierarchical' control but to actively enhance the development of a number of different interfaces between local and international actors.

The book can be seen as a first important step towards the future of more elaborate networks of international businesses where new regions will be important, if not dominating, ingredients.

Håkan Håkansson
Professor
BI Norwegian School of Management
Oslo, Norway

Preface

This book focuses on international business marketing in emerging country markets during the third wave of internationalization of firms. The fast change makes these markets more turbulent, more uncertain and risky than Western mature markets, at the same time as their high growth makes them lucrative. Relationships are of great importance, since emerging country markets can be characterized as 'network societies'. The firm is therefore connected to its business environment through its relationships, requiring a broad view of relationships found in the 'IMP' perspective on industrial networks. An international business marketing model is developed as part of the paradigm shift in marketing from transaction to relationship marketing. The book is about business marketing strategy, business marketing processes, internationalization processes and supporting network organization structures, mainly at the subsidiary level. The international aspect is given more depth by elaborating on the marketing environment; by integrating relationship processes and internationalization processes; and by taking up how the European business network is adapting to the characteristics of the Chinese business network as well as the Russian business network. The strategic aspect of business marketing is developed based on the institutional network approach and for three major international strategy issues: local adaptation, global integration and geographic spread. Four major factors are critical for the marketing strategy when entering a local market network, namely entry node, entry mode, entry process and entry role. The organization aspect is elaborated on by defining the MNC as a hierarchical network and going deeper into the importance of local and regional network organization for implementing business marketing strategy. Internal network capability profiles contain the main competences that MNCs need for marketing in emerging country markets.

The book has been written mainly for a broad academic audience, including students, lecturers and researches. Practicians such as managers and consultants will also find much to interest them, especially since there are few books that take a comparative holistic approach to international business marketing in emerging country markets. Since readers are assumed to vary in their interest and background, a suggested reading route is proposed below for each of four major groups of readers: the masters student, the teacher, the researcher/doctoral student, and the marketing and management consultant/general manager.

TO THE MASTERS STUDENT

If you are a graduate student with practical experience, a major reason for you to take a masters course is most probably that you have realized you need to develop your understanding of international marketing and to improve your analytical skills. Today's hectic business life in dynamic and complex markets provides few opportunities to develop skills in dealing with the long-term strategic marketing issues taken up in the book. In particular, it will provide you with insights into how emerging country markets work from a business marketing point and enhance your understanding of how marketing is done there. Besides providing you with models for your studies and research on marketing in such markets, you will learn more about how to apply theories to real-life situations.

Since the book is mainly written for the masters student, you are supposed to read the chapters in the order they appear. An overview of the book is given at the end of Chapter 1.

TO THE TEACHER

This book is intended to be used in graduate level courses in international marketing and international business. It is based on the premise that students already have basic knowledge in these fields, normally acquired from undergraduate courses on these and related subjects. The book is therefore best used for courses on business marketing in international markets, especially in emerging country markets. It is preferable that students have or first acquire a basic knowledge in business marketing, business-to-business marketing or industrial marketing. A good basic book here is the second edition of *The Business Marketing Course – Managing in Complex Networks* by Ford et al. (2006).

The book has primarily been written for masters students and for the learning situations they face. It is mainly aimed at seminar-type courses, where students work more independently on their own or in a small group. The focus is on interactive dialogue between students and teacher. The book is therefore best used in application-based courses, where learning from doing live cases or analysing ready-made cases are preferred to traditional root-learning and formal written examinations. The purpose is to develop the masters students' understanding of the particular circumstances in which business marketing is done in emerging country markets. The purpose is also to develop their analytical skills. Describing, understanding, analysing and recommending are viewed as the key processes in developing this analytical capacity. The book contains a research-based framework meant for understanding and analysing business marketing issues in these markets. Teachers at undergraduate level should benefit from the book mainly as a major source for their own teaching, providing models and examples.

The layout of the chapters is built on the major pedagogical ideas behind the book, as referred to previously. The major contents are introduced in Chapter 1. The international business marketing model is presented in Chapter 2 and three business marketing strategies suitable for emerging country markets in Chapter 3, namely network strategy, linkage strategy and competitive strategy. Chapter 4 is about how to prosper from the high investment pace in these rapidly growing markets by skilfully marketing large and complex projects. It is about project marketing cycles and team organization. In Chapter 5, the European business network is contrasted to the Chinese and Russian business networks, going into how adaptations take place between them. Chapter 6 is devoted to business marketing in the internationalization process, where network relationships are seen as the core of these processes. The internationalization of the firm is taken up in Chapter 7 as a basis for translating the organization of the multinational corporation into a hierarchical network supporting business marketing strategy. The final chapter takes the reader back to the local level by talking about how local and regional hubs are established and operated. Direct marketing to customers though subsidiaries is compared with indirect customer relationships via dealers and other intermediaries. The local and regional network organization of business marketing is analysed.

The book has primarily been written for graduate students, and they are therefore supposed to read the chapters in the order they appear in the book.

TO THE RESEARCHER/DOCTORAL STUDENT

This book will give you knowledge of major issues in international business marketing in emerging country markets and insights into the specific conditions under which business marketing is conducted in these markets. It will provide you with new ideas about international business marketing research, an integrated theoretical framework containing a number of models to base research on. In particular, the book highlights the subsidiary perspective of the MNC.

For the marketing researcher in general the book should be of special relevance if you are interested in new developments in business marketing in general, and international business marketing in emerging country markets in particular. The chapters are best read in the order they appear in the book.

TO THE MARKETING AND MANAGEMENT CONSULTANT/MANAGER

If you have business experience from emerging country markets, you are familiar with that a broader approach to marketing is required, for example other social skills to operate in these foreign business networks. As a manager, you have also most probably discovered that you have even less time to spend to understand the peculiarities of these markets and to ponder about long-term marketing issues. You have also realized the strategic importance of emerging country markets, especially the large ones like China and India which are dealt with in this book. This book will provide you with models and tools for being able to reflect on and understand business marketing issues in such countries. It is especially relevant if you have experience from more than one country market and want to compare these experiences. However, you should not be hesitant about reading this text, which is a little more demanding and abstract than found in most marketing and management books.

After having read Chapter 1, I propose that you proceed directly to Chapter 3 to read about the network strategy, linkage strategy and competitive strategy of a multinational corporation operating in India. The project marketing of that firm is then described and analysed in Chapter 4. After having read these two more practically oriented chapters, the reader is urged to go back to Chapter 2 and read the more conceptually-oriented presentation of the contents of the book. Those with a special interest in doing business in Russia, China and other countries with big Chinese and Russian minorities should find Chapter 5 interesting since it is about how European multinational corporations adapt their business marketing to these leading business networks in emerging country markets. Chapter 6 focuses on business marketing issues in connection with entering these markets and how to develop and maintain relationships there. It also takes up how internationalization processes evolve further, when firms move on to new markets. The last two chapters are finally about how business marketing strategy is implemented by organizing in an efficient way at the local level and the regional levels. An example is provided about how Volvo Construction Equipment is expanding in the Middle East and North Africa by establishing regional hubs.

1. Business marketing networks, institutions and MNC organization

INTRODUCTION

This chapter introduces the book. The importance of emerging country markets for the business marketing of multinational corporations is discussed for the third wave of internationalization of firms. In addition, the international business marketing framework based on the institutional network approach is introduced. The reader who wants to have a quick overview of the book is directed to the section on the outline of the book at the end of the chapter.

The fact that emerging country markets have become increasingly important grounds for the international business activities of multinational corporations (MNCs) can be regarded as indicating that a third wave of internationalization of firms is underway. MNCs originating from mature Western markets have during the last decade been establishing themselves on a large scale in China, India, Russia and Central and Eastern Europe (CEE), while firms from these countries are now starting to internationalize, possibly becoming new MNCs. This new wave is mainly a result of the opening up of China and India to international business as well as the integration of the CEE countries into the common market of the EU. In 2005, growth performance in the developing countries was generally good and East and South Asian countries, in particular China and India, acted as the second engine of worldwide growth after the USA (UNCTAD, 2005). The rapid growth of emerging country markets and their integration into the world economy creates a double effect of a strong global pull from growing demand and a push from growing competition. This double effect seems to be behind the third wave of internationalization involving market growth, re-location and outsourcing of production as well as shifting of supplier bases from Western Europe eastwards. How the responses differ between the key types of Western firms is developed in this book.

The third wave of internationalization of firms is then a result of the integration of former centrally-planned economies into the world economy, consisting of two major effects: the China/India or 'Chindia' effect and the EU-enlargement effect. The first effect is the most important since China and India together possess the potential to transform the 21st century global economy. They account for one third of the world population, which demand

and supply are now being integrated into the world economy, and which is a revolutionary change by itself. For the past two decades, China has been growing by 9.5 per cent per year and India by 6 per cent, and many economists believe that these countries have the fundamentals to keep growing by about 7-8 per cent for decades. The pace of institutional changes and industries being liberalized is very high and has in a rather short time turned China into the 'factory of the world' and India into its 'software center'. For example, this is seen in the much higher productivity in the manufacturing sector in China and the services sector in India compared to the overall productivity in each of these countries (UNCTAD, 2005)

The third wave concerns the so-called emerging country markets or transition economies and their relations with the mature market economies mainly in Europe and North America. According to certain projections of this development, it will drastically change the present relations between the EU and North America on one side, and Asia and South America on the other. For example, projections made by Goldman Sachs in 2003 about growth until 2050 in Brazil, Russia, India and China (the BRICs) show startling results. The BRICs represent the big emerging country markets, where most of the action takes place. So even if the international business marketing taken up in the book is relevant for all emerging country markets, the book mainly concentrates on international business marketing in the big emerging country markets, for example India, China and Russia. These three countries are already the dominating emerging country markets, and will be so even more in the future. Poland also plays an important role in the book, since it is the largest emerging country market among the new EU members, and the EU enlargement effect should be most visible in this market. To be comparable in size, other emerging country markets will be aggregated into groups of markets or regional markets. Here the book will also include international business marketing of Western firms in the emerging country markets of two regions: the ASEAN (the Association of Southeast Asian Nations) Free Trade Area abbreviated as AFTA; and the Middle East and North African region, abbreviated as MENA.

Regarding the globalization of companies, the formation of the Western MNC through the internationalization of big companies from Europe and USA constitute a first wave of internationalization from the end of the 19th century until the 1960s. This internationalization mainly took place between market economies in Europe and North America. A second wave of internationalization took big companies from first Japan and later South Korea out into the world market and an expansion of Western MNCs to East Asia. This added the Japanese and the Korean MNCs as well as the overseas Chinese business system to the group of global firms, while Latin-American firms only played a minor role in this globalization step. MNCs are also increasingly making money during the third wave:

> A survey of China by the American Chamber of Commerce and other data indicate that more than 65 percent of US companies in China are profitable and that their margins in China are equal to or greater than their global

margins. This market's challenge is that profits must often be reinvested to maintain market position. The sheer size of China, coupled with its rapid growth and competition, means that even market leaders must continually invest to maintain share. (Woetzel, 2004, p. 43)

Thus, the high growth of many emerging country markets and their integration into the world economy is increasing the interest for these markets by Western multinational corporations (MNCs) at the same time as it is rearranging the competitive forces for firms and economies. In the third wave of internationalization competition is increasing, involving industries where Western mature industrial countries traditionally have comparative advantages. In Sweden, for example, more and more production seems to be moving abroad, among other things being outsourced to Poland in Central and Eastern Europe (CEE), China or India. One major consequence is that the strong industrial base of the Swedish economy is likely to diminish as new jobs are not created at the same pace as jobs are lost. R&D investments and the number of new companies are going down. This indicates that the Swedish economy might not be able to sustain its comparative advantages built on capital/knowledge-intensive industries, no longer being able to gain from globalization to the same extent as before. One reason is that major markets in CEE have been integrated into the common European market. Another reason is the rapidly growing markets in China and India as well as intensified competition from companies in these new low-cost production bases. India and China in particular are also in the process of upgrading their comparative advantages to industries where Western mature industrial countries traditionally have comparative advantages, for instance in hi-tech industries. This creates a double effect of a strong global pull from growing demand and a push from growing competition that dramatizes the competitive situation, increasing the risk of Swedish firms being outperformed by foreign firms.

Ways to internationalize in the new Europe mainly seem to vary with how much experience firms have in operating in foreign markets, that is how far they have come in the global internationalization process. Internationally experienced firms are in a better position to take advantage of business opportunities in the new EU and Asia, both to sell more, relocate production and shift the supplier base eastwards. But there are other types of threats for the MNC. A major issue is how the traditional MNC structure of such firms can be kept in an even more globalized world. Is it possible to sustain the competitive advantage that originates from its present regional base, for instance when production costs are only a fraction of those in adjacent countries and when the supplier base in general seems to be moving to the new EU countries in Eastern Europe or to China/India? Are their owners willing to keep investing? This seems to vary with the type of industry and which type of MNC dominates the global industry.

Major Trends

Some major trends regarding how firms are influenced by and respond strategically through their business marketing to the challenge caused by the advent of emerging country markets during the third wave of internationalization are:

1. *Internationally experienced companies change their business marketing behaviour from mature markets to emerging markets.* Traditional internationalization processes in the first and second waves of internationalization mainly took firms to today's mature markets. European firms first went to markets in Europe and later to North America, and finally to emerging country markets in Latin America and Asia. The growing importance of this latter type of market in the third wave implies that internationally experienced firms are increasing their business marketing in such markets.

2. *More home-market oriented small and medium-sized enterprises (SMEs) are internationalizing their business operations, becoming more global.* The reduced physical and psychic distances make it less risky to operate outside the home market in foreign markets, for example initiating the business marketing processes of SMEs to neighbouring emerging country markets in Europe or Asia. The need to learn international business marketing is therefore increasing for such firms.

3. *Purchasing becomes a more important international activity, making imports a more essential part of international business marketing.* Internationalization processes are involving more activities in the value chain. Traditional internationalization processes are sales based and concern exports and foreign direct investment (FDI). The growing importance of outsourcing results in increasing reliance on foreign supplier markets, imports and the internationalization of supplies. This had earlier been a vital issue in certain industries and regions since the 1970s, for example regarding clothing and electronics in Asia, but it is now diffused to many more industries and firms. Internationalization of purchasing activities or inputs takes place through expansion to new supplier markets, either through replacing domestic production with imports or shifting from domestic suppliers to foreign suppliers. The first is the make or buy situation or the outsourcing issue. The second is a supplier selection situation or where to outsource, for instance with the intention to shift the supplier base from high cost to low cost countries. This is the off-shoring issue. This process is cost driven or market driven. In the latter case, the customer moves production abroad and the supplier follows. It could also happen that the customer faces cost pressures from customers abroad, and to avoid being replaced by cheaper sources the supplier moves production to keep the customer. Global sourcing is an example of highly internationalized purchasing.

4. *Internationalization of production changes character, new patterns of international production having different impact on business marketing.* According to the internationalization process, production is moved abroad rather late, being the last establishment form in a country market. In today's global world this might still be true for the firm that is internationalizing, especially when entering the first foreign countries. But with the increasing possibilities to take advantage of global economies of scale and low labour costs, this simple idea is only part of the picture. For the more internationalized firm, the situation is different and production mainly a matter of concentrating or restructuring production on a global basis. Traditionally, the location of production is a consequence of the gradual build-up of the foreign customer market. Such internationalization processes are still valid due to the rapidly growing markets in CEE and Asia. But lower costs for both blue and white collar workers increase internationalization of production, even making firms to only internationalize production without any direct linkage to sales.

Hence, responses to these changes in the global business environment vary between firms, among other things how they are affected by the intensified competition in world markets from more competitors from emerging country markets in CEE, China and India. For example, the accession of countries in CEE to the EU creates opportunities for going international for many European SMEs. For an already internationalizing firm, it could involve a repositioning of its international marketing efforts, while it might lead to restructuring of production for the even more internationalized firm, or it being able to take advantage of lower production costs in Europe rather than Asia and therefore outsource there.

BIG EMERGING COUNTRY MARKETS

The major consequence of the third wave of internationalization of firms is that emerging country markets have become increasingly important grounds for the international marketing activities of multinational corporations, in particular the very large countries with their big markets mainly dealt with in this book. As introduced above, this has meant a drastic and rapid change of the international business environment of the Western MNC and new conditions for business marketing. The general traits of emerging country markets discussed in Jansson (2007) are more pronounced in the big markets: economic growth, complexity and turbulence. They are undergoing liberalization and privatization of ownership, which is part of a general reformation of the whole society. The changing product/service market structures are characterized by different degrees of imperfection, which vary between different industries. At the beginning of the establishment of the market system, the market structure is still very much influenced by the former system, for example the centrally planned economy. The reformation of the state-owned enterprises seems to be rather slow to start with, meaning that the market structure is still rather homogeneous, rigid and closed. The concentrated market structure consists of a limited number of dominant big companies, mainly government-owned, resulting in low competition. This stage is then rapidly transformed through liberalization and privatization into a more developed and adolescent market structure, which is heterogeneous, fluid, fragmented and open. This is a stage of rather raw capitalism, which is finally consolidated into a more mature and organized stage similar to the markets found in the mature Western market economies.

A Market Transition Process in China

This transformation of markets is exemplified below for one industry in China based on an ongoing study of the internationalization of Chinese firms in a joint project involving researchers from the University of Kalmar, Stockholm University and Shanghai University.

The industry exemplified is a key industry in China, since it supplies a strategic component to many industries such as the power industry, construction industry, telecommunications industry and car industry. Initially, the state-owned companies were reformed and opened up through a rather slow process, mainly through being transformed into collectively-owned firms such as township companies, privately-owned companies, or mixes between such ownership forms. The market structure changed from a highly concentrated one at the end of the 1970s to a rather concentrated one at the end of the 1980s.

However, the key establishment of the market took place in the next stage, which lasted to about 2005. During this period, the market structure became highly fragmented with a very low concentration ratio. During this market expansion stage the most rapid change took place between 2000 and 2004 or during the tenth five-year plan. The share of the output from the state-owned enterprises was gradually reduced through privatization. At the end of this period the private enterprises had taken the lead. While the output of the state-owned companies amounted to 48 per cent at the end of the 1980s, it had come down to 4 per cent at the end of 2004. The output of the private firms increased from 40 per cent to 70 per cent. The competition in the second stage became increasingly intensive. With the growth of demand, the number of firms in the market grew to about 5000 during this stage, which resulted in overcapacity. Ninety-five per cent of these companies were small- and medium-sized companies, giving a very low concentration ratio compared to most other countries. The sales of the ten largest companies in 2004 amounted to approximately 5 per cent of the total sales in the country. The earlier big companies were broken up. The former largest company in Asia in this industry, for example, was divided up into parts, and major ones merged with or were acquired by foreign firms. The low entry barrier created a disorderly competition with variable quality, fierce price competition and a low business morale including counterfeiting, and rough making. Especially at the low end of the market the price competition was fierce with high risks for underpricing due to overcapacity.

The next stage has just started, being indicated by a stabilization of demand, which is also becoming more quality oriented. Some companies have started to rely more on the development of science and technology for their competitiveness. The cost pressure is unprecedented through heavily increasing raw material prices. This makes the very fragmented market structure start to change. The privatization of the public enterprises continued, their share being only 15 per cent in terms of assets in 2006. The three types of foreign-funded enterprises took 25 per cent and the private stock-holding companies 60 per cent. Among the top ten enterprises in terms of sales income, only one was a state-owned company. Even if a few local Chinese companies started to export during the former stage, the interest to go abroad became more real during the stabilization stage. One contributing factor was that governments began to urge and promote firms to export and to invest abroad.

This illustration is about an industry that has moved through an expansion phase of the market, where an oligopoly-like situation consisting of a limited number of mostly state-owned enterprises was replaced by a considerably larger number of mostly privately-owned large and small companies, creating and intensifying competition. The market is now found in a consolidation phase, where there are strong indications of a coming shake-out of firms. The 'wild' and fragmented market is beginning to be turned into a more 'tamed' 'Western' type of market consisting of a more limited number of competitors of both national and foreign origin. Rivalry has changed from being domestic to being global as well as from being supply-driven to being demand-driven.

Other Characteristics of Emerging Markets

The relationships of business networks change from being mainly personal to being impersonal. For example, Woetzel (2004, p. 44) discusses this development in China:

> Many executives are convinced that relationships are the key to doing business in China. That was certainly true in the early days of its economic opening to the outside world, when its decision makers had few ways of determining which companies could truly deliver what they had promised. Accordingly, lengthy discussions, often accompanied by extensive socializing, were the norm as the country's negotiators strove to understand their foreign counterparts. Now the Chinese, with more than 20 years of investment experience under their belt, are looking at the tangible business track records of foreign companies. Those that fail to bring tangible advantages, such as new capabilities, technologies, or business models – as well as a record of success – are unlikely to win the deal, no matter how good their relationships.

However, this does not mean that relationships are no longer important in marketing on the Chinese market, only that they have changed character. Relationships are still critical, but are becoming more and more professional and less and less social, approaching the business relationships found in Western Europe.

The unevenly distributed emerging demand is segmented into modern and traditional parts and mixes between traditional and modern consumption behaviours, a mix changing over time. This is illustrated in Table 1.1 for major segments of Indian consumers.

A main conclusion from this table is that the income classes require different degrees of adaptation in marketing. For the highest income class, 'Global India', no major adaptations might be necessary, since its one million households have a living standard comparable to Europe and North America. However, this is not the fact for the not so well off but much larger segment, 'Struggling India', consisting of 110 million households. The products consumed in Western markets might be hard to sell in this segment. In this case, marketing usually needs to be tailored to local tastes as well as local spending power, for example giving low price another meaning than in a Western market. If the MNC wants to go for a major part of this vast market, it needs to adapt marketing a lot, among other things charging prices that consumers can afford. Nevertheless, a major shift of demand in general is taking place in emerging country parts from price orientation to quality orientation, the more households that move up to higher income classes. In addition, commercial practices are different, being a changing mix of old/traditional and modern ingredients. They are generally more personal and socially oriented, as well as more influenced by corruption. The service sector is developing from a low service to a high service orientation with the rise of the service economy.

The uneven development of various industries makes it important to differentiate between them, for example regarding segmentation and marketing strategy. Both China and India, for instance, have sluggish and inefficient industries that are heavily regulated and lack competitive dynamism. They also have successful high-productive industries that are globally competitive. According to Farrell (2004a), the information technology, software and business-process-outsourcing sectors are the most successful industries in India, despite never having been regulated by the government. This and the low level of intervention in capital markets have created room for entrepreneurs. The sector is so far ahead that it will take more than 10-15 years for China to catch up. The liberalization of the Indian economy has led to a moderately successful auto industry, especially in the manufacturing of components. However, the tariffs on finished cars are still rather high. The consumer electronics industry is still protected, and is therefore not internationally competitive. The performance of the food-retailing industry is even worse as well as other highly regulated industries such as the power industry and transport industry, often related to the organization of the infrastructure of the country.

Table 1.1   Major income classes in India

Household income classes	Real annual household income [1] $	Segment size	Common occupations	Assets owned
Global India	>$10 000	1	Business people in small to midsize enterprises Corporate/government employees' Rich farmers	1-2 bedroom Colour TV, mobile phone, refrigerator, washing machine Car worth $5000-$10 000
Aspiring India	$4000-$10 000	40	Salaried employees New-services employees' (e.g. IT, media) Shopkeepers	Colour TV, refrigerator, telephone Scooter, motorcycle or small car worth ~ $4000
Struggling India	$1500-$4000	110	Shopkeepers Service workers (e.g. waiters, drivers, maids) Farmers	Bicycle Radio, black-and-white TV
Destitude India	<$1500	40	Subsistence farmers Farm workers	Watch

[1] *Note:*   *Average size of household = 5.4 Not adjusted for purchasing power parity; base years = 1995-96.*
Source: *Bharadway, et al. (2005)*

9

China also has some reasonably liberalized and highly competitive industries. In consumer electronics, the labour productivity is double that of its Indian counterparts. So India will not be able to compete seriously during the next ten years. The performance of the auto industry is moderately successful, mainly due to less liberalization. The productivity of foreign joint ventures, for example, is low compared with that of plants in Japan and the United States. The high amounts of FDI have established a big but still rather regulated industry, which has limited its competitive potential. Still, privately owned automakers such as Chery Automotive and Geely Automotive are beginning to thrive, now being able to put together cars of reasonable quality much more cheaply than foreign automakers can. According to Woetzel (2004), this has been made possible by local entrepreneurs who are using the skills and training provided by foreign MNCs. So even if there are small pockets of competitive products and firms, the auto industry in both countries as a whole is not yet internationally competitive. China, for example, imports from India high-value-added mechanized and electronic components, whose production depends more on known-how than on infrastructure.

A major characteristic of emerging economies is the deficient financial markets, which are gradually improved. Actually, the financial sector is seen as a major road block for further transformation of the product and service markets in China, India, Russia, and partly in Poland. China, in particular, has massive bad bank loans that will have to be accounted for. India, on the other hand, has more developed stock and bond markets that support private enterprise. The infrastructure constitutes another major barrier to industrial growth. India's poor roads and ports as well as insufficient water and electricity supplies raise energy- and logistics-related costs. China's infrastructure is much better, which has benefited manufacturing industries that depend on just-in-time production processes. India, on the other hand, prospers in software, biotechnology, or creative industries such as advertising, where such 'hard' infrastructure does not matter as much.

Non-Market Factors

Government plays a pivotal role in reforming the economy as well as the political system, the legal framework and the educational system, which is a complicated and sluggish process in all these countries as well as in emerging country markets in general. For this reason, the legal system, for example, is generally weak and 'people' oriented during most of the reform period, at least compared to the strong and formally developed system found in Western markets. Even if the situation varies between the three big markets, this is often shown by the lack of laws protecting property rights as well of the problems in enforcing laws.

India and China face daunting social, health and environmental problems. They have managed to reduce the number of poor people considerably. The share of India's population living below the poverty line, for example, was reduced from 55 per cent in 1974 to 26 per cent in 2000. The percentage of the population living on less than $1 per day was 35 per cent in 1994 compared to 42 per cent in 1974. Life expectancy has increased and infant mortality has been reduced. Even if spending on health and education is increasing, it is not enough. For example, about half of the Indian adult population still is illiterate. Environmental problems are pressing, especially clean water and sanitation, industrial pollution and deforestation. They also have a heavy health burden, where preventable diseases account for a large part of the disease burden, for example HIV/AIDS. Population growth is too low in China, while it is too high in India. India adds an Australia every 8th month and since 1947 has added more than two Americas without even half of its resources.

EMERGING COUNTRY MARKETS DEFINED

Emergence of markets is the major characteristic of the economies of the big country markets as well as many other country markets in Eastern Europe, Asia, Africa and Latin America. The use of the term market in this context means that the development of the market economy has reached such a state that it is possible to define the economic system as a market economy. Usually, these countries have an adolescent market economy in comparison with the more developed mature market economies of Western Europe and North America. The markets of these countries are therefore still undergoing change due to being reformed through liberalization and privatization efforts. They expand through a successful mix of market reform and societal reform. It is often unclear what is meant by 'emerging markets' and which countries to include in this group, especially since they are also called 'emerging economies', 'developing countries', or 'transition economies'. In this book, emerging markets and transition economies are viewed as being different but overlapping concepts. The difference lies in the starting point for the transition to the market economy. Transition economies refer to the countries of the former Soviet bloc in East Europe and Central Asia plus China, Vietnam and Mongolia in East Asia, which are being transformed from a centrally planned to a market economy. The base of other emerging markets is traditional economic systems, mainly in the developing countries that have never had a communist regime.

In accordance with Jansson (2007), emerging country markets are defined as growing markets, which are being transformed from a pre-market economy stage (either a non-pecuniary/traditional or centrally planned economy) to the market stage of the mature Western capitalistic economy, by way of integrated and successful structural reforms of companies, markets and society. This moving towards a market economy through a transformation process takes place through a number of stages and at different paces.

THE INSTITUTIONAL NETWORK APPROACH

The market system of big emerging country markets is growth-oriented, including strong and unevenly distributed local demand. However, it is also uncertain, turbulent and complex. This business environment is therefore relationship-oriented, embedded, holistic, social, reforming and institution-building. Relationships are always important. But they are even more so in emerging country markets, which therefore can be characterized as 'network societies'. The situation of 'everything influences everything else' is of particular importance in international business marketing, being a major distinction between emerging country markets and mature markets in the EU or in North America. This is characterized as 'embeddedness', which means that society is divided into various sections, which are embedded into each other. The MNC, for example, is embedded into the market, which in its turn is embedded into society at large. Another distinction is the faster change, which makes the business environment more turbulent and more uncertain compared to the environment of Western mature markets. This uncertainty is often felt even more strongly by Western firms that usually have less experience of markets in emerging economies both on a general basis and on how they differ among themselves. The embedded characteristic together with turbulence increases the complexity of these markets.

Thus, emerging country markets are relationship oriented, where firms are part of elaborate and complex networks. However, business networks are not unique to such markets, since firms all over the world are connected through networks. But business networks in emerging country markets differ culturally, organizationally and economically from those in the West at the same time as they undergo strong changes. This means that inter-firm network relationships in emerging country markets are more personal and embedded, that is overlapping with other networks in society. In Western markets they are more impersonal and confined to the business sector. Actually, on a very general basis, inter-firm relationships in emerging country markets tend to transform from the former state to the latter state. Changes of markets and relationship processes become important.

A network approach is therefore used to describe these emerging markets and how business marketing is done there: what the markets look like, how to establish and maintain relationships with various market actors, how to organize marketing activities and how to compete. On the whole, strategic issues become more important, where networking and relationship building become a strategic rather than an operational issue.

Another conclusion from above is that changes in emerging country market conditions are entangled with changes in the society. Markets do not develop by themselves, but basic support systems need to be in place, for example a legal system, a public support system and suitable values and belief systems. Such support systems and similar systems are viewed as institutions. The 'embeddedness' of market networks in institutions is a key characteristic of these markets, meaning that not only are markets emerging but more or less the whole society. The relation between environment and business marketing is therefore of the utmost importance to understand and analyse and consequently to be able to plan and execute business marketing. Actually, differences between emerging economies and Western economies expressed through variations in networks and institutions are of such a magnitude that they lead to very different marketing situations. International business marketing is therefore set within the institutional network approach as described in Jansson (2007).

MAJOR MARKETING PROBLEMS

The high growth often found in emerging country markets makes them lucrative or potentially lucrative markets for MNCs, especially the most rapidly growing markets. This book is about how MNCs can cope with major business marketing problems encountered in emerging country markets and the perception of them: how to market under the special circumstances discussed above and how MNCs handle international marketing problems in big emerging country markets, in particular. A major issue studied is how relevant their experience from Western markets is in these markets.

According to Zainulbhai (2005) successful foreign companies in India share three characteristics:

1. They have invested in the long term and made a strong commitment to the local market.
2. They have adapted to local conditions rather than forcing foreign models on India.
3. They have created and shaped the market, for example cheap products for the low end market.

Some major strategic marketing problems relevant for business markets faced in emerging country markets are then:

1. How to segment the market, especially how to relate to the low spending power of the major parts of the market.
2. What marketing strategy to apply in different sections of the transforming society. For example, a major issue concerns the trade-off between price and quality, which usually differs considerably in emerging country markets compared to Western mature markets.
3. How to relate to the emerging and reformed institutions influencing business, for example judicial system, political system, educational system and mixes of traditional local culture and modern global culture.

The MNC's ability to cope with such problems is critical for successfully managing business marketing operations in these markets. MNCs have gained experience from operating in emerging country markets and solving problems of this type as demonstrated by the many studies summarized in books by Cavusgil et al. (2002) and Jansson (2007), as well as the international marketing literature in general. However, research indicates that MNCs still base marketing in emerging country markets too much on their experience from Western markets, one reason being a lack of marketing models valid for emerging country markets. Even if there is no shortage of articles and books on marketing in these markets, there is a lack of literature providing firms with strategic business marketing models for emerging country markets, especially focusing on the specific marketing problems there. There is also a lot of literature about how to do business in specific emerging country markets from simple business guides to international marketing books. But there are few attempts to develop general models that can be used in most of these markets, for example making it hard to compare business marketing in these markets in various ways.

The basic tenet of the present book is therefore that traditional ideas and frameworks used for analysing, forming and implementing international business marketing in mature markets are in need of adjustment in emerging country markets. There is a need for a new framework to international business marketing, which is specified below.

BUSINESS MARKETING

This book is about industrial marketing or business-to-business marketing by Western MNCs to customer firms in emerging country markets. These international selling and purchasing activities involving firms from these major country groups are defined as international business marketing (IBM). Business marketing is therefore another term for business-to-business marketing or industrial marketing, being a kind of relationship marketing between firms.

In accordance with the institutional network approach the key factor of IBM is the relationships through which the MNC is connected to its local business environment. Networking becomes a critical issue, since a major part of the business activities in emerging country markets concerns building and maintaining networks of relationships to major commercial parties and other actors of interest to MNC success. Relationships are not only built with economic stakeholders but also with other stakeholders in society, for example government, local communities and interest organizations. One consequence of this interrelatedness is that marketing is interactive, where the firm responds to various activities from other organizations in the external framework.

Business marketing in emerging country markets therefore needs to build on a broad view of relationships, where the 'industrial networks' or 'IMP' perspective is found to be the most suitable (Ford et al., 2006). This is a business-to-business approach that has mainly been developed for industrial marketing and purchasing, building on major differences between the marketing of industrial products and consumer products. The main focus is on buyer-seller relationships, which often are well-established and of long-term duration. They are complex with contacts between the companies taking place on several different levels, particularly when complex products are involved. Business marketing is viewed as an inter-organizational matter and it is regarded as fruitful to treat both the marketing and the buying behaviour of firms as organizational issues. This makes it possible to apply the same theory of inter-organizational character to both types of activities. The two are seen as being opposite sides of the same coin. Together they represent the buyer/seller relationship. Interaction is viewed as taking place between the two parties to this relationship. The result is a more coherent theory for the field of business marketing generally. This inter-organizational approach is fundamentally different from most approaches to marketing in general as developed in Chapter 2.

The inter-organizational approach is limited to market relationships and rarely includes the non-market relationship aspect, for instance government and other stakeholders in the social environment. The main purpose in product/service markets is efficiency-based, that is to sell or buy products/services at a profit. The main purpose in the government field, however, is legitimacy-based, for example to get permits to do business in product/service markets. Thus, different rationalities dominate in different organizational fields, which, among other things, lead to variations in the type of relationship established with different types of stakeholders, for example government. This aspect is developed extensively in Jansson (2007) and is therefore not taken up in this book, which concentrates on business marketing in the efficiency-based product/service markets.

Still, even if this inter-organizational approach to business marketing is broad in comparison with most other approaches it is not broad enough to constitute the entire base for IBM in emerging country markets. It needs to be developed in four ways, namely the international aspect, the network aspect, the strategy aspect, and the organizational aspect.

THE INTERNATIONAL BUSINESS MARKETING MODEL

Based on the discussion above, the international business marketing model relevant for emerging country markets can now be presented. It builds on the institutional network approach and contains the following major points:

1. *The international business marketing strategy.* The IBM strategy consists of three basic sub-strategies: network strategy, linkage strategy and competitive strategy. In addition, first-mover advantages play a

critical role in achieving competitive advantages. The basic foundation is the interplay between IBM and institutions, where institutions are seen as constituting the framework for different marketing strategies as well as being influenced by the strategies.

2. *The international business marketing process*, that is how relationships are initiated, developed, maintained and terminated. Three major business marketing processes are distinguished: the marketing process, the relationship process and the product/service process. The relationship process is a major part of the internationalization process, while the marketing process and the product/service processes are mainly relevant in connection with marketing to large projects, of special relevance for the large infrastructural investments in the big emerging country markets.

3. *The adaptation of IBM to local networks.* This aspect is developed by looking closer at how Western business relationships are adapted to how the business networks in the Chinese context function as well as in the Russian context. The Chinese business network, which also dominates in Southeast Asia, is usually called the 'Guanxi' network and the Russian business network the 'Blat' network.

4. *The internationalization of relationships.* Relationships are seen to constitute the core of the internationalization process, whereas internationalization takes place through establishing and maintaining network relationships in foreign environments.

5. *The internal network organization of the MNC.* Implementation requires the business marketing strategy to be organized properly, whereas looking closer at how organizational structures extends organizational aspects on strategy further and controls relate to IBM strategy. The MNC organization is translated into a network organization.

6. *The local and regional network organization.* The MNC organization is looked at from below by taking up local organization in emerging country markets both at the country level and the regional level.

7. *The internationalization of firms.* Based on an extended analysis of the internationalization of major activities of the value chain and the gradually evolving international organization of the firm, a distinction is made between three major types of firms: the domestic firm, the internationalizing firm and the fully internationalized firm. The latter type is further subdivided into the Ethnocentric MNC, the Polycentric MNC and the Geocentric MNC.

FOUR MAJOR ASPECTS

The international business marketing model is based on four major aspects, which have been derived from comparing key characteristics of the particular business environment of emerging country markets with the usefulness of existing business marketing theories to such markets. As mentioned, the most suitable theoretical framework is the inter-organizational approach to business marketing. However, it needs to be adapted to the conditions of markets in transition which differ from the conditions of the West-European origin of this approach. These major aspects are:

1. The network-oriented society makes relationships the foundation of marketing activities. The 'embeddedness' of the firm into society also makes relationships with parties outside the market important; government and various stakeholders becoming central in business marketing.
2. This international environment is different, complex and volatile, or turbulent, which makes adaptations of marketing necessary. How to consider such major differences in international environments becomes a major issue in business marketing. The turbulent markets are tightly integrated into society, which increases the strategic importance of the macro environment, for example how this background environment is related to the more proximate business environment of the MNC.
3. Strategic issues in marketing therefore become more important. For example, the strategic importance of emerging country markets relative to other markets has increased for many MNCs.
4. Organizational issues also become more important. The quite different marketing situation prevailing in emerging country markets implies that business marketing needs to be adapted to these other market conditions. Resources and capabilities must be located there and coordinated with those of the whole MNC. Organizational issues in marketing then come into focus. In addition, the three issues above are very much related to the organization of the MNC and its environment.

These four factors are now discussed more in detail. First the network aspect is taken up, followed by the international aspect, and the strategy aspect and finally the organization aspect.

The Network Aspect

Most marketing literature based on the inter-organizational approach focuses on dyadic relationships but also on sets of links within networks. In the latter case, the relationship focus is mostly kept by looking at the network as a number of direct (the dyadic aspect) and indirect relationships (the network aspect) (for example Andersson et al., 1994). Dyads are connected to three major types of networks (activity patterns, resource constellations, actors bonds) according to Håkansson and Snehota (1995). The network aspect of this theory needs to be developed.

The International Aspect

Even if the international aspect is normally included as part of the industrial network framework, it is more taken for granted than being incorporated as a key theoretical construct (for example Håkansson, 1982; Hallén, 1982; Ford et al., 1998; Ford, 2002). This international aspect of business marketing is developed in three ways:

1. The book elaborates on the environment of industrial networks in different transition countries and studies how international business marketing is influenced by environmental variation. The external environment is defined as consisting of a number of rule systems or institutions (Jansson, 2007; Kostova, 1997). As a consequence, business marketing is assumed to be directed at identifiable actors in specific organizational fields such as product/service markets (mainly customers and competitors), financial markets and government. There is interplay between business marketing and institutions, where institutions are influencing business marketing as well as being influenced by it. Institutions represent broad categories or constraints for how business marketing is organized in different countries.

2. Integrating relationships into the internationalization processes of firms develops the international dimension of relationships. Firms are assumed to gain international experience by establishing and developing relationships to business partners. The more relationships that have been established in a foreign country and the more countries this has been done in, the more internationally experienced the firm then becomes. This is derived from research on internationalization processes, which has found that how firms respond to changes in international markets largely depends on where in the internationalization process they are found, that is their degree of internationalization.

    To know more about how firms respond to the market situation in emerging country markets, internationalization process theory is developed in four major ways:

    2.1 Developing the critical role played by relationships in the internationalization of the firm.
    2.2 Doing business in networks in emerging country markets is integrated into internationalization processes.
    2.3 Studying the end of the internationalization process. A lot of research has been devoted to the beginning of the process, while very little has been done about where it might end. It is reasonable to establish a finish line for this process, being about how firms are internationalizing from scratch to some final stage.
    2.4 Since relocation and restructuring of production plays a key role in this third wave of internationalization and new phase of global

restructuring, it is important to clarify and develop the role of manufacturing in the internationalization process.

3. The inter-organizational approach to business marketing has been developed and empirically tested to a large extent in Western European markets. Its vocabulary, thought patterns and logic can be used mainly to explain the relationship behaviour of firms from these markets, especially the 15 mature European Union markets (Jansson, 1994a, 2007). However, it cannot be taken for granted that relationships are developed and maintained in the same way outside these countries, whereas the business marketing of Western European MNCs in emerging country markets needs to be adapted to how local networks work. Looking closer at how business networks in the Chinese context function as well as in a Russian context develops this aspect.

The Strategy Aspect

Even if the inter-organizational approach deals with the strategic issues of business marketing (for example Snehota, 1990; Axelsson, 1992; Håkansson and Snehota, 1995; Ford, 2002), the strategy aspect needs to be developed further by incorporating how the resources and capabilities of the MNC are organized. This elaboration extends further industrial network models, where resources together with activities and actors are the basic factors (Axelsson and Easton, 1992; Håkansson and Johanson, 1992; Håkansson and Snehota, 1995; Ford et al., 1998; Ford, 2002). The strategy aspect of IBM is developed based on Jansson (2007) and Peng (2000). The framework developed for analysing international business strategies in emerging country markets is therefore founded on the institutional network approach.

When the four aspects are combined with the major marketing problems and issues of high strategic importance facing multinational corporations in emerging country markets discussed above, some critical strategic issues in international business marketing are identified. Actually, they can be summarized according to the three major strategic issues for MNCs identified by Tallman and Yip (2001): geographic spread, local adaptation and global integration. Most literature on strategic aspects of international marketing concerns these three issues, in particular the strategic dilemma that MNCs face between local adaptation and global integration. Bartlett and Ghoshal's (1989) well-established typology, for example, is about this dilemma. The multinational strategy focuses on local adaptation and the global strategy on global integration, while the international strategy and the transnational strategy directly concentrates on the dilemma by discussing various mixes of these two major strategic issues.

Geographic spread
The geographic spread aspect has to do with the spread of businesses beyond the borders of the home country, which is the original issue in international

marketing. It concerns strategic issues related to the internationalization process of the firm such as the entry strategy, for example by using various entry nodes and entry modes to establish relationships (Jansson and Sandberg, 2008). The new competitive situation characterizing the third world of internationalization seems to result in a new phase of restructuring of already internationalized firms, and an internationalization of firms with a low degree of internationalization, particularly small and medium-sized enterprises (SMEs).

Depending upon how far they have come in the internationalization process, firms respond differently to this new situation. At one extreme are firms that have completed the internationalization process and now are truly global firms or multinational corporations (MNCs). Such companies need to restructure on a global basis, innovating new products and businesses, being less dependent on their home base. At the other extreme is the still non-internationalized firm: the domestic market oriented SME. Firms at the early internationalization stages are slower to respond, because they lack the resources for and experience of international trade and investment and have a traditional home-market focus, being latecomers on the international scene.

Local adaptation vs. global integration
Local adaptation is about to what degree marketing is adapted to the specific circumstances of the foreign market being entered, for example, how much to adapt products to the different demands in the new market. Another strategic question in this context is how much knowledge that is needed about the local market environment to be able to make the right adaptations.

Global integration is about to what extent the MNC integrates its marketing operations between different national markets, for example in order to better leverage its locally-based resources. Usually, there is some integration, since the MNC does not have completely separate and localized activities. Examples of strategic options for this major strategic issue are the extent of global market participation, how much standardization of products and other marketing variables can be achieved, the location of various business activities, and how competitive moves are integrated between different country markets (Yip, 1992; Zou and Cavusgil, 1996, 2002; Tallman and Yip, 2001). The global integration aspect concerns the MNC as a whole, and is about how the company takes advantage of its geographic spread. The adaptation aspect, on the other hand, mainly concerns how an individual subsidiary locally exploits the resources and capabilities at its disposal.

This strategic dilemma between local responsiveness and global integration is also a key marketing issue in emerging country markets. It is a well-known fact that the products sold by an MNC on world markets vary a lot between different markets. Most products are adapted to the greatly varying market demands. This variation is also true for other MNC operations than marketing, for example in production, and purchasing, as well as for how the MNC acts towards governments in different countries.

As noted by Kotabe (2001) and others, management and strategy research is insufficiently integrated with marketing research in the way that management and strategy researchers mostly focus on the supply side of the relationships between firms and customers, while marketing researchers tend to focus on the demand side. The book will partly bridge this gap between strategy and management literature on one side and the international marketing literature on the other. For example, the book builds on research in international marketing strategy and management, developing further the three basic strategic issues discussed above, mainly the fundamental strategic dilemma of local adaptation versus global integration. The focus is on local adaptation and the global integration issue is therefore viewed from the perspective of local adaptation.

Due to variation in global environments, national responsiveness or local adaptation is a basic characteristic of international business marketing strategy in emerging country markets. This is also true for the need to globally integrate various strategic marketing activities, for example through standardization. This most basic of all strategic issues in international marketing is therefore developed further in this book by looking at what is behind these forces of differentiation and standardization. International business marketing operations and strategy are thereby fruitful to view from a relationship perspective, since a major issue in emerging and many other markets concerns building and maintaining networks of relationships to major actors. As a consequence, the organization of the marketing activities is also seen from a network perspective.

The Organizational Aspect

IBM is not only a matter of operating in external networks. The internal network of the MNC also becomes important, especially if the strategic aspect of IBM is stressed. The organizational aspect of business marketing therefore needs to be developed further.

A major factor of the strategic approach to international business marketing of this book is to include the organization of the internal network of the MNC. Strategic action and reaction are organized within an internal network, which consists of the group network organization as well as the local and regional organization.

Since the book is about international business marketing in emerging country markets, it has a local market focus by mainly concentrating on the marketing of subsidiaries and other local units of the MNC. This is a bottom-up perspective in comparison with the traditional top-down perspective. The emphasis on the business marketing strategy of the subsidiary implies that the fundamental perspective of the book is one of subsidiary choice. This perspective is not relevant in many developed countries today, since national subsidiary companies are not so common. However, developing countries or emerging country markets are often an exception to this rule (Jansson, 1994b, 2007; Birkinshaw, 2001). Since the subsidiary choice is restricted within the

MNC and by the environment, the subsidiary perspective is put in the context of the two other perspectives to research on the subsidiary suggested by Birkinshaw et al. (1998). According to the environmental determinism perspective, the subsidiary is seen as a function of its environment. This environmental perspective is mainly combined with the subsidiary choice perspective in this book, which will be contrasted to the third perspective of head office assignment, where the marketing strategy of the subsidiary is determined by head office. According to this perspective, subsidiary choice is studied as a spectrum of different degrees of self-determination, being a consequence of the structural context of the subsidiary, for example level of autonomy, control of resources and social control.

This book makes an important contribution to the knowledge on the MNC subsidiary, particularly with regard to its business marketing. First, a framework directly related to the business marketing strategy of the subsidiary is established. It builds on the assumption that it is the ability of an MNC to gain a subsidiary specific competitive advantage in the emerging country market that largely determines its success. The ability and the feasibility to combine the firm specific advantage at the group level (Rugman, 1981, 1986; Dunning, 1988, 1993; Jansson, 1994a,b) and at the subsidiary level, thereby creating a subsidiary specific advantage, is the source of the real strength of MNCs compared to the local as well as foreign competitors.

As observed by Birkinshaw (2001), the theoretical literature on the MNC subsidiary is rarely about individual units within the MNC but focuses on the MNC as a whole (for example Forsgren et al., 2005). This means that a theory directly designed for strategic marketing management of the subsidiary is missing. The bottom-up perspective of the book takes care of this problem of not having a theory directly designed for the subsidiary. Moreover, the theoretical framework developed focuses on the deficiencies in previous research on MNC subsidiary strategy discussed by Birkinshaw (2001). For example, the risk of having too descriptive a theory is taken care of by seeing international business marketing theory and international business theory combined through an institutional network approach as the main explanatory force behind the strategic marketing behaviour of the subsidiary.

CONCLUSIONS

This book focuses on strategic international business marketing issues in emerging country markets during the third wave of internationalization of firms, mainly from the perspective of the local MNC subsidiaries. The embeddedness situation of high integration between societal factors being likened to a system of 'a box in a box included in another box, etc.' is a major distinction between emerging country markets and mature markets. The fast change makes them more turbulent, more uncertain and risky than

Western mature markets. At the same time, the high growth makes them lucrative. Relationships are of high importance, since emerging country market societies are characterized as 'network societies'. The strategic environment of these markets is therefore relationship-oriented, embedded, institution-building and turbulent. The changing product/service market structures are characterized by different degrees of imperfection over time. Three stages of market development were identified. The differences between emerging economies and Western economies result in very different marketing situations for the MNCs, making traditional ideas and frameworks used for analysing, forming and implementing business marketing in mature markets less applicable and in need of adjustment. The main purpose of this book is therefore to develop and apply a new IBM model, mainly relevant for emerging country markets, and focusing on strategic aspects. It is set within the institutional network approach. A point of departure is the fundamental dilemma in international marketing of local adaptation versus global integration, where the former aspect is stressed of how IBM is adapted to the particular circumstances of the emerging country market.

The international business marketing model builds on major business marketing theories and key characteristics of emerging country markets, which are condensed into four aspects: the network aspect, the international or environmental aspect, the strategic aspect and the organizational aspect. These aspects are integrated into the IBM model, which consists of seven factors:

1. The international business marketing strategy.
2. The international business marketing process.
3. The adaptation of IBM to local networks.
4. The internationalization of relationships. Relationships are seen to constitute the core of the internationalization process.
5. The internal network organization of the MNC. Implementation requires the business marketing strategy to be organized properly.
6. The local and regional network organization. The MNC organization is looked at from below by taking up local organization in emerging country markets both at the country level and the regional level.
7. The internationalization of business marketing and firms.

Networking becomes a critical strategic issue, since a major part of the business activities in emerging country markets concerns building and maintaining networks of relationships to major commercial parties and other actors of interest to MNC success. One consequence of this inter-relatedness is that marketing is interactive, where the firm responds to various activities from other organizations of the external framework. Business marketing therefore builds on a broad view of relationships, mainly founded on the 'IMP' perspective to industrial networks or the inter-organizational approach as it is called in this book. This approach is fundamentally different from most approaches to marketing. It is developed in four ways. In addition to the network aspect the international aspect is deepened by elaborating on the marketing environment; by integrating relationship processes and internationalization processes; and by taking up how the European business network is adapted to the characteristics of the Chinese business network as well as the Russian business network. The strategy aspect is developed based on the institutional network approach and for three major international strategy issues: local adaptation, global integration and geographic spread. The organization aspect is elaborated on by defining the MNC as a hierarchical network and going deeper into the importance of local and regional network organization for succeeding with business marketing in emerging country markets.

Since the book focuses on international business marketing activities in emerging country markets, it is concentrated on the MNCs' operations in these markets, mainly the subsidiaries there. This means that the book mainly has a subsidiary focus to IBM – a bottom-up perspective in comparison with the traditional top-down perspective.

OUTLINE OF THE BOOK

The outline is described in Figure 1.1. The book is introduced in Chapter 1 on the *Business marketing networks, institutions and MNC organization.* The importance of emerging country markets for the business marketing of MNCs is discussed for the third wave of internationalization of firms. The international business marketing model based on the institutional network approach is also introduced.

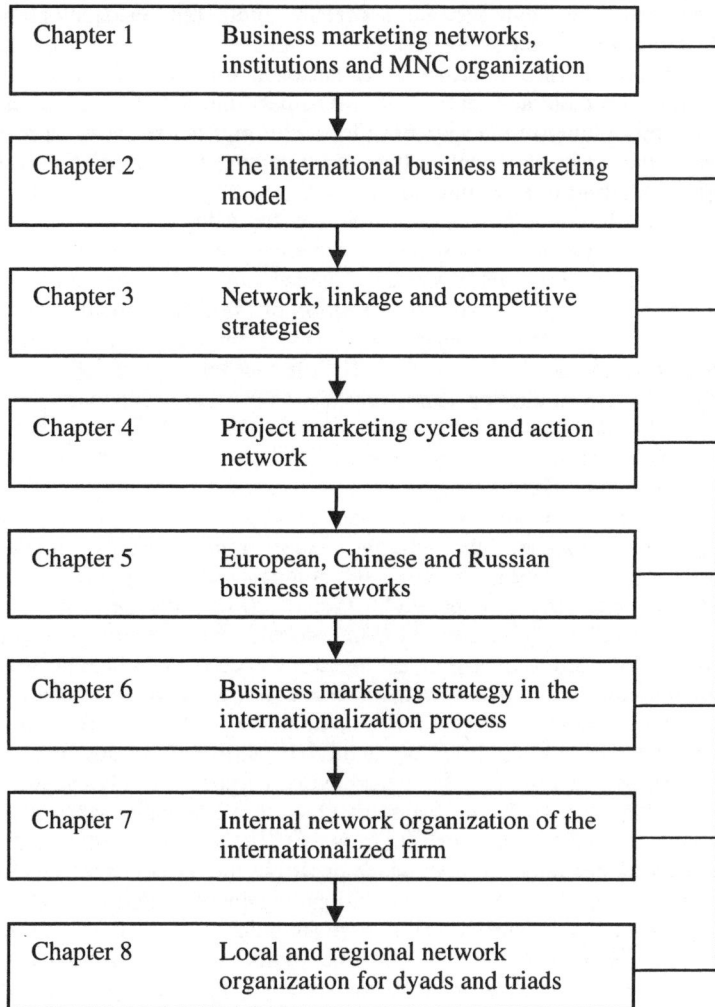

Figure 1.1   The outline of the book

Chapter 2 elaborates on *the international business marketing model* mainly relevant for emerging country markets, building on a broad view to relationships, and where the main foundation is the inter-organizational approach to business marketing or the IMP perspective. By incorporating strategy aspects, international aspects, network aspects and organizational aspects, the international business marketing model is established. The model consists of the business marketing strategy, where three major sub-strategies are working together to create superior customer value and first mover advantages. The model also includes three major business marketing processes and two major internationalization processes. In developing the international aspect, four major factors are critical for the business marketing strategy when entering a local market network, mainly entry mode, entry node, entry process and entry role. Another internationalization aspect concerns the globalization process. In addition, the network capability profiles of the framework contain the main competences that MNCs need for business marketing in emerging country markets. Trustworthiness is a major norm of the social capital that constitutes a capability to manage business relationships. It also gives a capacity to have and develop new relationships, since the execution of IBM strategy depends upon how the network is organized. The internal network organization of the firm is finally described as a hierarchical network, where the focus is on the local and regional network organization. Developing the IBM model takes place as part of the paradigm shift in marketing from transaction to relationship marketing. In particular, its focus on the integration of business marketing with the firm's resource base makes it possible to generalize the IBM framework to general developments in marketing theory.

Chapter 3 is about how superior customer value is created in product/service markets through the international business marketing strategy, or more precisely the three sub-strategies of *network, linkage, and competitive strategies*. The network strategy utilizes the network map to decide which actors to focus on, how to combine them and how to sequence the business marketing over time to the various actors. The linkage strategy or a suitable mix of sub relationships is then determined for each major party included in the network strategy. The competitive strategy concerns how to compete, for example on price or quality. In addition, getting first-mover advantages play a critical role in achieving competitive advantages. The outcome of these business strategies depends on a thorough mapping of the external and the internal network environment. The strategies are conditioned by the network capability profile, which describes the mix of capacities found at a local company for a certain international business marketing strategy. A customer specialist has the capability to make tailor-made customer solutions by operating through specialized networks, while a product specialist solve problems customers have in common through having direct and more standardized network linkages. A distribution specialist deals with customers both directly and indirectly through an own distribution network, while a network distributor specialist caters more for the problems of independent distributors, through which there is an indirect and rather distant coupling to the customer.

Chapter 4 extends the business marketing strategy further by focusing on international business marketing processes in connection with marketing to large projects, and how such network processes are organized. More precisely, the chapter is about *project marketing cycles and action networks.* The process is divided into four cycles – the scanning cycle, the tendering cycle, the completion cycle, and the follow-up cycle – which are connected through a number of transition points, and further sub-divided into a number of phases. Various project teams handle the marketing process or action networks, which are organized differently depending on process stage, size of the project, and other factors. This marketing process is related to two other processes, namely the relationship process and the product/service process.

In *Chapter 5* three major international business networks are analysed, namely the *European, Chinese and Russian business networks.* The institutional aspects of business marketing in emerging country markets are taken up by relating the European business network mainly expressed in the inter-organizational approach to the Chinese and Russian business networks. The inter-organizational approach to business marketing is defined as the European business network, since it is mainly represented by MNCs from Europe, especially the 15 mature European Union markets. Since it cannot be taken for granted that relationships are developed and maintained in the same way outside these countries, relationships need to be adapted to how local networks work. This aspect is developed in this chapter by looking closer at how international business networks in the Chinese context function as well as in a Russian context. These are dominating business networks in emerging markets. Differences between them are discussed more thoroughly and explained by viewing them as adaptations to institutional differences based on the institutional network approach. The focus is on the influence from one major institution – the country culture – or the basic rules of this informal rule system, that is norms, values, thought styles and enforcement mechanisms.

Chapter 6 deepens the international aspect of business marketing further by relating it to the internationalization process of firms. Relationships are seen to constitute the core of the internationalization process, whereas internationalization takes place through establishing and maintaining network relationships in foreign environments. Therefore, this chapter focuses on two aspects of the *business marketing strategy in the internationalization process.* The first is the entry strategy or how firms get access to new customers in new geographic markets by marketing their products there. Second, the internationalization strategy takes up how business marketing is globalized by the expansion of the firm to a larger number of countries. Four major strategic business marketing issues are taken up for the entry strategy. They are the major entry modes of trade and FDI; the entry nodes of dyads and triads; the entry roles of seller (exporter), buyer (importer) and producer; and the entry processes of the five stages of handling relationships. This relationship process is integrated into the internationalization process through forming a five/five stages model. Two major strategic aspects of this model of importance for IBM in emerging country markets are thereby developed further: organizational learning of experiential knowledge and psychic distance into institutional distance.

In *Chapter 7*, the organizational aspects of international business marketing are developed more by looking closer at the internal network organization of the MNC. The chapter focuses on the implementation of international business marketing strategy through the *internal network organization of the internationalized firm*. Implementation requires the strategy to be organized properly, whereas organizational aspects on strategy are extended further in this chapter by looking closer at how organizational structures and controls relate to international business marketing strategy. The MNC organization is translated into a network organization. To understand the different types of network organization identified, it is necessary to go more into how the international organization of firms has evolved, that is into the internationalization of the organization. Behind this, in its turn, lies the degree of the internationalization of the company. Thus, continuing from Chapter 6, the responses in the third wave of internationalization noticed between key types of firms are developed further by investigating the end of the traditional internationalization process. Taking up the internationalization of production complements the internationalization of sales and purchases from Chapter 6. Based on such elaborated aspects of internationalization of the major activities of the value chain and the gradually evolving international organization of the firm, a distinction is made between three major types of firms: the domestic firm, the internationalizing firm and the fully internationalized firm. The latter type is further divided into the Ethnocentric MNC, the Polycentric MNC and the Geocentric MNC. Illustrations are given of the internationalization processes of Ethnocentric

Chapter 8 takes up the *local and regional network organization for dyads and triads*. The subsidiary is seen as a central node or hub, through which the subsidiary is connected to the internal MNC network and to dyads in local external networks. To be able to match local IBM strategy and local organization, the MNC organization is studied from below by taking up local organization in emerging country markets both at the country level and the regional level. The trade-off between local adaptation and global integration is analysed as two aspects of the internal network position: loose or tight coupling and direct or indirect control of local external networks. The formation of local network organization for triads is taken up as a growing business marketing organization, being a response to an enlargement of business to an increasing number of countries. The chapter ends with a discussion of three major types of regional network organizations, namely the incorporated regional hub, the administrative regional hub and the diffuse regional hub.

2.   The international business marketing model

The main purpose in this chapter is to establish the international business marketing model to be used for business marketing in emerging country markets. Before the model is introduced, the relevance of existing industrial and relationship marketing theories for business marketing in such markets is evaluated. Initially relevant theories are introduced, the purpose being to give the reader an overview of the business marketing field. Next it is discussed whether such business marketing theories developed for mature industrial markets in Europe and North America can be utilized in emerging country markets.

The two dominating approaches to business marketing theory will be taken up, namely the micro-marketing approach, and the inter-organizational approach. The two approaches will be described and analysed: what they look like today, and how they developed. Recent developments in relationship marketing theory and marketing theory will also be included to evaluate if relevant theories can be found in those fields that are possible to combine with the traditional industrial marketing theories into an integrated business marketing model relevant for emerging country markets. This complementary third field is defined as the relationship marketing approach.

Thereafter, the most relevant group of theories – the inter-organizational approach – is adapted to the markets-in-transition situation by developing it along four aspects: the network aspect, the international aspect, the strategy aspect and the organizational aspect. Finally, the international business marketing model is derived and presented.

MAJOR APPROACHES TO BUSINESS MARKETING

In this section, major business marketing and relationship marketing theories of relevance to emerging country markets are discussed based on the main characteristics of these markets introduced in Chapter 1. Three major approaches are discerned: the micro-marketing approach, the inter-organizational approach and the relationship marketing approach (Jansson, 2006b).

The Micro-marketing Approach

Most research on industrial marketing acknowledges that there are basic differences between the marketing of industrial and consumer products, the main reason often being to motivate industrial marketing as a separate field in marketing. Based on these differences, the industrial marketing research field is divided into two major areas: the micro-marketing approach and the inter-organizational approach. The former builds on the traditional American approach to marketing, while the latter is a more recent European branch of marketing. Based on El-Ansary (1983), this former approach to industrial marketing is defined as the micro-marketing approach (Jansson, 1994a). According to this approach, the differences between industrial and traditional consumer marketing are not so large as to motivate a separate research field in marketing with its own theory and methodology. Industrial and consumer marketing are closely related, and have a common scientific base in economics and behavioural sciences, mainly psychology. For example, both types of marketing are dominated by the marketing management approach or the managerial school (Sheth et al., 1988).

A major impression gained from industrial marketing literature is therefore that most industrial marketing research in the USA is not founded on any theory of its own, mainly because no major differences are seen between the marketing of consumer products and of industrial products. Micro-marketing theory in its conventional form is therefore used in connection with the marketing of both industrial and consumer products. According to El-Ansary (1983), micro-marketing theory involves separate theories on product-brand management, pricing, promotion, physical distribution management, marketing research, financial aspects of marketing and marketing programme productivity. Micro-marketing theory can be contrasted with macro-marketing theory, a theory of consumer behaviour, and with different theories concerning distribution channels. It emphasizes marketing management, which so much dominates research on marketing in North America.

The marketing-mix view

Two different branches of the micro-marketing approach are distinguished: the marketing-mix view and the business-to-business marketing view. The first of these treats quite differing marketing perspectives as being essentially similar, through focusing on what is seen as being universal in the aims of marketing, namely consideration of the individual or organizational needs of the customer; needs which are met through a marketing mix. This is the mainstream view in marketing research. It is defined as the managerial school by Sheth et al., (1988), which they see as one of twelve schools in marketing. The theoretical bases are micro-economic theory and economic psychology theory (Mattsson, 1997). This marketing-mix view dominated in the industrial marketing field up to the end of the 1980s, in particular in the USA. It is clearly seen in various textbooks on industrial marketing management from these days, which strongly reflect research and practice in the industrial field. Industrial marketing textbooks of this genre tended to identify major differences between consumer products and industrial products. Traditional marketing-mix models thus take no basically differing perspective on industrial marketing than to consumer marketing.

The business-to-business marketing view

One implication of the customers being fewer and larger in industrial markets is the importance of the buyer/seller relationship. Some researchers emphasized the importance of relationships early, for example, Webster (1979) and Jackson (1985). However, this view on business marketing started to develop from the beginning of the 1990s, when also the first major journal in the field was launched, namely the *Journal of Business-to-Business Marketing*. It is seen as a separate field in the highly specialized American research on marketing that includes both service marketing and industrial marketing. Even if the focus has changed from the marketing mix to the buyer-seller relationship, no specific relationship marketing theory has been developed. It is more a shift of approach, looking at marketing from another angle. The traditional focus of the micro-marketing approach is still kept on the customer, originating from the new marketing approach as well as on the marketing mix. It has mainly been refocused and altered to fit with the new relationship orientation, which is still largely valid today. As stressed already by Jackson (1985), industrial marketing is to be explicitly focused on the buyer-seller relationship. This involves the need of a special marketing mix, since customers are committed to a few main vendors rather than being able to shift purchases easily from one supplier to another. This industrial marketing literature is largely practically oriented, not being based on any special business marketing or relationship marketing theory. Since it draws heavily on mainstream marketing theory, it is placed within the micro-marketing approach, being clearly separated from the inter-organizational approach, taken up below. This is seen in today's textbooks on business-to-business marketing, which refer very little to or are based on the inter-organizational approach. The exception to this rule is Anderson and Naurus (2004), whose textbook on business marketing management summarizes the state of knowledge within the business-to-business marketing field today in combination with theories from the inter-organizational approach.

The Inter-organizational Approach

According to Håkansson and Snehota (1995) a firm's role, development and performance in industrial product/service markets is explained by its ability to develop relationships. Volumes, market share, profits and growth depend upon how the company handles its relationships. Also most costs and revenues stem from its business relationships. The inter-organizational approach builds on a broad view of relationships, which makes it fundamentally different from most approaches to marketing in general (Sheth et al., 1988), relationship marketing (Sheth and Parvatiyar, 2000) including relationship marketing of services (for example Grönroos, 1995, 2000), as well as business-to-business marketing, in which traditional marketing concepts and tools are applied. Thus, the inter-organizational approach differs much more from the traditional scientific base to marketing by being mainly based on sociology. This is motivated by the fact that differences between industrial marketing and consumer marketing are so large and decisive that another theoretical foundation is required, namely organization theory rather than marketing theory. The reader interested in the basics of the inter-organizational approach is directed to Ford et al. (2006).

Major differences between industrial products and consumer products
A major rationale for the inter-organizational approach is then that the differences between the marketing of industrial products and consumer products are so large and decisive so as to motivate another theoretical approach, and mostly also another methodological stance. The emergence of the inter-organizational approach is very well described in Johanson and Mattsson (2005). It was originally developed in Sweden in the 1970s in close contact between industrial marketing/purchasing research and business practice, where the main research methodology was case studies. The discovery that the prevailing marketing theory did not fit with the actual practice in the industrial marketing field led to a broad search for other theories, also outside the marketing field. One reason for this was institutional. The organization of the business departments at the Swedish universities was open, and was not split up into subunits such as a marketing department, a finance department, etc. Another reason was the Swedish research in marketing in those days. In the early 1970s:

> research on industrial marketing in Sweden was based on earlier research about inter-organizational structures and change in distribution systems and industries and emerging observations of the nature of supplier-customer relations on international markets. (Johanson and Mattsson, 2005, p. 6)

The major differences between industrial product markets and consumer product markets normally referred to within the inter-organizational approach are as follows (Jansson, 1994a). A first major difference concerns market structure, for example markets for industrial products mostly being more concentrated than markets for consumer products. A second major difference in the marketing of the two types of products is that dependencies between buyers, sellers and competitors are stronger in the case of industrial products, especially in the vertical dimension, for example it being important for a supplier to also know about the purchasing behaviour of the customers' customers. These dependencies are represented in industrial marketing theory in various ways, being expressed, for example, in terms of networks which involve both vertical and horizontal dimensions. The buyer-seller relationships are closer and the distribution channels more direct in industrial than in consumer marketing. A third major difference between the two types of markets is that for industrial markets interrelationships between parties are more stable and long-term. Various studies have shown that the industrial structure in many European countries is rather rigid, with a marked preponderance of large companies. For industrial markets, geographical concentration tends to be greater, the number of customers to be fewer, and the individual customer to be larger in size than for consumer markets, the competition often being oligopolistic instead of monopolistic. A fourth dissimilarity between the two markets has to do with the type of demand. Industrial needs are generally more complex and sophisticated, in particular from an engineering point of view, than are the needs for consumer products. The awareness of these needs and means of fulfilling them tend to be organized in a more professional way in industrial markets. The buyers are firms, not individuals. For this and the other reasons just mentioned, sellers are confronted with a different demand situation than in consumer markets, as seen, for example, in the buying process, which is far more complex in the case of the professional buyer.

The interaction aspect
Based on major differences like these, and the finding that the marketing practice of the large successful Swedish international industrial companies differed from practice according to the marketing-mix view, led to the development of a new approach to industrial marketing. It was originally developed by the industrial marketing group (IM-Group) at the Department of Business Administration, Uppsala University, and was later taken up by some researchers in England, Germany and France. These researchers soon came together in what was later to become the first joint European research programme on industrial marketing and purchasing (IMP1). The results of the industrial marketing research of this first period are best summarized in the interaction model found in Håkansson, (1982). The inter-organizational approach is strongly sociological in its orientation (see, for instance, Håkansson and Östberg, 1975; Håkansson, 1982; Johanson and Mattsson 1987a,b). Originally it was applied to buyer-seller relationships between European firms (Hallén and Johanson, 1989), but was later extended to firms from Asia, North America and Australia (Håkansson and Snehota, 2000). Still, the inter-organizational approach has not spread much beyond Western Europe, which is also confirmed by Johanson and Mattsson (2005).

While most of the initial frameworks developed within the inter-organizational approach are structural, a process model for how relationships evolve was developed by Ford (1980). Buyer-seller relationships over time are separated into five stages, where the first stage takes up marketing activities before the relationship begins. The next three stages show how direct buyer-seller relationships are established – their beginning and deepening – and the final stage is about the termination of relationships. This evolvement of relationships is described according to a number of factors, for example how the experience, learning, commitment and adaptations of the parties increase, and how the various distances and uncertainties between them are reduced. The variable experience indicates the amount of experience the respective parties have of each other. Both parties will judge their partner's commitment to the relationship. Commitment is to a large extent shown by the willingness to make adaptations. The variable distance is multifaceted and can be split into the following types of distance: social, cultural, technological, time and geographical distance. Uncertainty deals with the fact that at the initial stages, it is difficult to assess the potential rewards and costs of the relationship.

The network aspect

At the end of the 1970s, the need for a larger perspective on relationships was felt, since it was demonstrated over and over again that the direct buyer-seller relationships were influenced by indirect relationships, for instance the buyer's customer relationships or the suppliers' supplier relationships. The network aspect of industrial markets started to be developed, where relationships are seen to evolve through interactions within industrial networks. Instead of the research being mainly focused on dyadic relationships, it was extended to sets of links within networks. This development can be explained from the specific market structures prevailing in Western Europe in those days. One major characteristic was that they were more imperfect or closed than in the US market. Industrial economics theory, which became popular in the 1970s, was used to explain this difference. However, it was found to be insufficient, mainly because it is based on the analysis of one industry, while relationships took place between firms from different industries. Inspired by transaction-cost theory, especially Williamson (1975, 1979), and to some extent systems theory, the 'Markets-as-Networks Approach' (Mattsson, 1997) was developed as an intermediate market form between the neoclassical pure market and the hierarchy. In Swedish research, the first major publications with this new network approach to industrial marketing came in 1982 (Johanson and Mattsson, 2005).

The network aspect is described according to the three major divisions made in industrial marketing theory between networks as relationships, as structures and as a process (Easton, 1992). In the first case, the focus is on the relationships of the network, for instance what they look like, how they are established, or whether they are direct or indirect. Network structure concerns the number of links and the degree to which the organizations are linked to each other. Relationship processes are divided into sub-processes, where each process consists of a number of stages or phases. Network relationships also concern flows or processes, for example the sequence over time of particular activities or that the nodes are connected to each other over time in a specific way. The inter-organizational approach is limited to business relationships and rarely includes the non-market relationship aspect or ancillary connections as they are defined by Blankenburg and Johanson (1992), for instance government and other stakeholders in the social environment. Exceptions are Jansson et al. (1995) and Jansson (2002, 2006a, 2007).

The most developed industrial network model so far is the activities-resources-actors (ARA) model founded by Håkansson and Johanson (1992). The model mainly focuses on dyadic relationships but also on network structure in the form of sets of links within networks. In the latter case, the relationship focus is mostly kept by regarding the network as a number of direct (the dyadic aspect) and indirect relationships (the network aspect) (for example Andersson et al., 1994). Dyads are connected to three major types of networks: activity patterns of links, resource constellations of ties and webs of actor bonds (Håkansson and Snehota, 1995).

For network processes past conditions are essential for the understanding of present and future network relationships, and where a network structure at one point in time is a residue of diverse past processes. This is most obvious in emerging markets or transition economies, where change is more pronounced than stability. For instance, it becomes important to study various types of change in networks and at what levels they take place as well as different search and discovery processes for customers and suppliers (Johanson, 2001).

The main concepts of the inter-organizational approach
The main concepts of the inter-organizational approach can now be summarized and illustrated in Figure 2.1, which mainly builds on Johanson and Mattsson (1987b, p. 38) but also on Snehota (1990), Håkansson and Snehota (1995), and Ford et al. (2006). The buyer-seller relationship model involved concerns marketing and purchasing behaviour. Both the various exchange processes through which relationships develop and the adaptation processes that take place between parties in the continuous evolvement of relationships, for instance through product modifications, changes in production, delivery routines and other behavioural rules, are analysed. The central idea is that the establishment of relationships creates bonds and dependencies between the parties involved, which make relationships continuous and stable. The more intensive processes of exchange become, the stronger the reasons are for adapting to each other and not replacing the other party. A mutual orientation is created which results in a preparedness to interact in a dyad. Change takes place within the relationship rather than of relationships with other parties. A mutual knowledge of and respect for each other's interests is established, which leads to cooperation and solution of conflicts. Mutuality is thus clearly characteristic of business relationships. This reciprocity is largely shaped by social exchange processes but also by business and information exchange. One reason behind the complexity of relationships is these different types of exchange. Another is the many organizational units and large number of persons normally involved. Different forms of investments in relationships shape the future behaviour of the parties involved, since they affect the parties' access to resources. It is less expensive to trade with companies with which one has relationships than those with which one has none. Aiming at establishing linkages involves realization of the fact that resources are heterogeneous. The same line of

reasoning can be applied both to dyadic relationships and to networks of relationships. In the latter case, in particular, it can have a strong systemic impact on the marketing and purchasing possibilities of the firm involved. The firm's interactions are strongly affected by the access it has to resources from different types of networks. For example, how a seller interacts with its buyers depends partly on how the two-party relationships involved are connected to other, indirect linkages within the network or networks to which the seller has access, for instance influencing how the seller relates to its suppliers. Competitive strength is likewise affected by relationships. Within a given network different macro positions (relating to the whole network) and different micro positions (relating to given dyads) can be distinguished (Johanson and Mattsson, 1987b).

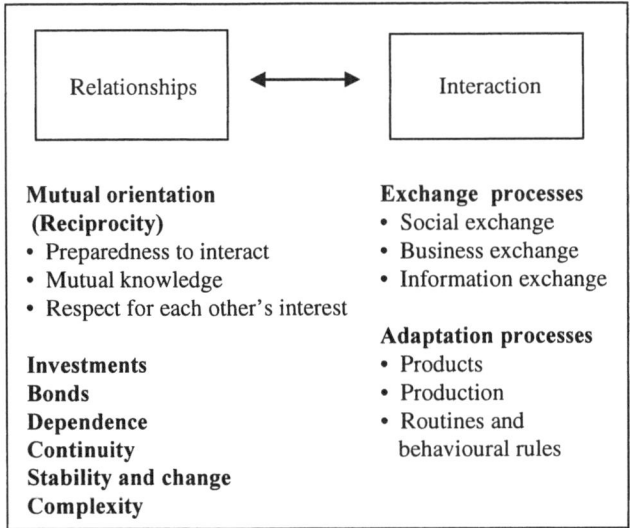

Figure 2.1   The main concepts of the inter-organizational approach (based on Johanson and Mattsson, 1987b)

A fundamental ingredient of the inter-organizational approach is social exchange theory (Blau, 1964). However, this theory often tends to be employed in the same way in analysing interpersonal as in analysing inter-organizational exchange. As Blau (1987) observed, it is dangerous to transfer concepts from a theory developed for social exchange between persons at the micro level to social exchange between organizations at the macro level.

Objectives of individual organizations are reached by participating in various networks. This leads to dependency on other networks and subjects an organization to the manipulations and influence of other organizations outside its sphere of control. This dependency creates uncertainty, inter alia concerning the organization's capacity to acquire reliable and adequate resources to attain its goals, for example to keep up its competitive position. Management of this uncertainty without losing organizational autonomy is a chief concern for individual units within a network.

Resources are a key factor behind these concepts of the inter-organizational approach, where they, inter alia, are used to explain power-dependence relations based on social exchange theory (Emerson, 1962; Pfeffer and Salancik, 1978; Cook and Emerson, 1984). This approach to resources still dominates the inter-organizational approach, which, inter alia, is seen in how strategic issues are taken up. The inter-organizational approach deals with strategy, for instance Snehota (1990), Axelsson (1992), Håkansson and Snehota (1995), Ford (2002), and resources are the basic factors of the ARA model. This corresponds to Gulati et al. (2000), who stress that the relationships in which firms are embedded profoundly influence their conduct and performance, whereas firms are more properly viewed as connected to each other in multiple strategic networks of resources and other flows. Still, the dominant strategy theory developed during the last 20 years has not been incorporated, that is the resource-based view. The main reason for this seems to be that this view is based on economics, which conflicts with the sociology base of the approach, for example expressed through its base in exchange theory and power-dependency (Axelsson and Easton, 1992; Håkansson and Johanson, 1992; Håkansson and Snehota, 1995; Ford et al 1998; Ford, 2002).

The inter-organizational approach has had little influence on business-to-business marketing in the USA. This is seen from the ten year index of articles published 1993-2003 in the *Journal of Business-to-Business Marketing*. Of the large number of articles published during these ten years, only twelve articles have an inter-organizational approach, of which six were written by American researchers.

The Relationship Marketing Approach

Business marketing according to the inter-organizational approach is a kind of relationship marketing. It fits well into Morgan and Hunt's (1994, p. 22) inclusive definition that 'relationship marketing refers to all marketing activities directed toward establishing, developing, and maintaining successful relationships'. It describes a certain approach to marketing focusing on cooperative relationships between the firm and its different marketing actors. Thus, relationship marketing encompasses business relationships in general and not only customer relationships, which is the more common approach (Parvatiyar and Sheth, 2000). Scholars involved in marketing of services often have such a narrow view of relationship marketing concentrating on customer relationships (for example Grönroos, 1995, 2000). The basis of marketing is the customer, irrespective of how many factors outside and inside markets are considered, that is how broad the marketing system is. Change in customer behaviour is a main factor behind the shift from transaction marketing to relationship marketing (Sheth and

Parvatiyar, 1995). This paradigm change is well summarized by El-Ansary (2004) as a change from transactional selling to relationship marketing (see Table 2.1).

Table 2.1   Transactional selling versus relationship marketing

Transactional selling	Relationship marketing
Emphasis on getting new customers	Emphasis on keeping customers as well as getting new ones
Short-term orientation	Long-term orientation
Interest in making a single sale	Interest in multiple sales and enduring relationships
Limited commitment to customers	High level of ongoing commitment to customers
Research on customer needs used to complete one transaction	Continuing research on customers needs to enhance relationship
Success means making a sale	Success means customer loyalty and low customer turnover
Quality in production concern	Quality is every employee's concern
Limited service commitment	High degree of service commitment

Source: El-Ansary (2004).

The description of relationship marketing according to this table matches well the emerging service-centred dominant marketing logic developed in Vargo and Lusch (2004). Six of their eight foundational premises match El-Ansary's factors in the table, namely:

1. Indirect exchange masks the fundamental unit of exchange (increased specialization of work means that fewer people have direct customer contacts, whereas direct interaction is more and more replaced by indirect exchange.) Still, money, goods, organizations and vertical marketing systems are only the exchange vehicles for services.
2. Goods are distribution mechanisms for service provision (they are platforms for meeting higher-order needs).
3. All economies are service economies (the common denominator of the economy is the increased refinement and exchange of knowledge and skills or operant resources).

4. The customer is always a co-producer (in using a product, the customer is continuing the marketing, consumption, and value-creation and delivery processes).
5. The enterprise can only make value propositions (a product, for example, is embedded with knowledge that has value potential for the intended consumer).
6. A service-centred view is customer oriented and relational (interactivity, integration, customization and co-production are the hallmarks of a service-centred view and its inherent focus on the customer and the relationship).

The two remaining premises add the resources behind marketing:

7. The application of specialized skills and knowledge is the fundamental unit of exchange (the focus is on the 'value in use' and not on the 'exchange value').
8. Knowledge is the fundamental source of competitive advantage (operant resources, especially the use of knowledge and competences, are at the heart of competitive advantage and performance).

These two latter foundational premises build on the integration of the resource-based view into marketing strategy, mainly inspired by Day (1994), and Hunt and Morgan (1995). The integration of relationship marketing with the firm's resource base in this emerging marketing logic opens up possibilities to relate the international business marketing framework developed in this book to developments in marketing theory in general. This possibility is especially promising when these approaches are related to the broad stream of research on relationship marketing, for example service management research on value constellations (Normann and Ramirez, 1993; Normann, 2001). Here, the main reason to establish and maintain relationships is to service the needs of various business partners, for instance customers, suppliers, government units and various non-governmental organizations. Wealth is obtained through the application and exchange of specialized knowledge and skills, and where the business partners are active participants in relational exchanges and co-production. This is a value constellation established for the temporary task of marketing a product/service package involving a certain combination of competences, for instance a group of actors representing different units that work together to create value for the customer. It implies that interdependent marketing activities link actors and their competences together.

Thus, the business-to-business marketing view fits with this relationship marketing development, even with the narrow stream of relationship marketing research. It matches both El-Ansary (2004) and Vargo and Lusch's (2004) foundational premises. For instance, this approach is customer focused and based on an integration of industrial marketing and service marketing in the same way as consumer marketing is integrated with service marketing. This is a major conclusion from Parvatiyar and Sheth (2000), who see relationship marketing as a new school in marketing or Vargo and Lusch (2004), who develop a new dominant logic for marketing. These developments can be seen as an addition to the twelve schools earlier identified by Sheth et al. (1988).

EVALUATION

Judging from Sheth and Parvatiyar (2000), El-Ansary (2004) and Vargo and Lusch (2004), relationship marketing mainly belongs to the narrow stream of research, since it builds on more traditional marketing thinking as represented by the managerial (marketing management) school and the (consumer) behaviour school. The inter-organizational approach, however, is more related to the systems school and the organizational dynamics school, which deal with relationships between organizations. It is founded more on inter-organizational theory focusing on the marketing issues between organizations and not on organizations and individuals as in the mainstream marketing theories dealing with marketing of products and services to consumers.

Mattsson (1997) identifies major similarities and differences between relationship marketing and the inter-organizational approach. The similarities are that the relationship is of value, that values are created through relationships and that the time dimension of the individual relationships are important. The basic difference is that the inter-organizational approach is characterized by relationships being embedded in a social structure, mainly a specific market structure in the form of networks (Granovetter, 1985). Relationship marketing, on the other hand, does not normally consider this macro dimension, but is a 'taken-for granted' marketing to actors in traditional markets, mainly related to the interests of the selling firm. Thus, relationship marketing is mainly a broadening of the micro-marketing approach to the major marketing theories identified by El-Ansary (1983), but which has not yet integrated with macro-marketing theory.

The strong focus on the customer of most of the other marketing theories discussed above is too narrow a focus for the inter-organizational approach, particularly if the purpose is to develop this approach to be more suitable to international business marketing in emerging markets. These country markets are not market societies in the European or North American sense. In embedded societies, where 'everything influences everything', it is hard to separate the marketing system from the rest of society. More stakeholders are involved in the system and relationships are more personal and embedded rather than impersonal and confined to business alone. The business approach to relationship marketing taken in this book therefore relates to other broad approaches such as the 'multiple markets' perspective that includes relationship marketing in a number of different markets: besides customer and intermediary markets also supplier and alliance markets, referral markets and influence markets, internal markets and recruitment markets (Peck et al.,

1997, 1999; Payne, 2000). A similar approach is also taken by Gummesson (1995), who identifies and analyses 30 different types of business relationships.

However, the approach to business marketing of this book relates mainly to the IMP perspective (Håkansson and Snehota, 2000). This inter-organizational approach to relationship marketing is preferred, since it stresses the general business relationship aspect rather than any particular type of relationship, for example customer or supplier relationships. The main reason is that it builds on both organization theory and marketing theory compared to most of the relationship marketing discussed above, which is an offspring from traditional marketing theory. Most relationship marketing theories are therefore not relevant for business marketing in emerging country markets. A broader approach such as the inter-organizational approach is needed, focusing on the marketing between organizations and not on organizations and individuals as in the mainstream marketing theories dealing with marketing of consumer products and services.

THE INTERNATIONAL BUSINESS MARKETING MODEL DEVELOPED

The inter-organizational approach is found to be the most suitable for business marketing in emerging country markets. Still, it is under-developed regarding the four aspects and needs to be complemented to fully consider them. The network aspect, the international aspect, the strategic aspect and the organizational aspect of this approach are therefore developed next as a strategy model for international business marketing relevant for emerging country markets. It is illustrated in Figure 2.2.

The network aspect is grounded in the basic networks model, where the MNC, markets and society are described from a network perspective (Jansson, 2007). The model illustrates international business marketing strategy taking place through network relations between the MNC network and some of its major external parties in local market networks such as the product/service market network and the government network. Financial market networks and labour market networks are also indicated in the model.

The international aspect that mainly concerns differences between business environments is also developed based on Jansson (2007). The business context influences how MNCs interact, thus providing underlying reasons for differences between relationships. According to the model, the MNC is operating in a number of local market networks, which in their turn are surrounded by macro factors. These factors specify the international aspect of the model. The international environment is turned into a playing field consisting of institutions, where markets and societies are looked upon as rule systems that the MNC and other network actors follow. The rules concern basic conditions for how marketing and purchasing relationships are organized. Networks are therefore influenced by 'macro rules', for example formal foreign direct investment rules decided by government; informal rules like customs originating from the culture of a country; 'relationships rights' expressed as systems of property rights and other legal rules such as judicial and penal systems. Other examples of important 'macro rules' originate from other societal sectors, for example family, clan, ethnicity, religion, culture, political systems in general, trades unions, business associations and business morale. The state holds a special position, since it participates both directly in the network and indirectly, by being seen as a separate rule system outside the network influencing relationships. In a similar way, religious norms might encourage or inhibit incentives for innovation and entrepreneurial activities. This is also true of rule systems more proximate to the firm in which actors are embedded, that is markets. The rule systems of a specific market might facilitate or hinder business marketing moves to be implemented.

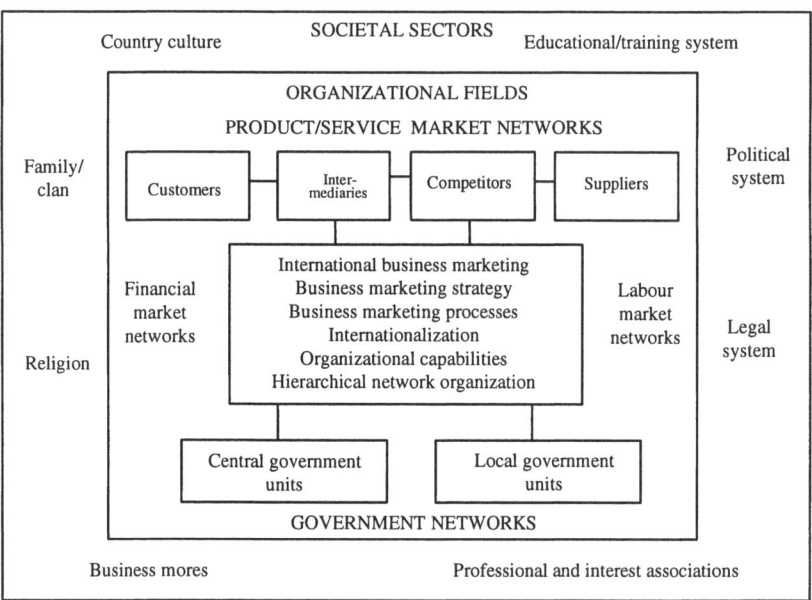

Figure 2.2   The international business marketing model

Thus, the external environment is defined as consisting of a number of rule systems or institutions. As a consequence, business marketing is directed at identifiable actors in specific organizational fields, for example product/service markets (mainly customers and competitors), financial markets and government. Such bridging strategies between actors, by establishing agreements through relationships, are influenced by institutional factors in organizational fields and societal sectors. There is interplay among business marketing and institutions, where institutions are influencing business marketing as well as being influenced by business marketing. Institutions represent broad categories or constraints for how business marketing is formed and implemented. Business marketing therefore bridges gaps at three levels: organizations, organizational fields and societal sectors.

Internal networks organize the resources and the capabilities of the interacting parties. Such local and regional networks condition business marketing by their ability to shape the outcome, for example competitive advantages in product/service markets. Resources together with activities and actors are then basic factors of the international business marketing model.

Institutions and Networks

Society is divided into different social groupings characterized by different regularities or rules. Such a grouping forms an institution of its own, where behaviour follows the specific rules inherent in it. This behaviour is not only influenced by such inside rules but also by those of outside social groupings. How one part of society is organized is therefore influenced by how other parts of society are organized. The institutional approach captures the major characteristics of emerging country markets: the embeddedness of groupings at different societal levels and how they are related.

According to Jansson (2007), institutions are carried over by being learned, consciously or unconsciously, by individuals. An institutional arrangement is chosen and, as a consequence, mediated through participation. Institutions therefore constitute a behavioural repertoire for individuals. Institutions are rigid collectives that largely change independently of what specific individuals know and how they use knowledge. A first main characteristic of institutions is therefore their rule-like or organizing nature. A second characteristic is their ability to facilitate and constrain the relations among individuals and groups. Third, institutions are signified by predictability. They standardize behaviour and transfer rules, norms and ways of thinking between individuals. Behaviour following on from them is repeated over time, meaning that behavioural regularities also are valid for future situations. Uncertainty is reduced by anticipation of repeated behaviour. These factors make institutions excellent instruments for describing, explaining and predicting actual organizational behaviour, thereby reducing uncertainty and risks in international business marketing. The reproduction procedure and the resulting established patterns of behaviour imply stability.

Since networks are impacted by institutions, different institutional environments cause different network forms to evolve. There are two levels of network environments or institutions in which companies and networks are embedded: organizational fields and societal sectors. Examples of societal sectors are the political system and the country culture. Culture is seen as an important institutional complex at this societal level, since it influences organizational patterns at the network level. Network relationships are therefore embedded in certain societal sectors, for example the educational system, the legal system, professional and interest organizations, and culture. The importance of cultural influences is shown in the model by dividing culture into four factors: country culture, family/clan, religion and business mores (morale). International business marketing is also influenced by different commercial actors in the product/service market and other markets as well as major interest groups in the broader societal environment, for example various actors in the government sector. These market networks and the government network are also seen from an institutional point of view as organizational fields. This means that actors in a market share certain values, norms (Heide and John, 1992), or ways of thinking (thought styles). For example a basic value for actors in product/service market network is profitability, while a common value in the government network is legitimacy. The main motive behind business marketing towards actors in markets is then mainly a response to profit motives, while the main motive with IBM towards actors outside markets such as in government is to respond to policy.

Institutions are viewed as different kinds of rules that govern business marketing in a certain country market. The MNC and its network actors in markets and government are influenced by 'macro rules' in societal sectors surrounding these networks, for example systems of property rights and other legal rules such as judicial and penal systems. Other examples of important rules systems are culture, political systems in general, trades unions, business associations and business mores and conventions. The state is a collective network actor that is in direct contact with the MNC, and an institutional structure outside the network, influencing IBM indirectly. An example of the latter case is national and local laws and regulations. In a similar way, religious norms or rules might encourage or inhibit incentives for innovation and entrepreneurial activities.

Basic rules
Behaviour is governed by four major rules found within an institution of the type mentioned above, namely norms, values, thought styles or cognitive factors, and enforcement mechanisms or regulations. They are defined as basic rules and are external to networks impacting IBM. Basic rules such as valuations, norms and cognitive structures in organizational fields are therefore influenced by such basic rules of societal sectors, for example the national culture of the country. Basic rules are a key part of the institutional perspective of the institutional network approach developed in Jansson (2007). The MNC is also defined as an institution. Because of its multicultural basis, it consists of many thought worlds, for example, where cognitive systems tend to vary between its various units. Those employees sharing thoughts, making classifications and labelling reality have a unified thought style. Their common frame of reference works as guidelines for sense making and action. These established thought styles therefore work as cognitive recipes for how people behave. They produce a self-activated regular organizational behaviour. Norms and values also influence how people think and act. Values are the root of cultures and behaviour, defined

as 'conceptions of the preferred' and as standards for comparison, for example good or bad, right or wrong. They set the priorities and function as guiding principles. Norms, on the other hand, specify how things should be done. They work as guiding principles for how to act, a kind of decree about how one should act or how something should be constituted or organized. Organizational behaviour is also controlled by incentives and sanctions. Such enforcement mechanisms concern how to construct the sanction and incentive system in order to reward or punish individuals and groups within the MNC together with establishing surveillance and assessment system to control its enforcement.

The Institutional Network Approach

The institutional aspect is included in the international business marketing strategy model to develop the international aspect. It is used as a classification system for the marketing environment, among other things making it easier to compare the business environments of various emerging country markets. These contexts can also be related to each other, for example by defining an institutional distance between buyers and sellers in different countries. The institutional aspect is also included, since it is possible to use to explain network behaviour. The direction, spread and substance of relationships in and between organizations are then determined by institutional factors. The institutional aspect is based on a new perspective to international business marketing, which is called the institutional network approach (Jansson, 2007). Networks could for example have a public aspect and be accountable to an audience of external actors through some kind of public 'score' or legitimacy. Efficiency is another rationality typical of certain actors in an organizational field. It is based on a profit rationale and is the main orientation in markets. This is expressed in the following way by Meyer and Scott (1983, p. 140):

> Networks operate in institutional sectors characterized by the elaboration of rules and requirements to which individual organizations must conform if they are to receive support and legitimacy from the environment. Technical sectors are those within which a product or service is exchanged in a market such that organizations are rewarded for effective and efficient control of the work process.

Thus, there are for example common rules for the whole market system in a country, leading to a certain type of competition. MNCs, for example, usually operate simultaneously in such a technical sector demanding efficiently produced outcomes as well as in other institutional sectors, for example government. General efficiency and legitimacy grounds often coincide, since efficiency is based on legitimacy-based rules. Networks of organizations, which are embedded in various organizational fields, are also influenced by other external institutional complexes 'higher up', mainly by societal sectors.

The Strategy and Organizational Aspects

The MNC is embedded in a great number of market-related relationships, whereas business marketing in product/service markets or financial markets deals with relationships towards market actors. One consequence of this relatedness is that marketing strategy is interactive, and the MNC responds to various activities of other organizations found in the external framework. However, business marketing strategy towards actors in the social environment is also important in emerging country markets, for example towards stakeholders outside the market. The goals of these stakeholders are not primarily economic but social, implying that they operate according to another rationale than market actors. For the firm's marketing, this means that in markets it is primarily a question of satisfying economic goals by promoting efficient relationships. Outside the market, however, the underlying issue is to satisfy social goals by being legitimate in the eyes of the stakeholders. Such legitimacy-based business marketing strategy is fully covered in Jansson (2007).

The definition of marketing strategy also builds on that book, where business marketing strategy plus matching strategies are deduced. The institutional perspective and the network perspective are combined to form an institutional network approach, in which the MNC and its environment are looked at as institutions and networks, stressing that the MNC is embedded in its institutional network environment. International business strategy is about finding a relevant mix between business marketing strategy and matching strategy to achieve a sustainable competitive advantage in the external setting of the MNC consisting of organizational fields and societal sectors. Competitive advantage can thereby be achieved in efficiency-based environments, while the advantage in legitimacy-based environments is defined as societal advantage.

A sustainable competitive advantage in emerging country markets is in turn accomplished through having a suitable mix of competitive and societal advantages. This mix is created from the internal setting of the MNC that consists of resources and capabilities organized through the internal organization composed of the local/regional organization and the global organization.

Major International Business Marketing Factors

The major factors of the IBM model based on the four aspects are specified further in this section based on Figure 2.3. One group of factors concerns business marketing strategy, where network strategy, linkage strategy and competitive strategy form three basic sub-strategies. A second group of factors relates to the business marketing process, which is divided into the relationship process, the marketing process, and the product/service process. A third group of factors relates to the international dimension of business marketing strategy, namely entry strategy and the internationalization of business marketing and firms. A fourth group of factors concerns the resources and capabilities behind the IBM strategy and processes, namely network capability profiles and trustworthiness. A fifth group of factors is about how business strategy and strategic processes are organized into various type of hierarchical networks at the group, regional and local levels as well as in the form of action and organization networks. These factors are described briefly below and used throughout the book.

Figure 2.3   Major factors of international business marketing

Business marketing strategy

The network strategy is about how the MNC relates itself to the whole market network, inclusive of buyers, distributors, competitors, suppliers and financiers. The linkage strategy, on the other hand, concerns how the seller creates and maintains direct relationships with individual parties within the network. The competitive strategy, finally, primarily focuses on networks involving competitors. Unlike the linkage strategy, it does not involve direct relationships with parties, rather the position the seller takes or possesses in the competitors' network. It concentrates on how competitive the product/service is. This means that the competitive strategy relates to the horizontal market network, while the linkage strategy involves the vertical market network.

Business marketing processes
Three network processes are distinguished: the relationship process, the marketing process and the product/service process. The relationship process is split up into various stages, starting with the pre-relationship stage and ending with the final stage. The marketing process concerns the time order of the type of exchange or the activities going on within the network, for instance marketing and influencing activities. This process is divided into a number of cycles and phases, where the number of cycles will vary with type of marketing activity. In such cases, how relationships develop and persist and what the marketing activities look like over time depend on type of product exchanged. This means that network processes also vary with what is exchanged; in product/service markets it is the main type of product. This major content of the relationships in turn depends on the need satisfied or the type of solution demanded. This is the product/service process, which is about how the exchange of solutions (products/services) for customer needs is organized over time. It is divided into a number of periods. The more complex the product/service, the longer this process is, and the more periods exist. The exchange process for large projects, for example, consists of four periods: the formation period, the bidding period, the execution period and the termination period. Marketing and product/service processes are mainly relevant in connection with the selling of projects.

Thus the relationship process is divided into a number of stages, the marketing process into a number of cycles and the product/service process into a number of periods. Collective action according to these three processes occurs through the mobilization of various actors and resources. In project marketing, for example, action networks are formed around project teams, through which the resources and capabilities are mobilized.

Entry strategy
Internationalization is divided into two aspects: entry strategy and internationalization process. When entering a local market network, four major factors are critical for the business marketing strategy. The entry mode has to do with what kind of organization the firm has during the initial period in the foreign market, for example a subsidiary, joint venture or using an outside organization such as an agent or distributor. The entry node relates to how the MNC plugs into the local market network, whether it sells directly to the customers or indirectly through a dealer or agent. The entry process concerns how relationships are established and maintained with actors of importance to the firm. The entry role relates to what commercial role the MNC plays the local network: seller, buyer and/or manufacturer.

Internationalization process
Internationalization processes take up how business marketing and firms spread between emerging country markets, regionally and globally, that is the overall internationalization process of the firm. Based on the experiential knowledge process, internationalization processes are often divided into

different degrees of internationalization or stages. During the first stage, firms have a domestic market focus. Next follows the pre-export stage, when the firm evaluates the possibilities to start exporting. The third stage is experimental export, when exporting is a marginal activity. The fourth stage is active involvement, when international business is a normal activity, for example an important share of the turnover is exported. A suitable organization structure is also in place for this activity. The fifth and last stage involves committed involvement in exporting. The firm can now be called international, since it is heavily involved in markets abroad.

Network capability profiles

Business marketing strategy is incomplete without taking up the resources and capabilities that the firm has at its disposal. What resources and capabilities can be mobilized in the emerging market to execute the IBM strategy? The key role for marketing and gaining competitive advantages played by the organizational capabilities of the firm was stressed above, for example as the key foundational premise of the emerging dominant marketing logic (Vargo and Lusch, 2004). The IBM strategy is effectuated through its organizational capabilities, shaped by its resources and constrained by its external environments. Four network capability profiles provide the connection between the external and the internal network. A customer specialist has a competence to tailor make customer solutions by operating through specialized networks, while a product specialist solve problems customers have in common through having direct and more standardized network linkages. Two major types of competence relates to intermediaries. A distribution specialist can deal with customers both directly and indirectly through a distribution network, while a distributor network specialist has a competence to cater more for the problems of distributors, through which there is an indirect and often distant coupling to the customer.

The network capability profile influences the possible range of entry strategies open to an MNC, for example if it should enter through an agent or a subsidiary, that is what entry mode to select. In the former situation, it is a question of establishing indirect relationships to the customers via the intermediary, for which a distributor network specialist capability is required. In the latter situation, it could be a question of going for direct relationships with customers through establishing an own entry node in the form of a distribution network, for which a distribution specialist capability is required.

Trustworthiness

Establishing trustful relationships is a critical part of IBM strategy, whereas trustworthiness becomes a key ingredient of every network capability profile. The term trustworthiness signifies that trust is defined as a capability of the firm (Jansson, 2007). Trustworthiness is a major norm of the social capital that constitutes a social organizational capability established from the resource base of the firm in the form of relationships. It also gives the capacity to have and develop new relationships with other parties. This norm or behavioural rule expresses an established ability to behave in a certain way. This is relational trust, which is defined as one party's trust in the other party, who is perceived as trustworthy. This distinction between trust and trustworthiness builds on Hardin (2002). Trustworthiness is a major norm in the social organization of the network. Being a trustworthy seller, for example, creates expectations by the buyer that the seller behaves in a specific way, for example producing reliable products. That the seller can be trusted also makes the buyer act in a certain way towards the seller. Trust and trustworthiness are mutual, since the trustworthiness of one party results in the other party trusting that party. Trustworthiness is therefore possible to define as a capability. The behaviour following from this ability to be trustworthy takes place through network relationships. Since relationships are used for trustful actions, they can be defined as kind of resource. Thus, the social capital consisting of relationships-based norms is divided into social resources in the form of relationships and social capabilities in the form of trustworthiness.

Trustworthiness is related to the social organization of the network, where a distinction is made between organizational trustworthiness and individual trustworthiness. Organizational trustworthiness concerns the organization, while individual trustworthiness occurs between persons.

Hierarchical network organization
How IBM strategy is executed depends upon how the network is organized. The internal network organization of the firm is described as a hierarchical network. A distinction is made between the basic organization of the MNC, which is defined as an organization network, and the organization of projects, which is defined as action networks.

A network where the authority is directly present within the network controlling it, is defined as a hierarchical network. The opposite is the arms-length network, where relations are formed to facilitate concerted action on the part of autonomous organizations in situations where there is no formal authority to impose coordination, for example relationships between buyers and sellers in market networks. When the authority is the backbone of the network, type of authority and execution of authority becomes vital. This approach, where the MNC consists of exchange relationships among organizational units, is a relatively recent phenomenon (Ghoshal and Bartlett, 1990; Forsgren and Pahlberg, 1991; Jansson et al., 1995; Forsgren et al., 2006). One main advantage with a network approach, stressed by Ghoshal and Bartlett (1990), is that the contingency aspect of the MNC organization can be developed considerably by combining an internal network with its various external networks. This is a main departure from the tradition of seeing the MNC as a unitary organization operating in highly simplified environments. It is also important to study how specific external networks are connected to the internal MNC network. This is a further development of how institutional environments influence the structure and behaviour of organizations (Meyer and Scott, 1983).

One main argument for using a network approach to study MNC organization is the importance of informal organization or emergent network organization. Several studies have demonstrated organizational variables or internal management processes to change more often than formal structure (for instance Prahalad and Doz, 1987; Bartlett and Ghoshal, 1989). This might be so. However, the organization structure prescribed by impersonal authority forming a hierarchical authority system is still the most important control of subsidiary action. A corollary is that both this type of formal structure and internal management processes are important, which is also a logical conclusion from a network perspective. Such an approach broadens the study even more by including the external network. Such a combination of internal and external networks is a most neglected aspect in organizational studies of MNCs (Ghoshal and Bartlett, 1990).

Due to how various types of hierarchical networks have developed internationally, a distinction is made between three types of internationally developed hierarchies: the Ethnocentric MNC, the Polycentric MNC and the Geocentric MNC. These fully internationalized major types of firms are contrasted to the internationalizing firm and the domestic firm, which is entirely operating on the home market. Still the focus of the international organization of the firm is not on the group network but on the local and regional organization networks, in particular on the development process of the regional network organization.

A distinction is made between action and organization networks (Aldrich and Whetten, 1981; Jansson et al., 1995). The action network is a temporary set of units or a project organization which has been established out of different units in the organization network for a specific purpose, for example to solve and transfer a customer solution. The organization network is thus a larger more permanent social structure or the 'ordinary' hierarchical network of the firm, from which members are drawn for participation in temporary action networks. When the task of this arm's length network is completed, the action network is dissolved, the units remaining in the organization network awaiting formation of future action networks.

CONCLUSIONS

The major result of the evaluation is that the inter-organizational approach is the most relevant basis for developing the business marketing framework valid in emerging country markets, since it builds on a broad view to relationships. Business marketing is here viewed as an inter-organizational matter and both marketing and buying behaviour are treated as organizational issues. Interaction takes place between the two parties to this relationship or between several parties in a market network. The network aspect is described according to three major divisions made between networks as relationships, as structures and as processes.

The inter-organizational approach and the business-to-business marketing view are part of the fundamental change in marketing from transaction to relationship marketing. They are developed further in this chapter in accordance with the emerging service-centred dominant marketing logic, since the eight foundational premises of this marketing logic are also valid for these frameworks. For example, the integration of relationship marketing and the firm's resource base makes it possible to generalize these frameworks to such general developments in marketing theory. The broad stream of relationship marketing is more relevant for emerging country markets than the narrow stream. The reason is that it focuses on a wider set of relationships and thereby marketing issues, also including the business-to-business marketing view. However, the inter-organizational approach, as a whole, is harder to fit into this evolving relationship marketing framework. The main difficulty behind the integration of the theories is that the inter-organizational approach is characterized by relationships being embedded in a social structure, mainly a specific market structure in the form of networks. Relationship marketing, on the other hand, does not normally consider this macro dimension. However, some major trends in the global markets might lead to more convergence, mainly the globalization of marketing involving emerging country markets, and the integration of European markets. Although the international business marketing model is mainly based on the inter-organizational approach, it can be seen to be part of the paradigm change in marketing from transaction to relationship marketing.

An IBM model is developed, building on the major characteristics of emerging country markets, for example of being relationship-oriented societies. When these characteristics are compared to existing business marketing approaches, the outcome is a requirement to consider four aspects: the network aspect, the international or environmental aspect, the strategic aspect and the organizational aspect. The model is based on seeing the MNC as an inter-organizational network consisting of exchange relationships among organizational units. The MNC, markets and society are described from a network perspective, where the network relations between the MNC network and major external parties in product/service markets are illustrated. The IBM model is built on the institutional network approach. The internal network of the MNC and its external network in markets are influenced by institutional structures ('macro rules'), determining what goes on inside the networks.

The network aspect is thus considered by viewing the MNC as operating in a number of external networks: product/service market network, financial market network, labour market network and government network. The international aspect is included by looking on markets and societies as rule systems under which marketing and purchasing relationships are organized. Networks are influenced by 'macro rules' in societal sectors. There are four major contents of these organizational fields and societal sectors, namely thought styles, values, norms and enforcement mechanisms.

The strategic aspect of business marketing is developed in a number of ways. A first group of factors concerns strategy and network relationships. A second group of factors combines strategy and the international dimension of strategy, namely entry strategy into emerging country markets and the internationalization of business marketing and firms. A third group of factors concerns the resources and capabilities behind IBM strategy, namely network capability profiles and trustworthiness.

The organizational aspect is developed by combining the internal network aspect and strategy aspect by taking up how business strategy and strategic processes are organized into various types of hierarchical networks at the group, regional and local levels as well as in the form of action and organization networks.

The IBM strategy consists of three basic sub-strategies, namely the network strategy, the linkage strategy and the competitive strategy. The three business marketing processes are the relationship process, the marketing process and the product/service process. These processes are divided into sub-processes, where each process consists of a number of stages, cycles or periods involving different degrees of change and mobilization of resources and capabilities. Further developing the international aspect, four major factors are found to be critical for the business marketing strategy when entering a local market network, namely entry mode, entry node, entry process and entry role. Another aspect concerns the internationalization process. Trustworthiness is a major norm of the social capital that constitutes a social organizational capability established from the resource base of the firm in the form of relationships. It also gives a capacity to have and develop new relationships with other parties. This norm or behavioural rule expresses an established ability to behave in a certain way. How IBM strategy is executed depends upon how the network is organized. The internal network organization of the firm is described as a hierarchical network. A distinction is made between the basic organization of the MNC, which is defined as an organization network and the organization of projects, which is defined as action networks. Due to how various types of hierarchical networks have developed internationally, a distinction is made between three types of globally developed hierarchies: the Ethnocentric MNC, the Polycentric MNC and the Geocentric MNC. These fully internationalized major types of firms are compared to the internationalizing firm and the domestic firm. The focus of the international organization of the firm is the local and regional organization networks.

3. Network, linkage and competitive strategies

This chapter takes up international business marketing strategy in industrial product/service markets. According to Håkansson and Snehota (1995) a firm's role, development and performance in industrial product/service markets is explained by its ability to develop relationships, that is the networking process in the market. Volumes, market share, profits and growth depend upon how the company handles its relationships. Most costs and revenues also stem from the business relationships. This ability to develop relationships in order to exploit the resources of the MNC as well as other resources of the network is developed further in this chapter. International business marketing strategies concern activities with the purpose of bridging gaps of various kinds. In this chapter strategies are taken up to bridge gaps between organizations, mainly by making agreements through inter-organizational relationships. These network relationships are influenced by factors in organizational fields and societal sectors external to the network. This means that business networks in their turn bridge international gaps between organizational fields and societal sectors in different countries. These two latter types of bridges are mainly taken up in Chapter 6, while chapters 3 and 4 mainly deal with how to bridge gaps between organizations. The IBM strategies taken up in this chapter are primarily directed to customers and distributors. However, relationships to suppliers and other identifiable parties are also touched upon.

Analytical models helpful for the identification and description of international business strategy are developed. First an international business marketing strategy model is developed, which consists of three sub-strategies: network strategy, linkage strategy and competitive strategy. Here, a main purpose is to get first-mover advantages as a major condition for achieving competitive advantages in emerging country markets.

Second, a model for mapping networks is presented containing three dimensions along which the different parts of the network are grouped: the vertical dimension, the horizontal dimension and the diagonal dimension. This network mapping methodology is used to analyse the marketing situation of MNCs in the emerging country market.

Third, a typology of suitable types of capabilities for developing and maintaining network relationships in emerging country markets is developed in this chapter, namely four major network capability profiles. This typology is grounded in the situation that resources are a key factor in the inter-organizational approach to business marketing. Resources and capabilities play a key role both in conditioning this relationship process and in creating a favourable outcome, for example future competitive advantages. Based on Jansson (2007), resources are defined as the basic assets of the MNC, for example divided into physical, financial, human and intangible resources. Such resources are separated from capabilities, which are the abilities of the company to use its resources for specific purposes. Thus, the internal conditions for IBM are also analysed to a certain extent.

India is chosen as the case country to illustrate international business marketing strategy in this chapter and business marketing processes in Chapter 4. The main reason is that India went through an interesting phase of liberalization at the end of the 1990s with a large number of MNCs growing their business in the country. This took place in the initial period of higher growth, which was a major result of the liberalization of the economy from 1991 and onwards. The case story is about business marketing strategy in the Indian power industry. The MNC illustrated is one of five major Western MNCs with both product and project sales in India studied at that time. As a condition for obtaining full access, the names of the companies could not be openly revealed, which means that it is referred to as Indpow. See Appendix 3.1 for a presentation of the MNC and the business marketing situation in India.

INTERNATIONAL BUSINESS MARKETING STRATEGY

The three basic sub-strategies of the IBM are illustrated in Figure 3.1: the network strategy, the linkage strategy and the competitive strategy. The network strategy is about how the MNC relates itself to the whole market network, inclusive of buyers, distributors, competitors, suppliers and financiers. The linkage strategy, on the other hand, concerns how the seller creates and maintains direct relationships with individual parties within the network. Through linkage strategies, for instance, the seller both cooperates and competes with the buyer for the resources involved in the exchange. The competitive strategy, finally, primarily focuses on networks involving competitors. Unlike the linkage strategy, it does not involve direct relationships with parties, but the position the seller takes or possesses in the competitors' network. It concentrates on how competitive the offer is. This means that the competitive strategy relates to the horizontal market network, while the linkage strategy involves the vertical market network.

A crucial aspect of IBM strategy is to get a first-mover advantage. One way to achieve this is to transform the market condition from a large number of parties to a small number of parties by gradually reducing the number of competitors, for example by out-competing competitors, acquiring them, etc. Another way to get a first-mover advantage is to be an early mover on the market in order to pre-empt it, whereas the goal is to reduce the number of competitors by locking out potential entrants from the market. This is not only a question of entering early into the market but also of seizing the customers before the international competitors. From a network strategic point of view, the means behind this fundamental transformation process to change basic market rules can be described as the spinning of a network so that the buyer is enclosed in the relationship at the same time that competitors are locked out.

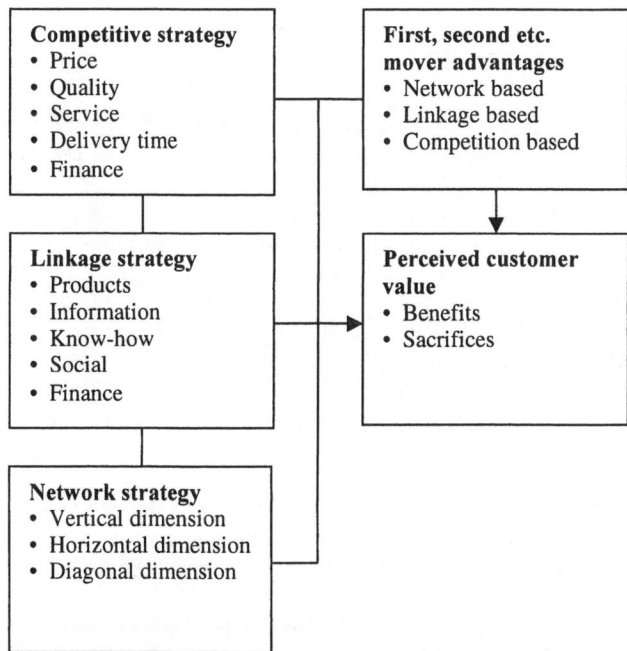

Figure 3.1   International business marketing strategy

Customer value
The main purpose of the international business strategy is to provide superior value to customers. This value is created jointly between the supplier and the customer through the network of relationships. To be able to create a superior customer value, the supplying MNC needs to be familiar with the value-generating processes of the customers, that is what solutions or packages customers want to purchase and use so that value is created for them. Values are subjectively perceived by the customer, meaning that different groups within the buying organization may have different perceptions of the supplier's value offering. Perceived value is defined according to Monroe

(1991) as 'the ratio of perceived benefits relative to perceived sacrifice'. The customer therefore makes a trade-off between benefits and sacrifices in the supplier's offering. Examples of perceived benefits are physical attributes related to the product, for instance the productivity and durability of the product or ability to change features and applications of the products according to the customer's special requirements. Other benefits concern service attributes such as technical support, availability of spare parts and ease of use for operators. Examples of perceived sacrifices are purchasing price, expected costs for maintenance and repairs, and risk of failure or poor performance.

NETWORK MAPPING

Before the MNC starts to build relationships with its customers and distributors to create superior customer value, for example, preparations are necessary, mainly by mapping the marketing network situation and establishing the basic strategic foundation for the IBM strategy. A major result of the mapping of the network situation is network maps with possible 'routes' described and analysed. Network mapping is a way to handle the complexity of international business marketing. To be able to know where to focus marketing efforts it is important to map the strategic network situation of the MNC, for example concerning the product/service network, the financial network and the labour market network. After having identified relevant market networks they need to be described and analysed. In this analysis of the market environment, the following questions may be raised:

1. What does the network look like? Which are the relevant nodes and linkages? Should only direct linkages to the customers be included or should indirect relationships also be considered, for example to customers' customers?
2. How much of a network of a specific organizational field needs to be 'laid out'? Where is the network horizon? This outer border question is difficult to solve, since there are no objective ways to delimit a network. As a consequence, the map of the network will vary with the marketing problem at hand.
3. What type of network is it? Is it a hierarchical or an arm's-length network?
4. What does the network consist of? Which are the major bridges between the different parts of the network?
5. How should the network be structured? Does it consist of clusters? Is the network loosely or tightly coupled?
6. To what degree does the MNC reach out to different parts of the network, that is, what is its degree of connectivity?

Three main network dimensions are distinguished and illustrated in Figure 3.2: the vertical dimension, the horizontal dimension and the diagonal dimension. The vertical dimension takes up the parties included along the valued added product chain: first-tier customers and second-tier customers such as customers' customers, etc.; first-tier suppliers and second-tier suppliers such as suppliers' suppliers; various kinds of intermediaries. The horizontal dimension includes competitors, while the diagonal dimension concerns connections to other organizational fields such as the financial market network and the government network.

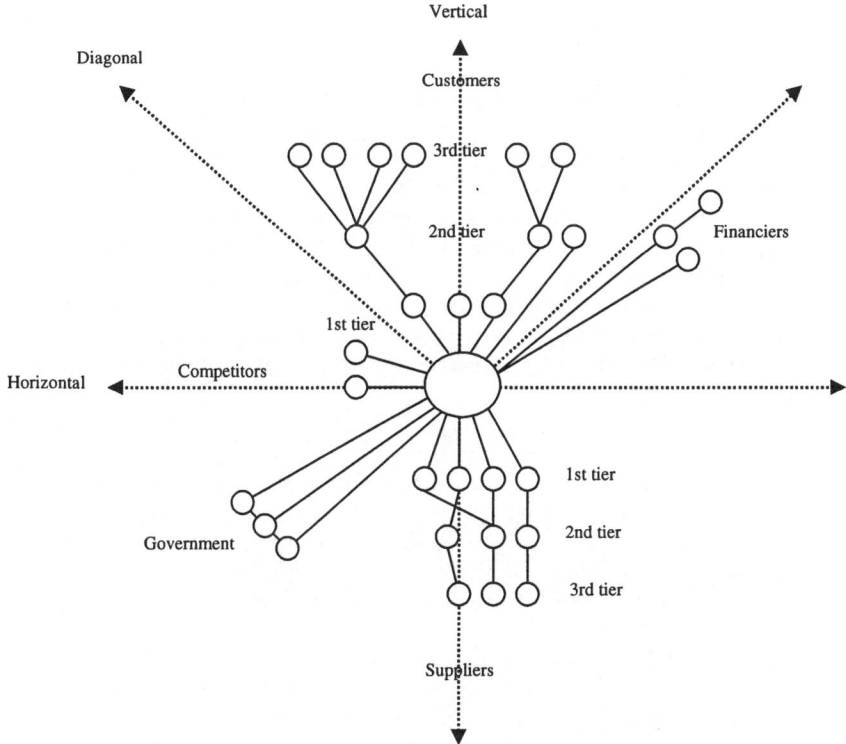

Figure 3.2   Network map

The organizations along the three dimensions are grouped at different levels or tiers. The primary part of the network or the first tier of relationships consists of direct business marketing relationships, which are manifested linkages with external parties such as customers, suppliers, competitors, financiers and government authorities as well with internal units outside the country within the MNC. The secondary part of the network consists of the second tier of indirect relationships of the MNC, for example, suppliers' suppliers. They are only considered when they are of critical importance for business marketing in the primary network. Sometimes a third tier of relationships are included, for example when the MNC as a seller wants to know about the customers' customers of its dealers.

In structuring the network, it is often necessary to assemble companies in different groups. A distinction is then made between macro and micro clusters. A macro cluster consists of individual first tier companies or a mix of companies from different tiers, for example end users, main contractors and consultants. A micro cluster consists of organizational units within a company, for example different departments involved in marketing a certain product or project.

Network Mapping Illustrated

The complexity of network mapping is illustrated for Indpow, which is involved mainly in the business marketing of projects. The reason is that the more complex the product/service sold, the more complex is the process of linking up buyers and sellers. Usually, it also takes a longer time to handle change in networks involving complex products than those exchanging simple products. The primary network of the MNC in marketing to projects is exemplified below based mainly on Figure 3.2. The MNC exemplified – Indpow – is a dominating MNC in most of its business fields throughout the globe. With its long and large experience of operating in transition countries, it is especially suited to illustrate the marketing of industrial goods in emerging country markets.

The first tier of relationships illustrated consists of direct business marketing relationships with external parties such as customers, consultants, suppliers, financiers and government authorities as well with internal units outside India within the own group. Although no relationships are established with competitors they are included in the primary network, the reason being that there is dependence through market competition. The second tier of indirect relationships of Indpow consists of customers' customers.

The vertical dimension: customer clusters

Direct relationships with customers are considered to be the most important of all relationships with external parties. For the project business exemplified here, they are characterized as long-term, broad and flexible. Although the customer structure varies, it is rather concentrated in big companies. These customers organize the purchasing situation in different ways, for example whether a power station is built from parts supplied by the customer or whether a turn key solution is demanded. These different purchasing situations directly influence the configuration of the customer cluster. In both these marketing situations, the customer macro cluster consists of two major buyers: the end user and the main contractor, who assembles the project. Here, Indpow has created a strategic flexibility by developing a capability to act as both a main contractor and as a subcontractor. This makes it possible for the MNC to adapt to various marketing situations by operating both as main contractor and as subcontractor. When Indpow is a subcontractor, the major strategic issue is to develop a relationship mix between the end user and the main contractor. When the end user only wants to deal with one party, Indpow teams up with the main contractor in front of the customer.

Other times, marketing is concentrated on the end user linkage, in which case this customer makes a separate deal with Indpow and then tells the main contractor to buy from Indpow. Whether clusters consist of public or private customers is an important strategic issue. Regarding the composition of the macro cluster, for example, Indpow has a problem in getting public sector customers to understand the value of the turn-key arrangement, which is not the case in private industry. Public customers traditionally believe that it is less expensive to act as main contractors themselves by breaking projects down into pieces, buying parts separately and assembling the plants themselves. However, this is usually more expensive, since public customers overestimate the technical competence of their engineers. Such assembled systems often turn out not to work so well in the long run. This situation of having the main contractor facility in house is slowly changing with the liberalization of the industry. A difference regarding the micro cluster is that public customers operate their plants differently. Private customers therefore better appreciate the value of technical solutions, and do not only focus on price. Relationships with private customers are also characterized by a more relaxed atmosphere involving more or less continuous discussions between the parties during the project process. Linkages with public customers, on the other hand, are more formal or strictly rule-bound, for instance involving sealed tenders where purchasing is organized in committees which follow formal procedures by the book. This means that offers are picked at the lowest price conditional upon passing the requirements of the tender. Despite this formality, the contract often becomes only one station on the road to the final order, with many changes and renegotiations taking place after the contract has been signed. This blend of formal and informal relationships is essential within the micro clusters of public customers. Even if purchasing committees are strictly rule-bound, members have some discretion, and friendship can smooth things out. They might become less rigid to the letter, more understanding, give time for meetings and presentations, and become more open to giving and taking information and influences. In Indian private industry, on the other hand, micro clusters are dominated by the authority of the owner, whom takes quick decisions when required.

Another important division of customers from a network perspective is between established and new customers. It is considered to be much easier to deal with established customers, although they might not be as profitable as new customers. The most important influencing factor with an existing customer is a good relationship. Competitors will usually bid very low, but if the relationship works well it will work as a barrier for the customer in accepting the bid. With new customers, the cost of capture is much higher. A reasonable price is more important with new customers, since it is difficult to justify a higher price with them.

For another project-selling MNC, technological issues are not an important part of the business marketing any longer, being looked upon more as a basic requisite or standard for competing in an area. The reason is that all major competitors have similar competence, which makes technical solutions equal. Software therefore becomes more decisive for getting competitive advantage, for example service offerings, delivery security, resources and capabilities such as contact nets and relationships, as well as the ability to comprehend the purchasing decision processes of the micro clusters. The informal parts of the relationships with the micro clusters have become more important, for example social calls, dinners, and associating with customer personnel outside work. Overall, linkages are more privately oriented than in Scandinavia. Price is also more important. The customer often wants additional service, but is not willing to pay for it.

The behaviour of the customer changes with the stage of the purchasing process, which is discussed later on in the chapter.

The vertical dimension: consultants

Consultants are often crucial actors in product/service markets. They are critical members of the macro clusters, where they play different roles. Long-term relationships with consultants are therefore of special importance when selling to projects, especially to large projects.

In most local Indian industries, where Indpow is involved, there are ongoing contacts with a rather limited number of consultants, usually 2–4 firms. Most of them are technical or engineering consultants. But there are also some agent-type consultants, who provide commercial assistance on the basis of broad contact nets in India. Often their role in large projects is limited to being consultants: taking care of, or coping with technical diversity and double-checking the conclusions reached by the customer staff. In one industry segment, for example, a project normally starts with the customer identifying a suitable consultant, who is then hired to investigate locations, work out technical specifications and handle various political processes. Therefore, consultants become important information sources about new projects. One important task is to make feasibility studies, especially for government projects financed by the World Bank or aid organizations. Consultants are also often involved in the writing of specifications and in the evaluation of bids. Sometimes they also more directly influence purchasing by giving recommendations about how to divide the project among suppliers. It could also happen that they are involved in the engineering design that takes place after the contract has been signed, as well as in the execution phase by being used for inspection, controls and supervision. Thus, sometimes consultants only participate during the initial phase of a project, and sometimes they participate throughout the whole project.

The vertical dimension: suppliers

The MNC also has long-term relationships with key suppliers in India, which are usually developed by means of education and training. Indpow considers these suppliers of strategic equipment as long-term strategic alliances, which take years to develop. Relations are normally kept up, even if projects sometimes are rejected and business lost. Many of them also supply competitors, but that is not a problem. Such world-class suppliers will not play tricks. As discussed below, these key suppliers, compared to ordinary suppliers, also participate in the marketing of projects.

The horizontal dimension: competitors
Indpow has three main groups of competitors. There are MNCs, with which competition takes place on equal terms. The second group consists of wholly or partially state-owned enterprises, which through their strong government connections get various favours. The third group consists of small companies, which compete on price. Indpow India keeps itself informed about the activities of the competitors through published information, rumours, 'people', surveillance within the Indpow group or customers, former company employees. Social and informal relations are important media. The competitive situation is often concentrated or highly concentrated with a few buyers and sellers. Certain positions have developed among competitors in another MNC's major fields of operation. American companies are strong in political influence, and German companies in having good cooperation with Indian industry. French companies are clever, but it is hard to know why. Japanese companies toil, but they are far too careful and detailed.

The diagonal dimension: financiers
There is a trend towards finance as a major competitive tool. Indpow has therefore established a finance function in India. The company provides own financing to customers but also acts as an intermediary by having contacts with banks in India in order to provide customers with project financing, especially private customers. Some financial solutions are local, but most financial packages include a considerable element of foreign financing. Here relations are international and are taken care of by the group, for example with the World Bank group and when aid organizations are involved in the financing of the project. With government projects, the financial aspect is not important, since public customers raise money internally or externally from the World Bank or aid organizations. Because of the large sums and risks involved in very big projects for Indpow, two or three banks cooperate in a syndicate with one of the banks as lead bank. As part of investigating the future cash-flow of the project, banks demand that they approve key contracts. In that way financial organizations are involved in evaluating very large projects, but not usually 'normal' projects. Indpow also has a project and trade finance company of its own, which can arrange finance for large projects and leasing arrangements for smaller projects. Through another group unit dealing with ventures, Indpow may also provide equity finance to a project. Banks are important information nodes, inter alia, to get information about the financial strength of potential customers at an early stage of a project.

The diagonal dimension: governments

The importance of relationships with government officials decreased gradually during the 1990s due to liberalization, for instance license issues became more and more unimportant (cf. Jansson et al., 1995). The discretion of officials at all government levels was reduced and more clear-cut rules led to greater transparency. However, there are still ongoing contacts with municipal and/or state level authorities regarding practical issues related to manufacturing.

The Group

The relationships the subsidiary has with different group units vary. Since the project business is mostly handled by the Indian companies of Indpow, there is less contacts with internal units outside India. Because of the high independence and long history of being established in the country, these subsidiaries are Indian in character. Since the subsidiary receives little internal technical and marketing support, there are few contacts with various units within the group. With the build-up of local competence, independence from the group is large.

THE NETWORK STRATEGY

Based on the network mapping, the network strategy takes up how the MNC utilizes the network in its marketing efforts, for example the parties influenced in the product/service network, and the parties included in the financial network and the labour market network. One major aspect concerns how many parties are focused on in the network, that is whether the MNC has a broad or narrow strategic approach. Another major aspect concerns the size of the network, that is how much of the network is included.

Illustration

Marketing of projects, for example, is very much a question of coordinating various relationship activities. Even if the edge in marketing is directed at the customer cluster, several other parties are involved in the marketing activities. The network delimited in the mapping process is activated in the network strategy, where the leading role is played by the customer.

The philosophy of Indpow is that different units should go together as much as possible in order to pull resources together and to have a united front towards the customer cluster. The marketing is organized in project groups, where members change with the evolution of the marketing process (see next chapter). If Indpow's customer is an Indian company, then the local subsidiary has the customer interface network. Sometimes, the picture is more complicated. If the customer is a joint venture, there is a customer micro cluster with a foreign partner and an interface abroad as well, for example in the UK or US. This is a sensitive situation that needs to be evaluated carefully. It is necessary to know about the relationship between the partners: how they get along, if they have different or even conflicting drivers. The experience of this MNC is that one party dominates the joint relationship, and it is necessary to find out who that is in order to have the right network strategy.

For Indpow, how the consultants are included in the network strategy depends upon the role they play in the marketing process. Sometimes, linkages to them are only used as part of an intelligence network to get information. When consultants are utilized to investigate new projects, relationships are formed with consultants to learn about new projects. Consultants will also float inquiries to various companies. A most important capability then is a good relationship with both customer and consultant, which needs to be constantly maintained, for example by keeping good relationships with these parties even between projects. When consultants are directly involved in influencing purchase decisions, the solution is sold both to the customer and to the consultant. Often consultants are used to go through the specifications, whereas it is important to have good connections with them in order to influence this process to the advantage of the company. Since the consultants' recommendations are not binding to the customer, it is also possible to influence the customer directly to change the specifications, if these recommendations are unfavourable to the seller.

When Indpow needs to organize finance, banks and other finance organizations are also linked up. Banks are used to arrange loans, since procurement of finance gives a competitive advantage. They are also used to get important information about new projects, particularly in the World Bank and aid organizations. But usually there is no lobbying with banks, since they are not involved in technical evaluations. An important competitive weapon is to help the customer to find good financial solutions. Indpow uses its capability of having well-established contacts with banks to achieve this. Sometimes, the MNC's internal finance unit based in Europe also provides project finance. When equity financing is required, many times up to one third of the investment, Indpow sometimes agrees to own a minority equity share (about 10 per cent) for a period of about five years.

For Indpow, the few key suppliers of important components are not only suppliers. As subcontractors, they are already involved in the pre-tendering phase and stay active throughout the project. Some go along with the company representatives on customer calls. Information is also shared with these long-term partners very early in a project. The supplier will assign representatives to participate in the project, who are usually well known to the customer. There is pre-tender understanding between the main contractor and the subcontractor. When there is a list of acceptable suppliers, agreed upon with the customer, subcontractors are not normally brought along for joint customer visits. Indpow has a lot of contacts with federal government authorities to facilitate imports of key components to projects. Meetings are held for discussing specific issues. Sometimes assistance is also received from the customer on such matters.

THE LINKAGE STRATEGY

While network strategy covers the whole network of the MNC, the linkage strategy relates to a part of the network, for example customers or suppliers. In the latter cases, linkage strategy pertains to vertical competition and concerns how to establish and run relationships along the vertical value chain in product/service markets. The linkage strategy considers both the complexity of building and maintaining different types of relationships with a certain group of parties as well as the time dimension of network formation and development, for instance how long it takes and when various linkages are used to establish, develop and decide on the value offering together with the customer.

A combination of five major types of linkages is involved along the vertical value chain, forming a specific mix of relationships:

1. The product linkage
2. The financial linkage
3. The information or know-what linkage
4. The knowledge or know-how linkage
5. The social or know-who linkage

The general objective with the linkage strategy is to build long-term and mutually beneficial relationships with customers, dealers and distributors in order to add value to the end product along the vertical product chain. Through the linkage strategy, a bond is established between the parties. For example, when developing a new product, buyers and sellers might work together closely for an extended period of time. Through this process, they become enveloped in their relationship, making the substitution of either of them by another party difficult. The seller, for instance, becomes involved in various concrete problems of the customer. The distance to be covered between the start of commitment and the results in the form of an exchange of products is often long. Commitment grows gradually as the parties become more and more absorbed by the relationship. Strong mutual interdependence involves considerable dangers for both parties. The strong tie-up and the long-term character of business deals results in considerable trouble, if anything goes wrong. If each solution to a customer problem is specific, most of the expenses are wasted if the business is taken by a competitor. In such cases, the degree of linkage specificity is high and switching costs are high, since it is hard for the parties to replace each other. Here, it is thus important that the parties protect themselves from the dangers inherent in this type of business dealings. This is usually done within the relationship through building up a mutual balance of gradual commitment of resources, which is done in terms of the linkage. The decisive judgments for both parties concern the degree of commitment to be made in each phase of the business process.

Thus, linkages in industrial product/service markets are often characterized by a limited degree of substitution, investment in linkage-specific resources and capabilities, and a long-term character. In many dyadic relationships, for example, the parties have become so united that other parties are excluded, competitiveness being maintained and the costs being kept low through a certain standardization of procedures, which serves as a barrier to competitors. It is essential to not lose this competitiveness and first-mover advantage by letting the relationship become set in a fixed mode. Flexibility is kept up by adaptations to a changing context. How relations develop between parties is discussed and illustrated in more detail below.

Linkage strategies for projects concentrate on social linkages being built up and maintained with various key persons. The establishing and maintaining of contacts often represents the largest and most important part of the marketing investment which project selling involves. In Southeast Asia, personal contacts are often the most important aspect at every project phase (Jansson, 1994a).

There is a trade-off between main types of linkages. The information linkage is often most important in the initial stages, where the parties build up knowledge of each other. Both this greater knowledge of each other which the parties gain and the linking process itself make it increasingly possible to organize the relationship better, making it possible to simplify and even sometimes routinize it. The social linkage seems to be important throughout the whole process. Creating trustworthiness through social contacts is often important in many emerging economies in the initial stages and even a pre-condition for starting the commercial exchange. Later on, when parties have come further in their relationship, they learn to know each other, which further strengthen the relationship.

As more and more transactions are carried out, parties are able to reorganize for further improvements. With the stabilization of relationships, knowledge of prices and of other conditions tends to reach a steady state. Parties have learned much about each other and about competitors, and this in turn makes it expensive to change prices. Interest in prices has gradually decreased and price competition has been replaced by non-price competition.

When establishing relationships in new markets, there is always the danger of repeating behaviour from other markets, which might not suit the new market. Such habits of following invisible, taken-for-granted norms from the 'old' markets of Western Europe was noted in Southeast Asian markets (Jansson, 1994a), especially in the first years of operation. Local needs, for example, were taken more or less for granted, assuming them to be essentially the same as in Europe. Such 'easy ways out', however, could reflect poor local responsiveness, and an unsustainable long-term competitive position. This could amount to the marketing situation not having been properly analysed. Through necessary adaptations thus having been delayed, later costs may be considerably greater (for example due to lost sales) than such costs would have needed to be with better adaptation to local conditions.

Trustworthiness

Establishing trustful relationships is a critical part of the linkage strategy. Trustworthiness is mainly related to the social organization of the relationship, where a distinction is made between organizational trust and individual trust (Jansson, 2007). Organizational trustworthiness concerns the organization, for example a buyer trusting the selling organization to keep promises given on quality and delivery time. This is a relation between an individual and an organization, that is impersonal and formal.

However, it does not mean that it is less emotional than other person-to-person relationships, since an individual may be highly involved with an organization, identifying with it through its brand in a very personal way. Reputation is an expression of this trustworthiness. Individual trustworthiness is about people and the friendship among them. One type of individual trustworthiness is related to coalitions and concerns the individual as a representative of his or her company. This type of trustworthiness is defined as professional trustworthiness, since it has to do with how tasks are completed together with other individuals, and is more instrumental than emotional. An employee can, for example, be expected to complete his tasks in a certain way, not being biased from undue influences. This relationship is personal and formal. Another kind of trustworthiness is related to cliques, that is to other individuals as persons. It has another friendship base than business, for example personal traits, membership of a social or cultural group, or the like. This is called social trustworthiness, since persons associate because they like each other, or because they belong to the same social or cultural group.

As found by Jansson et al. (1995), the relation between social trustworthiness and emotions in India is complex. When trustworthiness is based on personal traits, friendship is mostly based on emotions and the relation is therefore personal and informal. This is the true personalized relationship. However, when social trustworthiness comes from a common social or cultural background, a low degree of emotional affiliation may be involved. Business relationships in Southeast Asia are signified by a high importance of individual and social trustworthiness as compared to organizational and professional trustworthiness in the Nordic countries. Cultural influence is a major factor behind the critical role of the social linkage in the Chinese business network. Guanxi behaviour goes deeper than professional friendship, and therefore the Chinese display traditional ways of behaving in the business world. Nordic firms have a rigid concept of trust and honesty, indicating for instance that people are typically trusted until they have proven they cannot be trusted. In the overseas Chinese context it is typically the other way around: people are distrusted until they have proven they can be trusted. Business relationships between Nordic and Chinese firms therefore most often start with a good personal relationship; only thereafter does the business relationship start. (Jansson and Ramström, 2005).

THE COMPETITIVE STRATEGY

The competitive strategy, the third part of the international business marketing strategy, is more closely related to horizontal competition. The seller offers a technical solution to a buyer's problem, which creates a favourable position in the competitors' network. The offering is contained in a package consisting of various offers, for instance of hardware in the form of products of a certain quality and of software such as service, transfer of know-how and financing. The package is delivered within a specified time at a specified price. It is modelled in such a way that it distinguishes itself favourably from the competitors' offers.

An important part of competitor analysis or benchmarking is to analyse the competitors' business marketing strategies, for example what projects they are involved in, how these sellers are evaluated by the customers, how they influence decisions, how they follow up on contracts, how they are paid, and how they deliver and install projects.

Price

Since it is usually hard to sell on quality in emerging country markets, price is the dominant part of the competitive strategy in these markets (Jansson, 1994a). Therefore, it deserves to be analysed in more detail. The market creates the conditions under which a competitive strategy is carried out between the sellers and the buyers. Firms acting within certain market structures use price as the main strategic component. In other market forms, price competition is not the dominant component, although it is still important. An important function of the market is to establish norms for the functioning of price, which form critical constraints for the MNCs' competitive strategy.

How prices are fixed in various market networks is important for competitive strategy. In traditional forms, prices are determined by the market and the market actors therefore being mainly price takers. In other forms, on the other hand, the parties are the chief price makers. In most industrial product market networks, prices and products are not seen as given, as they are in the more classical markets such as many commodity markets. Rather, it is the other way around, prices and products being viewed as being first negotiated and then determined (product and factor prices). Market actors are considered as price makers and not as price takers. This is usually a very difficult and risky task, the outcome of which determines the distribution of economic benefits between the parties. Prices are considered to be not only discovered but also to be influenced by the parties, as well as to be dependent upon the resource situation of the buyer and seller and of their competitors.

This situation is faced in the imperfect emerging country markets, where it is expensive to find out about the price of a product, both for the buyer and for the seller. The seller, for instance, collects information about the segment of the market of relevance (customers and competitors). In the well working Western markets, price provides a good approximation of efficient resource allocation. However, this is not the case in emerging country markets. Price is still though the main approximation of an efficient allocation of resources between the parties to a linkage and between competing parties in the environment.

Thus, price is the most important component of competition, since it determines the economic outcome of the business for the parties involved. It can be seen as the very basis of competitiveness. However, as already indicated, it is particularly difficult in emerging country markets to establish the relation between price, costs, efficiency and competitiveness. Pricing is more complex in these markets. First, it is difficult to calculate prices and to know whether they reflect an efficient resource allocation between parties. Second, non-price competition is also important. This type of competition largely dominates marketing of advanced industrial products by MNCs, relegating price to the background there in competitive strategy. Even if price agreements finally determine the resource allocation between the parties, quality, service and other competitive factors may be stressed by buyers and sellers. Complexity of needs makes it difficult to price an offer. The price must be related, for example, to a certain quality and service level as well as to delivery time. These parameters are determined collectively within the framework of the network. Price is one of various factors determined through such a process.

The high uncertainty involved in marketing in emerging countries and the ensuing problems of fixing prices, making them less transparent, can be taken advantage of by an opportunistic seller. The buyer can be influenced to buy a product that is less than suitable to actual or future needs. Similar problematical results could come about through neither party having sufficient knowledge about the needs in question and the potential alternatives in the market. The non-transparent role of price as a competitive factor under such conditions may thus result in biased business.

Price tends to be evaluated in terms of expectations and promises or norms regarding such matters as quality, service and delivery time. Exchange only takes place if price is acceptable to both parties.

FIRST-MOVER ADVANTAGES

A crucial part of the international business marketing strategy is to achieve a first-mover advantage. It has to do with the timing in achieving the competitive advantage. One way is to be first in the field. An MNC that enters a new market before its competitors increases its chances of winning the game by being the first to offer its solutions to the customers. This means that the supplier that manages to establish the first linkage with a customer more easily gets a competitive advantage. Another way is to become the first supplier of a customer. This happens when the seller gets some kind of advantage over the competitors by becoming the primary supplier in the industry or on the market. When the business is renewed with the satisfied customer, parity between sellers no longer exists, since it is cost saving for the customer to do business with a company it already knows and trusts. Getting a first-mover advantage is then both a question of when the business marketing move is made (picking the right time) and how it is made (making the right move), for example by finding the mix and sequence of network linkages over time.

First-mover advantages may be achieved either through the information linkage, with the customer being influence by and dependent upon information from the seller. It could also be achieved through the social linkage, by the customer becoming socially committed to the seller. In addition, such advantages may be achieved through product or financial links, the customer becoming dependent upon the seller's products and financing. Specific linkage mixtures may be found to be particularly advantageous at various stages in the building up of the relationship. In the marketing of projects, for example, social and information linkages are very critical at the initial establishment phases.

A first-mover advantage can also be achieved through a competitive offer. The strategy here involves a combination of a linkage mix and a competitive mix, which are interconnected. The linkage mix creates a framework for the transfer of the competitive mix, but is also influenced by what the MNC as a seller can offer. An advanced technical solution far above the customer's present capabilities, for instance, requires a more long-term build-up of information and of social contact networks for transferring know-how. Likewise, if financing is an important marketing element in the package, a financial linkage will become established.

If one MNC has already achieved a first-mover advantage, the strategic alternatives are more limited for the other MNCs, any of which can at most achieve a second-mover advantage. This is achieved by entering the market before the other remaining competitors, or by being a second supplier of a customer. Third- or fourth-mover advantages may not even exist in small emerging country markets, for example in the small formerly centrally planned economies in Eastern Europe. The MNC that manages to acquire an earlier state-owned monopoly company in an industry also acquires its entire local customer network. By being able as a first mover to control the whole local industry, a large, sustainable and durable competitive advantage is created in the form of large entry barriers for competing firms. Thus, due to the normally limited size of emerging country markets during the initial development stages, the chances to establish a sustainable number of customer relationships are reduced, the later the company moves into the market. In case there is only room for two suppliers in a market, newcomers need to out-compete the incumbents by taking over their customer relationships. This is more difficult than being a primary supplier on the market. However, such third- or fourth-mover advantages may arise at later stages of market development with the fast growth of some of these economies. There is also a downside to being a first-mover. The first to enter a market, for example, often has to make a higher market investment. Making way for others is costly. Furthermore, later arrivals may benefit from lower learning costs by being able to learn from the first entrant about what works well and what does not.

NETWORK CAPABILITY PROFILES

Behind a competitive international business marketing strategy lies the MNC's resource/capability constellation in the country or within the group outside the country. Local IBM strategy is conditioned by the capability profile. The MNC needs to have certain resources or capabilities localized in the country to be able to effectuate the IBM strategy there. The capability profile describes the mix of capabilities found at a local company for a certain IBM strategy, for instance knowledge and skills. An IBM strategy in a certain market environment, for example, may require either specific knowledge about a few customers or general knowledge about many customers.

The business marketing capability profiles show a company's ability to handle various types of networks and linkages. The grouping of the profiles is illustrated in Figure 3.3. First a distinction is made between two main types of solutions: those that satisfy specific customer needs and those that satisfy general customer needs. In the former case, solutions are made and adapted to individual needs, while they are not adapted in the latter case. Behind each type of a solution are found problem-solving capabilities. There are capabilities such as certain employee skills and technical systems as well as management systems in the form of certain problem-solving routines. Those capabilities that make it possible to solve the problems of the individual customer are defined as a customer specialist profile, while the case of more general capabilities is called a product specialist profile. The reason is that, when linkages are managed at solving such common customer needs, they tend to converge at the product instead of at the customer. Hence, in this case the product is the key focus and not the specific individual customer solution.

Second, a distinction is made between how needs and solutions are bridged, that is if it takes place through direct linkages between buyer and seller or indirectly through a third party. The profiles of product and customer specialists are both oriented towards problem solving through direct contacts between two major parties. Where intermediaries are involved, the linkages of the supplying company with customers are indirect. Two strategic profiles directed at an indirect bridging of the gap are distinguished, where intermediaries are involved in problem solving. One profile is based on the situation where an independent intermediary is the major customer interface and plays a major role in solving customer problems, for example a dealer. To handle this situation, the MNC needs to have a capability to market the product/service through the intermediary. Such a capability to handle linkages primarily through intermediary networks rather than with final customers directly is called a distributor network specialist. A profile, on the other hand, that is specialized at the MNC being the intermediary itself by having the distribution network 'in house', is called a distribution specialist.

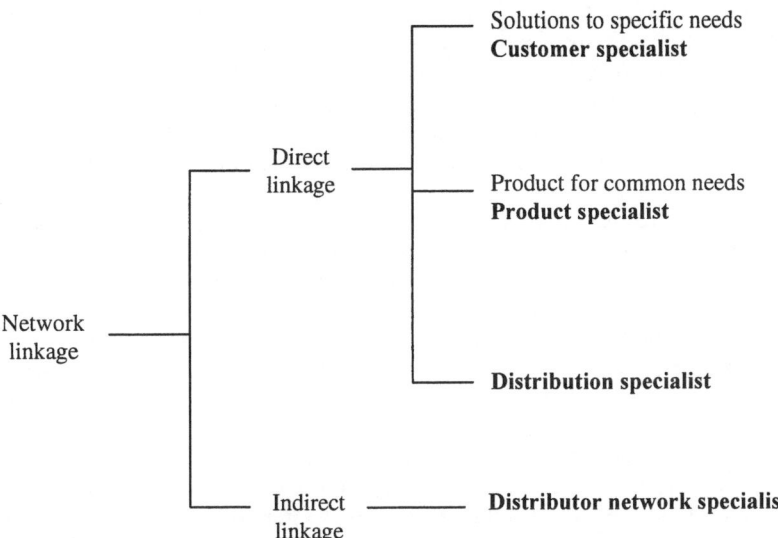

Figure 3.3   Network capability profiles

A distinction is further made between marketing and manufacturing capabilities. Often manufacturing is important from a marketing point of view, since an efficient production of a solution and/or a product is a condition for a good marketing result. For instance, some MNCs call attention to local production as an important factor of the competitive strategy. When the profile is oriented towards production, there is a manufacturing specialist. Otherwise, there is a purchasing specialist. Sales companies are, of course, also purchasing specialists while manufacturing companies are manufacturing specialists or have a mix of both. If a company is classified as a manufacturing specialist only, it has no capacity for marketing, for example a subcontractor of machine capacity. Trading companies which specialize in sourcing products for the group are pure purchasing specialists. When the capabilities of a firm are classified according to this scheme, one profile or a mix of profiles is obtained.

Customer Specialist

The ways customer problems are solved implies that each of the business marketing capability profiles introduced above represents a specific problem solving capability. The capability typical of the customer specialist profile has the following characteristics. Each customer is treated individually, business marketing activities are specialized at the individual customer level, and information is collected about specific customer needs. Most tailor-made products as well as package deals such as various types of equipment typically belong to this category. The main feature of the customer specialist's capacity profile is that the problem solving is directly oriented at the specific needs of certain customers. The emphasis is on the software aspects, chiefly design of and adaptation of technically advanced products to individual customer needs. Engineering is the key word. The business marketing activities denoted by this profile are signified by long lead times and high sales costs in long-term relationships and broad contact nets. Production capabilities are subordinated to marketing capabilities and are to be flexible to make possible production of the specific individual solutions. The scope of the problem-solving capacity varies with how many different kinds of particular needs are catered for. As analysed below, customer specialist capabilities tend to emerge through the continuous contacts with the customers, learning and adapting to their changing requirements. A deliberate planning of activities built on such capacities is difficult; hence continuous contacts are very important.

The degree of specialization of the problem-solving capability is high. The specialization of resources and capabilities are usually high because of the tailor-made products sold. This implies that the costs of switching between customers are substantial for customer specialists. Competition is need-positioned and oriented directly towards customers, to which solutions are provided. Competition takes place between networks of specialized linkages.

Product Specialist

Companies selling technically advanced industrial products with low or no adaptation to individual customer have another problem solving capability and are therefore classified as product specialists. Networks and problem-solving capabilities are concentrated on the product rather on the customer directly. These products are sold to customers who have a common need for a functionally high and consistent quality. For example, most components and steels sold directly to original equipment manufacturers (OEMs) are found in this category. A high engineering capability is prominent, if the competitive advantage of the first mover is to be maintained through the technical quality of the product. A product development capability is also critical. These engineering capabilities are high throughout the company, in marketing as well as in manufacturing and purchasing. The co-ordination of these capabilities is important to achieve a successful strategy. Economies of scale are important in all these activities. The need for flexibility in marketing as well as in production, and of the problem solving capabilities behind it, is less than for a customer specialist. The specialization of resources and capabilities to specific linkages is lower than for customer specialists. This means that the stability of networks is often more important than change. The networks of product specialists are characterized by being stable for long periods, but which tend to change rapidly during rather short time periods. Network strategies are therefore more of the deliberate kind, since a certain strategy can be maintained for a longer period. A product specialist, contrary to a customer specialist, lives from exploiting an established network rather than from changing it. Competition is product-positioned and oriented directly towards customers. Products are offered and competition takes place between standardized networks.

Distribution Specialist

Large ball bearing manufacturers, for example, sell both large volumes of products directly to OEMs like car companies and market small quantities through intermediaries to repair shops in the after market. When the bearing producer is also a retailer taking care of its own sales in the aftermarket, it is a distribution specialist. If, on the other hand, it outsourcers the distribution to independent dealers, it is a distributor network specialist. Sometimes the high costs of establishing an own distribution network are justified provided that pure distribution is important and that a sufficient number of customer linkages are involved. The number of customers and industries as well as product varieties cannot be too limited, since they must allow an investment in capabilities for an own distribution network. In addition, other capabilities besides distribution are important, especially those required for direct customer contacts.

Therefore, establishing a company as a distribution specialist is the same as establishing both a distribution and sales company, thereby becoming a distribution specialist as well as a product specialist. If the MNC is earlier represented in the market by an external distributor, this could mean taking over this network. This is different from the case of establishing a sales company with a product or customer specialist profile by taking over an agent network. In both cases, however, the aim is to integrate forwards all the way to the customers in order to have direct linkages with them. The main difference lies in the type of marketing capabilities required. Product and customer specialists specialize their problem-solving capabilities directly to customer problems, while distribution specialists concentrate on abilities to transfer these solutions to the customers, for instance skills in assembly of an assortment of goods, and capabilities related to physical supply, transportation and storage.

Distributor Network Specialist

Many products are not economical to sell and/or distribute directly to customers. Being a distributor network specialist means that transfer capabilities related to distribution are outsourced to other parties. Distributors are set apart from agents. They are middlemen that buy and sell industrial goods. Besides sales and warehousing they could also offer customer service and financing, for which they need relevant capabilities. Agents, on the other hand, only represent sellers, normally a limited number of sellers, and specialize their capabilities to a certain geographical area and number of industries. Even if agents can have resources for carrying stocks they mainly have capabilities concentrated to selling. The main marketing capacity of distributors, on the other hand, is distribution. Agents are therefore seen as an alternative to an own sales subsidiary.

Resources and capabilities for distribution are usually profitable to externalize to distributors when there are long and extensive networks, that is small quantities are sold of a broad variety of often rather technically simple products, for which there are numerous customers spread out over a rather large area. The same goes for the capabilities behind selling the products. In such cases, an intermediary makes a more efficient use of the resources than the producer. An already established distribution network can be utilized for these marketing functions as well as a channel for information about customers and competitors. The costs for such information are usually lower when using an existing network. Negotiating with intermediaries is also many times less expensive than negotiating with the customers directly. Moreover, the costs of controlling the prices of the intermediaries is lower than enforcing them directly with the customers, or through an own distribution network. Informing oneself about the market and the intermediaries in order to control the prices of the distributors is one of the main costs for a distributor network specialist. These costs are lower for simple standard products, since prices are mainly controlled by the market.

Availability of the products in the various parts of the industrial distribution network is a critical competitive factor for a distribution specialist or distributor network specialist. It is very vital that the right product is delivered to the right customer at the right time. Then, resources and capabilities relating to delivery systems, inventory management, service levels and location of warehouses become critical. But in industrial distribution other functions such as sales, service and maintenance are important as well. An important issue is then how to divide up the capabilities behind these functions between the manufacturing MNC and the local distributors. A minimum requirement for the supplier is to have the capabilities that make it possible to control the marketing process of the distributor.

At a certain stage, it might even become more economical to integrate forward, that is acquiring the distributor network or setting up an own distribution network. Since this solution is very expensive, cost savings must be considerable. The establishment of such specialist structures involves high fixed costs. Another alternative is then to partially integrate forwards to set up an own sales company to participate in and control the distribution network on the spot. Then the MNC moves closer to the customers with its stocks and marketing capabilities. Still, this capability makes the MNC a distributor network specialist, since products are supplied through distributors at the same time as most contacts take that way. A distinction is instead made between this type of distributor network specialist, where there is more of joint action towards the customers, and the other type of more pure distribution and divided-up capabilities, where distributors operate more independently in a country. The MNC invests more in the distribution network in the former case than in the latter.

CONCLUSIONS

International business marketing strategy is based on the inter-organizational approach, where marketing, buying and other relationship-oriented behaviour of firms is viewed as an organizational issue. The main factors of importance for the analysis of IBM strategy were taken up in the chapter. After having identified relevant market networks they are described and analysed using a network mapping methodology, for example concerning the product/service network, the financial network and the labour market network. Of the three main network dimensions distinguished, the vertical dimension takes up the parties included along the valued-added product chain: first-tier customers and second-tier customers such as customers' customers, etc.; first-tier suppliers and second-tier suppliers such as suppliers' suppliers; and various kinds of intermediaries. The horizontal dimension includes competitors, while the diagonal dimension concerns connections to other organizational fields such as the financial market network and the government network.

The complexity of network mapping is illustrated for an MNC selling projects. The reason is that the more complex the product/service sold, the more complex is the process of linking up buyers and sellers. Usually, it also takes a longer time to handle change in networks involving complex products than those exchanging simple products. The configuration of the macro cluster varies with the purchasing situation. When the customer buys turn key projects or buys and builds the project himself, the macro cluster consists of one major customer. When the buying process is divided up between different parties, this is also reflected in the macro cluster, for example the end user and the main contractor, who assembles the project. The organization of the macro cluster as well as the micro cluster, and as a consequence IBM strategy, was shown to be influenced by two major factors: whether they consist of public customers and new or established customers. The composition of the macro cluster and the network strategy, for instance, is influenced by the fact that public customers prefer to buy and build the projects themselves. The micro cluster and linkage strategy is influenced by the more formally organized purchasing committees and the particular way of establishing and maintaining the social linkage, while the competitive strategy is influenced by the focus on price in purchasing. Similar differences were found between new and established customers. This is mainly explained by the fact that they are found at different stages along the relationships cycle, which is developed further in the next chapter. Consultants are crucial members of the macro clusters, where they play different roles, for example pure consultants, influencers, or information sources. The vertical dimension of the network map also includes the suppliers, where certain key suppliers participate in the supplier cluster when marketing to projects. The mapping of the competitors forming a horizontal network shown that there are three major types of competitors: other MNCs competing on equal terms and favoured state-owned enterprises, which are found in rather concentrated oligopoly-like market structures. A third category includes price-oriented small and medium-sized companies. Three actors found in the diagonal dimension of the map are important members of the network: financiers, governments and group units outside the emerging country market.

The network map coming out of the mapping procedure lays the foundation for the IBM strategy. The network strategy utilizes this map to decide which actors along the three dimensions to focus on, how to combine them and how to sequence the relationships marketing over time to the various actors. Then, the linkage strategy is determined for each major party included in the network strategy. Dependent upon the characteristics of the customer micro cluster, for example, the product, financial, information, knowledge and social linkages are blended in a specific way. In emerging country markets, it is of utmost importance to build trustworthiness, which is mainly done through the social linkage. Considering the network map at hand and keeping the network and linkage strategies in mind, the IBM strategy is completed by adding the competitive strategy. As discussed above, the critical trade-off in emerging country markets is between price and quality, and simultaneously considering other competitive parameters such as service level, delivery time and finance. In addition, first-mover advantages play a critical role in achieving competitive advantages. Depending upon the size of the market and the competitive situation, later entrants to an emerging country market could also gain sustainable competitive advantage through having a second- or even third-mover advantage.

As demonstrated above, the outcome of the IBM strategy depends on a thorough mapping of the external network environment of the MNC. This is also true for the internal environment, which was shown to consist mainly of some major types of organizational capabilities, particularly four IBM capability profiles. A customer specialists has the capability to make tailor-made customer solutions by operating through specialized networks, while a product specialist solves problems customers have in common through having direct and more standardized network linkages. A distribution specialist deals with customers both directly and indirectly through a distribution network, while a distributor network specialist caters more for the problems of distributors, through which there is an indirect and rather distant coupling to the customer.

APPENDIX 3.1 INDPOW IN INDIA

Indpow in 2000 had 10 500 employees in India. Since most of the resources and capabilities required for the local business had been established in India, little support was received from Europe. Forty-one per cent of the local Indian group was owned by the mother company, 6 per cent by a product company within the group and 22 per cent was owned by Indian financial organizations held by government. There was a local legal requirement that 25 per cent must be offered to the public. The factories were established a long time ago. The number of staff had grown slightly over the last few years of the 1990s, but the operations had grown very much more.

Organization Network

Indpow India had a matrix organization, where one line of command is based on the product dimension and the line of command on the geographical dimension. The product part was divided into three major business segments based on type of customer demand (power, transmission and industry). The business segments in India were divided into business areas (BAs), which in their turn were divided into business units (BUs). Four zones or regions represented the geographic dimension, which was also the operational sales organization. The regional office for the Northern region was located in Delhi, the office for the Southern region was found in Chennai (Madras), and the office for the Western region was located in Mumbai (Bombay), while Kalgata (Calcutta) was the base for the regional office covering Eastern India. The operations were handled by branch offices with front sales people in various locations and a number of factories spread out over India. This matrix was managed from the country headquarters in Delhi, where the president and his staff were located together with two of the vice presidents for two of the business segments. The third segment – the industry business segment – was headquartered in Bangalore. This matrix in India was connected to the worldwide matrix of Indpow at the group level.

Each regional office covered the whole product range found in this Indian part of the MNC. The people at a regional office assigned to the various business areas reported to the business area HQ in India. The area marketing manager was responsible for the whole product range in his area. Inter alia, this system of marketing managers worked as a kind of information network covering all India, for instance where the local sales representatives received 'early warnings' by talking to potential or existing customers. This is very important in India, where social nets are close with many meetings face to face. In eight of ten cases, earlier information was received from these sources than from other sources like media channels and consultancy reports. At the 150-people-strong regional office in Mumbai, for example, product experts were available locally. When assistance was required from other units, most of it came from New Delhi. In some projects help was also needed from foreign units, especially during negotiations. The Mumbai office was not much involved in implementation of projects, which was managed by the central organization in New Delhi.

The power segment

The power segment consisted of business areas, which were profit centres. These business areas had different capabilities for projects, for example. Some of them were almost fully self-sufficient, which applied to cases where the local market was considered big enough to carry many projects. In some cases, business took place on a global scale with production of various parts all over the globe. For large projects, for example steam or gas turbine plants, there was usually both local and overseas participation. One of the business areas within the power segment concerned the selling of complete rehabilitation packages (including equipment and work) for old power plants, mostly coal-fuelled. Four persons were working with marketing of rehabilitation projects, one in each geographical region. Most of the knowledge needed for this rehabilitation network was available within the Indian group, where each unit had some specialties or advantages, which were drawn upon when needed. The rest of Indpow was only used when some specialty products/equipment were required. The Indian BA was specialized on local equipment and the types of rehabilitation and new equipment that fit them. There were also a factory for equipment rehabilitation and repairs belonging to this network. Another Indian specialist capability in this area was system design. When old plants are rehabilitated, their old equipment is used as much as possible to attain the output performance required by the customer. The extent to which clearance was required from other group units for making an offer depended on the technology involved.

The industry segment

The industry segment was organized according to customer industry, which gave a good understanding of the needs and wants of the client. The seller learned about the customers' processes, which made it possible to make the customers' equipment more functional and more valuable, leading to leaner processes. This organization gave the customer a total solution across various business areas within this segment, one advantage being that the customer did not need to deal with a number of different persons from the MNC.

To facilitate contacts between Indpow units involved in project business, there was a global information system for projects called PROMIS. Any job getting yes in the screening and worth more than $3 million was fed into this system, where the status of the project was reviewed every 15 days. The technical support was managed by product responsible persons within the Indian unit. Support or information could also be received from product responsible persons in PRUs (Product Responsible Units or lead centres) spread out over Europe. PRUs also arranged trips to a suitable country on favourable terms for a customer who wanted to inspect some reference facility. PRUs did not interfere in local business but gave support on request from the Indian organization, mainly to the various action networks involved in marketing the projects. Support was not paid for by the hour, but part of the revenue was placed in a pool for services available. PRUs were generally knowledgeable about India and they knew the realities there. There were no 'besserwisser' attitudes, though they might have difficulties in keeping up with day-to-day things. Marketing support was coming from a marketing centre in Japan.

For R&D operations there were different labour practices in India and in Europe. The main difference was that work was much more automated than in India, where it was more labour intensive, which means that adjustments might be necessary. When the Indian company was capable of doing its own R&D, decisions regarding such issues lied with the respective Indian unit. If R&D was located in Europe, however, units there took care of it. Local Indian units then had a decision meeting every year on R&D issues. For example, if development of local products was not of local but global worth to the Indian company, development costs are shared with the European R&D unit.

The transmission segment
The transmission segment was a typical product business and was therefore quite independent from other group units abroad. The reason was that 95 per cent of the goods sold were manufactured in India, which meant that there was more local responsibility compared to the other segments in India. Only low-value items were imported and then resold to the customer, who only wrote a contract with the Indian company.

Regional/Local Organization in India

At the regional offices, there were different groups assigned to different segments. The transmission segment in the regions, for example, had most of the local expertise it needed and was therefore independent of the segment's headquarters in New Delhi. Transmission business, being a typical product business, was the most decentralized activity. Similarly as the transmission segment in India was independent from other group units abroad, regions were quite independent from the Indian headquarters. Regional units were self-sufficient for standard products, but not regarding customized products, for which support was given by headquarters. Sometimes priorities differed, but most of the time the headquarters listened to the regional office because it was located closer to the customer. Even if there were different points of view, some kind of consensus was usually reached.

In the other segments, where there was more project business, foreign units were more involved. For tax reasons, for example, contracts were often split in a domestic and a foreign part, where the customer handled the imports from foreign units. Regarding contract changes, regional units were allowed to make changes as long as a reasonable profit was maintained. If not, approval was required from the Indian headquarters. However, changes afterwards were not very common. The responsibility for an action network like a core team was regional and the different groups within the team worked out different packages to offer. This was a way of ensuring a joint approach to the customer. Very large projects were usually handled from New Delhi, and they were also involved in forming a project team and assigning a project leader when the contract had been signed.

Of the goods sold by the industry segment at one of the regional offices, 50-60 per cent was imported from internal units abroad. The Indian part of the contract was signed with this regional office, at least for small projects, where the independence of the region was high. For large projects ($5-10 million) support was needed from the headquarters of the segment. For tax reasons, the customer of imported goods usually signed a contract directly with the foreign unit involved. Even if the foreign unit then assumed responsibility in a formal sense, the moral responsibility remained with the Indian unit, whereas the foreign units did not usually interfere in these local deals. This part of the regional office did not have much contact with the group outside India, since most of the help came from the segment headquarters in Bangalore.

The regional office, in its turn, supported the branch offices in various locations, which also received some support from BUs and BAs at the segment headquarters. The larger, the more important and the riskier the project, the higher up it went, meaning that the size and number of teams grew. For complex products there was support from BU or BA, which prepared the actual offer. In these cases there was a transfer of responsibility to BU or BA, but the field person stayed involved as an interface to the customer. The decision-making was informal and there was usually a consensus between branch, region and BA. Sometimes assistance from abroad was also involved, but not much. There was some import of items to the industry segment, but whether this import was direct or not was up to the customer. Often they felt more comfortable when the regional office handled the imports, since it was located closer to them.

4.   Project marketing cycles and action networks

The previous chapter took up the international business marketing strategy without going so much into the change processes, whereas this chapter is devoted to these processes. The IBM strategy takes time to plan and execute, involving varying types of activities and number of actors over time, especially in the particular environments of emerging country markets. Customer problems to be solved and ensuing network, linkage and competitive strategies in the initial phases of the relationship formation process usually differ from those at the later stages, when the purpose is to maintain or dissolve relationships and networks. For example, first-mover advantages are of special importance in the initial stages. The process of linking parties through relationships changes continuously and runs through different stages. This business marketing process varies for different customer needs and solutions, and the more complex the product/service offering, the more complex usually is the process of linking up buyers and sellers. Thus, international business marketing strategy processes are best studied for projects, especially for large projects, which are extremely complex and time consuming. And such projects are plentiful in the big emerging country markets. Building many roads, airports, ports, houses, dams, power stations and industrial plants are a pre-condition for their high economic growth.

Capital goods are examples of such complex industrial products, often sold as a project in the form of a package deal consisting of products and services. Take a power plant for example, which can be designed in many ways fulfilling a large variety of needs, creating a complex value generating process. The equipment for the plant takes a long time to manufacture and put together by a large group of manufacturers and contractors. It is expensive to buy and therefore involves financing matters not valid for most other types of industrial goods. To succeed with such a project numerous issues have to be solved together by buyers, sellers and other parties involved. Buying and selling activities as well as other activity investments made in building up infrastructure and industry in emerging country markets creates vast business opportunities for MNCs skilful in marketing complex business projects. This is taken up next.

INTERNATIONAL BUSINESS MARKETING OF PROJECTS

There are important differences between industrial marketing in general, which mainly concerns products, and project marketing, which mainly concerns a package of products and services. The complexity is larger in many ways. First, business marketing is of a more imaginary kind in selling projects due to the special mix of physical and service attributes of the package deal, and how they are manifested over time. The physical facility, for example, cannot be inspected until the project has essentially been completed, which means that project marketing most of the time consists of a presentation of ideas and images. Such an imaginary type of marketing increases uncertainty for both parties, implying that successful marketing more than in most other business marketing situations depends on the reduction of uncertainty and hence on the establishment of trustful relationships, that is strong social and information linkages between buyers and sellers.

Second, project business is of a more temporary character compared to the more continuous product business. It is often found that business marketing and exchange activities related to the specific project take place within a limited, often well-specified time-span. However, this is questioned based on the experience of other MNCs, which have been shown to have a more long-term approach to project business, building relationships with the same customer that cover more than one project cycle. This chapter contributes to solving this contradiction.

Third, it takes a much longer time to form and develop customer relationships for projects than products. Between its initiation and completion, a project passes through a sequence of events. In fact, this extensive evolution path of the relation is considered to be the major difference between marketing of 'ordinary' industrial products/services and marketing of projects, therefore being the focus of this chapter. More precisely it is about the strategic aspects of this relationship process. The focus is on how links or activity chains are initiated, developed and organized, meaning that actor bonds and resource ties are relegated to the background (Håkansson and Snehota, 1995). Although being concentrated to the development of the strategic aspects of relationship building, the specific resource-based aspect of how relationship-based competitive advantages are created through the development and maintenance of cooperative value networks is left out of the chapter (Morgan, 2000).

Three major issues in international business marketing of projects are taken up:

1. The business marketing process is studied. Due to the long time-spans involved in project marketing, relationships take on a particular character, being of long duration, complex, and divided into three different sub-processes. This develops considerably the normal way of dividing the project sales process into various stages, where the number

of stages and the names given to them vary between authors. There is therefore a need to define them better from a marketing point of view, being grounded in a specific theoretical framework.

2. Some specific strategy issues in the business marketing of projects will be focused on. It has been established that mutual adaptations in long drawn relations create strong interdependences and high switching costs. But how do these take place during the various cycles of the marketing process? For this and other reasons, project business is risky with the high stakes involved. How are these uncertainties dealt with throughout the project cycle, particularly those created by tie-ups among the parties throughout the process? Furthermore, the winning sellers often emerge in the early stages of the process, even before tenders, for example, are published. It seems to be that the winners are those MNCs that manage to influence the tender specifications in their favour. This essential strategic issue is discussed below.

3. The organization of project marketing is taken up, since a neglected issue here regards how marketing is organized along the evolution path.

The chapter focuses on the business marketing strategy in this project process, where marketing is mainly a question of establishing and maintaining a network of relationships with customers and other parties of relevance to get the order. An important basis is research on the life cycle of relationships for industrial products (Wilkinson and Young, 1996; Ford, 2002), which mainly builds on the inter-organizational approach. Research on the dynamic aspects of relationship marketing is also relevant (Dwyer et al., 1987; Gordon, 1998; Rosen et al., 1998; Peck et al., 1999) as well as research on the evolvement of inter-organizational relationships (Ring and Van de Ven, 1994). The business marketing process framework within which this project marketing process takes place builds on previous research on project marketing in emerging markets (Ghauri, 1982; Jansson, 1989b, 1994a) and other relevant research in the project marketing field (Mattsson, 1973; Bansard et al., 1993; Cova and Hoskins, 1997).

A framework for the international business marketing process regarding projects is presented below, followed by an illustration of this process for Indpow – the large MNC active in India. This is a continuation of the analysis of strategic issues in business marketing of this MNC from the previous chapter. See Appendix 3.1 for a presentation of the MNC and the business marketing situation in India.

INTERNATIONAL BUSINESS MARKETING PROCESSES

To facilitate analysis of international business marketing processes, they are grouped into three separate processes: the product/service process, the relationship process and the marketing process. The product/service process concerns the fact that business marketing is different for different solutions offered by the seller. It is divided into a number of periods. The more complex the product, service or package offered, the more periods it consists of. For the large projects studied in this chapter, there are four periods from the initiation of the project to its finalization: the formation period, the bidding period, the completion period and the termination period. The relationships process originates from Ford (1980, 2002) and Ford et al. (1998) and consists of five stages: the pre-relationship stage, the early stage, the development stage, the long-term stage and the final stage. These stages in the relationship process are only taken up briefly in this chapter, and discussed in more detail in Chapter 6 on how they relate to the internationalization process of firms. There, the relationship process is merged with the internationalization process to establish a common background for IBM during the different stages of internationalization. This chapter is focused more on the marketing process, which is divided into a number of marketing cycles and phases relevant for the life cycle of a project made up of these relationship stages, and periods of the product/service process. These three sub-processes are related to each other in Figure 4.1. Before the chapter is devoted to the marketing process, the product/service process is presented as a background to this process.

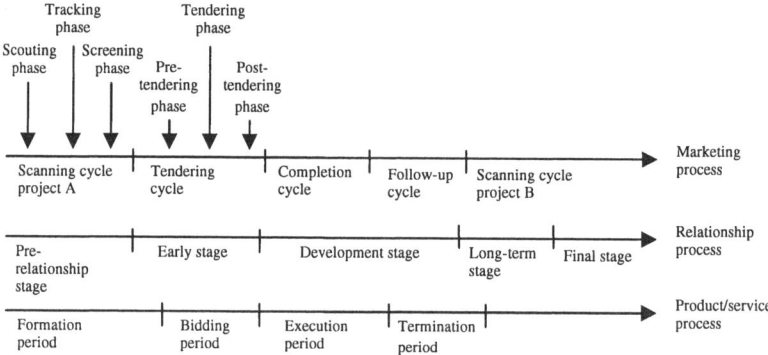

Figure 4.1   The international business marketing process

The Product/Service Process

The product/service process in selling projects normally consists of four periods. The project emerges and is specified during the *formation period*. Due to its complexity, it takes time to specify the need and how best to fulfil it. Often the customer is not capable of determining this by himself, but must seek help from experts such as technical consultants. Other issues than marketing and manufacturing issues also emerge, for example finance matters. Even if exactly what is needed can be established, the buyer might not be able to finance such an expensive need. When a general need has been established, it is time to study the need in more detail as well as comparing it to what is available on the market. For the buyer, this means translating the need into more specific requirements for equipment and service, which takes place through writing the tender specification. This is an elaborate process with many people involved. For the seller, it is a question of influencing the buyer to select his product/service or package. The publication of the finished tender finalizes the formation period and starts *the bidding period*. Based on the specification, sellers are normally asked to submit tenders, either sealed or open bids. These tenders are evaluated by the buyer and the order then given to the seller supplying the winning bid. This period ends with the signing of the contract. Now the *execution period* starts, when the ordered project is implemented. The equipment is manufactured, delivered, installed and tried out. Next, the equipment is ready to be run for many years to come. The project is finally transferred from the seller to the buyer, which means the end of their relationship for this project. This is the *termination period*.

The Marketing Process

The marketing sub-process of the business marketing process is the key process in selling projects (Jansson, 1989b, 1994a). This process is viewed from the perspective of the seller as a network strategy, where the seller tries to influence the buyer to select his offer. From a marketing point of view, the process is divided up in a number of major marketing activities. Each major activity tends to follow a cyclic pattern with gradually increasing and decreasing activities before the cycle is phased out and the next cycle starts along a similar pattern. These marketing cycles are illustrated in Figure 4.2.

In the formation period, the seller identifies the project and evaluates its profitability. Since most of these activities concern scanning, this cycle is called the scanning cycle. This marketing cycle takes place during the pre-relationship stage, since it is too early to influence the buyer cluster. However, sometimes the seller starts to influence the buyer already during the end of this cycle, where it overlaps with the tendering cycle and shifts the relationship process into the early stage. Most influencing activities take place during the tendering cycle, when the seller also makes and submits the tender. If the company gets the order and a contract is signed, the marketing process continues with the completion cycle, when the equipment is manufactured, delivered and installed. This cycle also marks the beginning of the development stage of the relationship process. Finally, during the termination period, the project is finalized by making trial runs. Two major types of marketing activities take place in connection with this period: the follow-up cycle and a new scanning cycle, which marks the beginning of the marketing process of a new project. If there is a follow-up cycle, the seller does not finish the marketing activities for the ongoing project upon entering the termination period. The project is followed up by, for example, servicing it and selling complementary products. So even if the project process has come to an end, it does not necessarily have to mean that the relationship with the buyer is terminated, since more projects may come up in the future. Rather, the relationship process enters the long-term stage with the start of a new project process, during which the relationship is kept alive by making courtesy calls, for example.

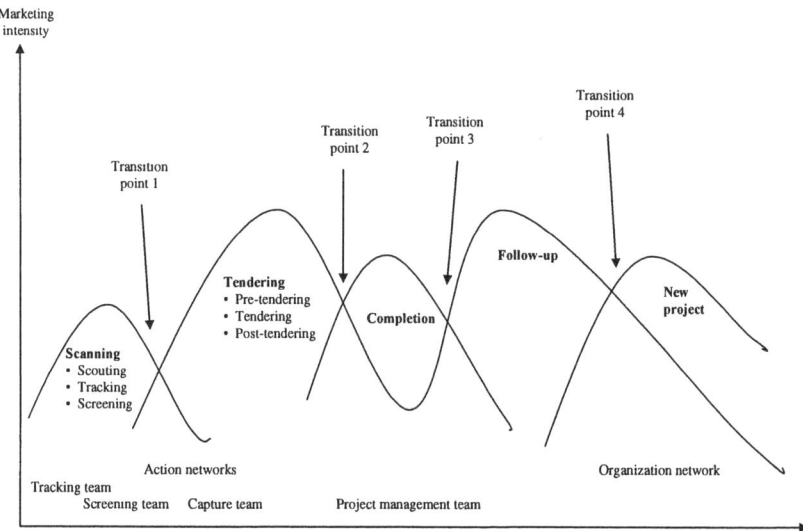

Figure 4.2   Project marketing cycles

Throughout this lengthy marketing process described through four major marketing cycles, a relationship with the customer has been institutionalized or an already established relationship strengthened further and reproduced. For a first-time project, most of the marketing activities during the scanning cycle take place in the pre-relationship stage, namely all activities until transition point 1, when the outward marketing activities start in the form of influencing the buyer cluster. The early stage of the relationship process has now been reached. The relationship might have reached some kind of habitual stage, where network relationships have become routine, and appropriate habits developed. The relationship could then function in accordance with certain customs, which can be taken advantage of in future business.

The scanning cycle
The marketing process is divided into four cycles. The activities during each of these cycles are further divided into some major types of activities. During the scanning cycle three major activities or phases occur: the scouting phase, the tracking phase and the screening phase. In *the scouting phase*, the MNC collects information from the environment in order to identify upcoming

projects. During this phase, the seller surveys different organizations of the broader network that initiate projects. After having identified projects, their business potential is evaluated. First a preliminary evaluation is done in *the tracking phase*, followed by a more detailed assessment of a more limited number of projects in *the screening phase*. During the scanning cycle the buyer is also engaged in investigating and evaluating the needs of the project and the suppliers being able to fulfil them. In this process, the buyer searches for information of different kind, inter alia from potential suppliers. A feasibility study is often done by the buyer or by a consultant. Some sellers also offer such studies free to the buyer.

Based on the information and evaluations of the profit potential of the project during the scanning cycle, it is decided at the end of the screening phase whether the MNC should go on with the project and submit a bid or close the project. This is a crucial decision point. So far not many resources have been invested in the project, while a continuation means that the MNC really involves itself in the project, investing many more resources than before. This is a crucial point in the project. The first marketing cycle has come to an end and may continue into a new cycle, if the project is not aborted. This instance is defined as *transition point 1*, since the marketing process continues through one marketing cycle being changed into another.

Mapping of project networks
An important pre-relationship activity during the scanning cycle is to identify the project network. Purchasing of projects normally is a very complex type of business, implying that the network identification often produces a complex grouping of clusters. This is illustrated in Figure 4.3, where a network consisting of four main types of clusters is illustrated: buyer cluster, seller cluster, competitor cluster and government cluster.

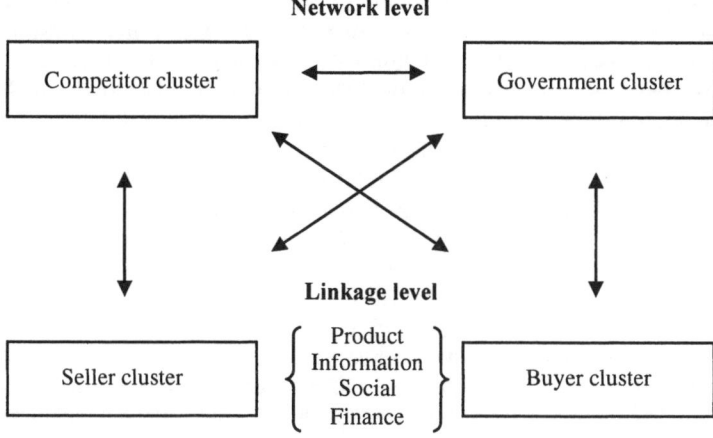

Figure 4.3   Map of project network

Several parties are usually involved in the buyer cluster such as end user, consultants, main contractor and subcontractors. Complex projects consist of a large number of different products and services, which are supplied by several units that could either be separate companies or belong to the same MNC. These sellers form different seller clusters that compete with each other (competing clusters). Various parts of the government are often involved as a government cluster either in the buyer cluster, for example as a public end user, or as outside parties. Individual clusters are connected within themselves, for example a micro customer cluster, and with one another through the five main types of linkages of the linkage strategy: the product linkage, the information linkage, the knowledge linkage, the social linkage and the financial linkage.

Intelligence networks
To map the project network or other activities during the scanning cycle, it is a question of using intelligence networks rather than influencing parties through the customers' network and the competitors' network. Moreover, in line with trying to achieve first-mover advantages, it is important to obtain information about a business opportunity, for example a project, as early as possible so as to be able to start influencing the buyer cluster. An intelligence network could then be formed encompassing a variety of major organizations involved in a project in one way or another, allowing first-hand information about emerging projects to be obtained.

An intelligence network is exemplified in Figure 4.4. It has been established at the group level to get information about emerging new projects that could mean business for the group. The main idea is to cover those organizations that finance large projects, and which evaluate project proposals at very early stages. The network involves relevant UN organizations, World Bank organizations and aid organizations as well as foreign embassies. An information broker specializing in contacts with these organizations is also hired and information about suitable contact persons for interesting projects bought from him. The Swedish Trade Office in New York is also used for such purposes. This network is also linked to local information clusters at the regional offices and market companies in various countries, which scan local organizations for possible future projects and feed such information into the network. Effective surveillance within the network demands regular visits to the various organizations of the network, as well as an organization for receiving persons from the network, for example foreign missions and other important visitors. Such activities are either carried out internally by the parent company and different subsidiaries, or are managed externally by consultants and trade offices.

One way for a company to take the initiative at as early a stage as possible is to create a project for a customer and then try to influence the latter to accept it. The company must have considerable knowledge of the country so as to know which projects could be in demand and what the project networks look like.

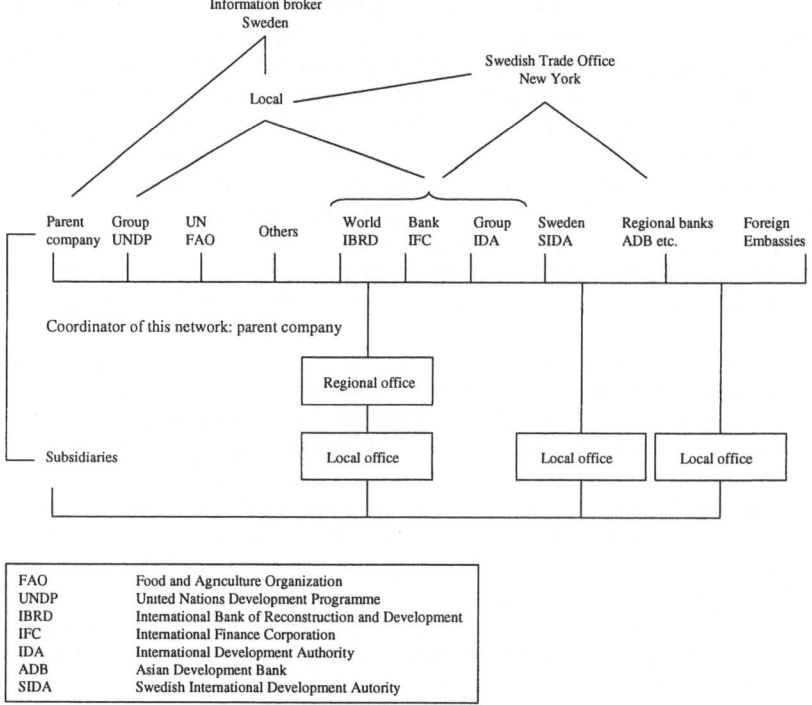

Figure 4.4   An intelligence network

The Tendering Cycle

During the tendering cycle, the influencing of the customer mainly takes place. This cycle is also broken down into three major activities or phases: the pre-tendering phase, the tendering phase and the post-tendering phase. The pre-tendering phase is centred on the writing of the tender specification, and where the seller tries to influence the specification to be adapted to suit his own products. In the tendering phase, the seller is preparing the bid, which is then submitted to the buyer on a specific pre-determined date. During the post-tendering phase the various bids are opened (if there are sealed bids) and evaluated by the buyer.

During *the pre-tendering phase*, the seller approaches the buyer with the start of outwardly-directed and canvassing communication activities. The seller now knows about the different potential projects and project purchasers and begins trying to influence them. During this phase, the different parties do not yet know much about each other and still experience high uncertainty. As for the buyer, this may concern the seller's production capacities and solvency, as well as propensity to keep agreements. The marketing activities during this phase begin in a general way and later become more specific.

Thus, the company mostly starts to influence the specific parties of the clusters already in the pre-tendering phase, which is mainly done through the linkage strategy. Two such important parties, which influence the network strategy, are often the end user and the consultant. A common tactic in this phase with the end user is to try to affect the tender specifications through a suitable linkage strategy. To facilitate this, the company endeavours to be on the spot long before a tender comes out, even before it is known when the tender will be made. The aim is to recognize what products the firm could supply in terms of the specifications. To achieve this, visits are made to key persons in the micro cluster, mainly the end user's technicians. The purpose is to create a contact net with them through promoting the information and social linkages. Sometimes, certain persons are employed by the seller cluster to make trips for scanning purposes, and where the contacts made are maintained for many years. Thus, it is important to find out who writes the tender specifications to be able to supply them with information. Since very complex projects are usually specified, outside information is required, which makes those writing the specification receptive to visits from suppliers. Consultants are often important in this context, since they take part in the writing of tender specifications. Moreover, they make feasibility studies on which specifications are based. It is therefore essential to include them in the network strategy and build up good relations with them. To get a first mover advantage at a very early stage, the seller may decide to prepare a feasibility study himself, thus bypassing the consultant. Such studies, on the other hand, are very expensive to make and there is, of course, no guarantee of getting the order.

Since the project does not materialize during the pre-tendering phase, marketing is very much a matter of selling ideas or project concepts. First-mover advantages are often created in this phase since, when the tender is published in the next phase, many competitors enter the business process with their bids. Thus, the aim is to pre-empt the business by coming in earlier than competitors in an effort to get the specification adjusted to the company's products. Since competitors act in the same way, this is a difficult and delicate task. Customers vary in their inclination to be affected by attempts to influence them in this early stage of their decision-making. Arranging seminars is a common marketing activity in this phase.

The *tendering phase* starts with the buyer publishing the tender and the seller supplying a bid. A critical decision in this context is how much to invest in a bid, that is to what extent the seller should become further involved in the relationship with this particular buyer or buyer cluster. The stakes are rather high, since it is expensive to produce bids, particularly for large projects. The chances of getting an order very much depend on how much the seller has managed to tie up the buyer in previous stages.

Sometimes the first part of the tendering phase, the evaluation of the bids, is open rather than closed, making it possible to influence the buyer. In such circumstances there is no clear demarcation line between the tendering phase and *the post-tendering phase*, which tends to be rather fluid. Under these conditions the bids are usually short-listed and a few sellers are selected, these being invited then to discuss various types of clarification. Such meetings tend to be extremely important. Since not everything can be formulated on paper, oral specifications may be decisive for the outcome of negotiations. Technical matters often dominate. Final negotiations of the contract for large and complex projects often take place even after an order has been accepted. Often it is possible to influence the buyer during the post-tendering phase, meaning that the submitted tender is not final. The tendering cycle ends with the signing of the contract. Negotiations are a critical part of this cycle, especially if the bidding process is open, and if two or three sellers are selected for further bargaining. During these negotiations, the sellers are familiar with the need in question and the buyers are familiar with the various offers. Bargaining takes place in order to reach an agreement. Bids are evaluated in both technical and economic terms. Bidding usually starts with a preliminary bid followed by informal meetings to specify the final offer. After that, negotiations become more formal, before the buyer finally decides on the suppliers. The agreement reached is influenced by the state of the broader institutional framework. If for one reason or another the legal system cannot be made use of here, stipulations not normally present in business contracts may be included, or a less formal agreement may be made based on trust.

Usually, it takes a long time before attempts to sell projects result in orders, and the tendering cycle itself sometimes can last for up to two or three years. The overriding purpose during this cycle is to get the order. If this happens, the relationship changes again, this time from the tendering cycle to the completion cycle. This point in time where the relationship passes from the second to the third cycle is defined as *transition point 2*.

The Completion Cycle

If the MNC wins the race and gets the order, the project process continues with the execution period, when the deal is implemented. The completing cycle of the marketing process has now been reached, and the hardware and software contracted for are manufactured, delivered and installed. Thus, after the equipment has been tried out and proven to work, the completion cycle is over and the operation of the project begins. This is the final point, or *transition point 3*, if the completion cycle shifts into a new marketing cycle, the follow-up cycle. After the equipment has been tried out and proven to work, the completion cycle is over and the running (operation) of the project begins. Since the seller is usually not involved in this stage, the project at hand is over as well.

The Follow-up Cycle

The follow-up cycle is an important marketing cycle, since spin-offs from the project can be taken advantage of. Software, for example, may be sold as service contracts. The buyer may also supplement the previous order or buy other equipment related to it. So even if the project process is over, the contacts built during the early stage and so far in the development stage can be used for getting future business. A first-mover advantage might have been achieved which can be used to sell additional equipment and service through the follow-up cycle. Also, even if a company has lost a contract, there are sometimes possibilities for sales later, during this cycle. A common heuristic is to try to bind the customer to the purchase of spare parts and service through a combination offer. The guarantee for the machines may be formulated in such a way that it is no longer valid if spare parts from other suppliers are employed. Orders for supplementary equipment might also be received. All these follow-up sales demonstrate how an initial order for main equipment can be worth much more later on. This is often taken account of in marketing strategy through the selling of basic equipment at a low price in order to gain access to a profitable after-sales market. In addition, the seller cluster may want to utilize the recently completed project as a reference object for future business, to enter a new scanning cycle that might lead to new project business. During this new scanning cycle, it is important to maintain contacts with the buyer so as to obtain information about new projects. The relation is maintained by courtesy calls and other similar activities.

Thus, even if the project process has come to an end, the marketing process goes on. This is also true for the relationship process. This new scanning cycle bridges and connects the individual project processes, meaning that the relationship process enters the long-term stage. This point in time, when the old project process turns into a new project process, is defined as *transition point 4*.

Integration of Marketing Activities

The marketing activities during the four cycles vary as regards such project characteristics as project size, purchase form and how well-known the seller is. A successful result requires the integration of the various marketing activities along the project process. There are, for example, crucial marketing problems already in the formation period, even before it is possible to identify what projects will be available. The seller tries to obtain first-mover advantages as early as possible. It is thus important to make a strong marketing effort early on, so as to get a lead over competitors. In that way, more is also learned about the business situation and about how to act in the various cycles. The own commitment increases, and with it the size of the linkage-specific investment, as more and more periods and relationship stages are passed. As stressed above, there are two crucial transition points or milestones. The first one occurs between the scanning cycle and the tendering cycle at transition point 1, when it is decided if the MNC should close down the project or go on. The second critical decision takes place at the end of the tendering cycle (transition point 2), when the winning bid is selected.

THE MARKETING PROCESS ILLUSTRATED

The marketing taking place during the various cycles and phases of the linking process will now be described further with the help of the experience of Indpow operating in India.

The Scanning Cycle

During the scanning cycle projects are identified during the scouting phase, the identified projects investigated further during the tracking phase and the projects evaluated mainly during the screening phase.

The scouting phase
Some of the most important sources are daily newspapers, government bulletins, market surveys done by the MNC, government general policies and big business houses. Other sources of information are customer talk, consulting firms and units within the MNC abroad with contacts with the World Bank or with foreign suppliers/subcontractors. There are also industry associations and information is subscribed from special consultants, who gather and sell information. Information might also be available from the principals and from other parts of the world having contacts with the World Bank.

It is important to track at an early stage, to be able to forecast. There is a pooling of information from within the company. A first hint of a new project is often recieved when representatives read between the lines in newspapers and magazines. Papers and magazines are scanned regularly and especially when there is a specific industry focus. The reason is that for a substantial project, or a greenfield investment, money must be raised. The representatives also get information – 'early warning' – by talking to potential or existing customers. This is very important in India, where close face-to-face meetings are emphasized. In eight out of ten cases early information is received from these sources, which gives better 'timing' and earlier warning than other sources used, for example media channels and reports by consultants. One way is to look at suitable government units for license applications submitted, which are published monthly. There it can be seen which customers have applied for licenses and for what. Other sources are customer talk and technical consultants, who are known well and with whom long-term relationships are kept. Such a consultant, of which there are only a few in each area of expertise, is usually hired by the customer to work out the project. A project in one business area usually starts with the customer identifying a suitable consultant, who will then investigate locations, work out technical specifications and handle various political processes. Big groups might not need consultants. They usually have enough in-house expertise. A new project is usually heard about from these consultants, with which the company is in constant touch. The consultants will also float inquiries to various companies.

Watch is kept at branch offices, regions, business areas and business units. There is a circulation of newspaper clips scanned into the computers and e-mails among units. For the spotting of new projects, there is a marketing organization spread out, extracting information from customers. Indpow has organized the scouting for new business opportunities to be done by business development groups.

The tracking phase
When the MNC has identified a new project and found the 'tracks', a series of evaluation processes take place. At first, there is a preliminary screening or tracking, when as much information as possible is searched for. This is important because of the large uncertainty with a project at this early stage. The tracking is usually done locally in India by a team consisting of a regional sales manager and representatives of the business area at HQ, where the regional sales manager has the main responsibility. In some cases, when the customer is a partially foreign joint venture, help from foreign units of Indpow in evaluating the foreign partner is received. The information found is fed into databases, both local and global, which, inter alia, help global headquarters to see trends in different markets, also being of use for manufacturing units and technology centres all over the world. The tracking team is to come up with a 'yes or no' decision for investing in further screening, which is very important in emerging markets like India. There is a huge gap between supply and demand in the industry, which has the consequence that many inexperienced companies want to diversify into the power business by setting up power stations. Among these, there are many unrealistic projects with a high drop-out rate.

So before the customer goes public with the plans, the company follows up the track by phoning different financial organizations or some four to five consultants doing feasibility studies in this field. If the customer is entering a new field of business, he will need a feasibility study and the expertise of consultants. Otherwise he will not get the finances. If it is a major venture, some reshuffling can be expected to take place among the top executives of the firms, which changes can be followed in newspapers and in monthly news monitors. A project with a major public customer usually starts with a feasibility study by the government to find out about the possibility of a plant. This is necessary, since the World Bank and other aid organizations need to approve of the projects they finance. In the feasibility study it is also stated whether a turn key or split contract is to be used, something that can be influenced through good connections and relationships both with the customer and with the financiers. You have to locate where to 'hit the nail'.

The screening phase
There is an 'opportunity tracking system', which produces an 'opportunity list'. Then follows a screening process, where the appropriateness of the project and risks involved are assessed. Before it is decided to go for a project, there is a screening process to study mainly the financial conditions

of the project and the past record of the customer. These studies are less important with well-known companies and public sector units.

One important aspect that is analysed, together with other fundamentals, is if the project will find financing. With government projects there are usually no financial problems. Public customers raise money internally or they might borrow from the World Bank and similar financiers. With private industry, on the other hand, the financial issue is crucial. Even if Indpow can lend to the customer, other financiers also need to be included.

Since the financial standing of a project is of great importance, an element of the screening process is to compare the track record of share prices with some industry index. The development of share prices gives an indication of the financial standing. It is considered important to pursue good performers, which means less risk and more timely payment.

Screening is organized differently depending on how demanding the task is, varying from being handled by teams of different sizes or by one individual. For example, if an official announcement of a large and potentially profitable project is likely, which means that the project is reasonably serious, a screening team is assembled. This follows from a decision by the tracking team to go on with the project. Since business units abroad are usually involved in a large project, it also has to be approved by the lead centre to which the business area reports.

Transition Point 1

For evaluating all inputs of these three phases of the scanning cycle, a 'sales pursuit tool' software is used. The objective is to come up with a decision whether to carry on, or not. If the software clearly indicates a yes, no further approval is needed for starting the spending of money on the project. The job of the screening team is to come up with a 'yes or no' decision on preparing a bid. On the basis of that decision, a capture team is set up, which then follows the project all the way. They make further competitor and strategic analyses, where they evaluate the weaknesses and strengths. This is important, since this preparation process during the tendering cycle for a large project might take two to three years, involving a cost of $1-3 million.

Thus, after influencing the project concept, and after working out a capture strategy and the partnering/financing concepts, the tendering cycle starts with a close analysis of all available information. Until this cycle, few resources have been needed, but now the MNC has decided to go ahead with bidding, increasing the resource allocation to the project considerably. The decision to go ahead depends on how good the chances are to win and if the returns are reasonable.

The Tendering Cycle

There are important differences between a single tendering and a two-step tendering process consisting of a technical part and a commercial part. In the two-step process, the technical specifications are fixed after the technical tendering and are not possible to influence afterwards, whereas the outcome will depend on the price of those bids fulfilling the specifications. However, the specifications might be upgraded in the process, for example if the customer becomes aware of new technology, which might then lead to a new round of bidding.

A single-tendering process is mostly used for technically simple items, often purchased repeatedly. This situation is easier to influence. The customer will arrange the qualified bids according to price, and the general rule is to take the lowest priced bid. There is usually a buying committee with two to three more influential members, who all have their preferences. The final decision rests with the board, which does not always go for the lowest price. Some private customers do not float tenders. If they find an acceptable solution, they will sign a contract with that supplier. These customers know which suppliers have the best and newest solutions, and contact these companies directly.

Public customers are obliged to float tenders, where the micro cluster in the form of a tender committee often consists of technicians, finance people and some senior managers. The purchasing process and as a consequence the composition of the micro cluster depends on the nature of the customer. With private customers, one to two people often take the final decision. In family-run businesses the owner is the decision-maker. In professionally run firms, the management is authorized to decide. With a public customer, different departments work out the specifications for their respective parts of the project. Often they use vendor specifications of available equipment, since they cannot prepare better specifications themselves. Most of the time consultants participate in the macro cluster, where they are used to going through the specifications, sometimes adding qualifying requirements such as 'previous experience' or 'manufacturing in India'. If the seller's connections with the consultants are good, the process can be influenced to the advantage of the seller. Consultants usually want a project to go on forever, since they will earn more money that way. However, since their recommendations are not binding to the customer, it is possible to influence the customer directly to change the specifications.

The pre-tendering phase
When a project is coming up, a sketch of a solution is presented to the customer. Important ingredients of the solution are then manufacturing, project management, after-sales and financing. Customer representatives are visited in teams consisting of both technical and commercial people, where support is received from the group when needed. The technology of the seller, and what can be done with it, is demonstrated to the seller. If a tender process is used, the goal is to influence the contents of the tender.

If the value of the project is large (about $5 million), a national capture team is set up at this point. The team consists of at least three persons but often more: a team leader, usually from the business unit at the Indian HQ, a group leader from the region and some technical experts from the business unit at the HQ. A project manager, who will take charge after the contract has been signed, might also be involved at this stage. The team members start interacting with the customer, presenting image and products as well as references from other customers. They give a solution, trying to influence the customer towards that solution. The purpose is to make the tender specification more favourable with respect to the solution presented. The initial customer visits are with technical people, followed by contacts with commercial people in order to get more favourable terms. The leader of the business unit, the group leader of the region, experts from business unit, and the project manager make these early visits. The customers' organization of the micro cluster is important to analyse, for example which persons favour the seller and which favour different competitors.

It is much easier to set a deal with established customers. Although a little less money might be received, it is easier to justify a higher margin with them. Normally they are satisfied with a less costly solution than the one originally proposed, if their needs are fulfilled. The most important influence factor with an existing customer is a good and trustful relationship. Competitors will usually bid very low, but if the relationship is good, the customer will usually not accept that bid. With new customers, the cost of capture is much higher. Stiff competition might lead to several rounds of bidding before price has been adjusted to specifications. Since it is difficult to justify a higher price based on value and performance, a reasonable price is most important as a factor with new customers. There is a trend towards financing as a major competitive tool, and a finance function has been established in India. The large projects sellers often go in with equity, but this MNC usually arranges consortia of banks which can give loans on favourable terms. In this, the MNC uses its good contacts, inter alia, based on its globally well-known name.

Regarding contacts with other group units, there is a global system called PROMIS, to which all group units have access. Any job getting yes in the screening phase and worth more than $3 million is fed into PROMIS, where the status of the project is reviewed every fortnight. With long-term partners such as key suppliers, information is shared very early in a project in order to have a pre-tender understanding. Actually, there is a list of acceptable suppliers agreed upon with the customer. These key suppliers often assign representatives to participate in the project, who then also are well known to the customer. Sometimes they are even brought along on customer calls.

The tender specification
After the strategy and action plan has been developed, the influencing of tender specifications starts, where technicians deliver technical arguments, finance people financial arguments, etc. The sales manager is the key person of the network, being the generalist who brings other resources along. In these activities, it is important to know the decision-making process of the customer. If the customer is Indian, then the Indian unit has the customer

interface network. But sometimes the picture is more complicated. If the customer is a joint venture with a foreign partner, there is an interface abroad as well, for example in the UK or US. This is a sensitive situation. The relationship between the partners needs to be known: how they get along, if they have different or even conflicting drivers. However, at the end there is always someone who is dominating the relationship, and who that is must be found out.

Since the pre-tender discussions mostly concern technical matters technicians at two to three levels are influenced. A key success factor for influencing is a good relationship with different members of the buying committee, to have a number of promoters. Another success factor is the previous experience of these members with the selling MNC as a company. Still another important factor concerns offering various personal gifts to the decision makers, which is done in about 30 per cent of the cases. In the selling process, it is important to act in a coordinated way. Marketing people, for example, might make promises to the customer regarding prices and delivery times that could be hard to live up to. Such unrealistic promises are harder to run away from if the responsibility for the contract terms remains with marketing all through the project. Since consultants are usually involved in the tendering process, it is equally important to influence them.

The tendering phase
Often the bidding, especially with public customers, is a two-stage process, starting with technical bidding and followed by commercial bidding. Regarding the contact frequency with customers and suppliers, it increases during pre-tendering but then stays even throughout the project. However, the nature of the contacts changes, since implementation people replace the marketing people who are important in the early cycles. Thus, the marketing department does not function as the customer's channel to the MNC after the contract is signed. The subcontractors are involved already in the pre-tendering phase and stay active throughout the project.

To make the actual bid or offer is a rather standardized process. Some balances are checked and some approvals obtained. A project team is assigned to work out the offer to be delivered to the customer. In this team members from the capture team often participate to keep themselves informed about the process. Generally speaking, the information gathering activities go on continuously during the entire sales process, both in Delhi and in the regions. It is necessary to keep track of the developments all the time. How much clearance that is required from other group units when making an offer depends on whether technology from other units is used or if they participate in negotiations. The division of work between units is set when the deal is signed and not when it is settled.

If the specifications are unclear or the lowest bid deviates somewhat from the specifications, the customer has to consider whether the lowest bid is still good enough or whether he should strictly follow the specifications. If Indpow's bid is higher but the quality better, the established relationship could be used to convince the customer of the usefulness of the own higher-priced offer. It is mainly argued that the equipment is a little more expensive for the moment, but that it is of greater usefulness in the future. If this tactic succeeds, the customer might add an extra amount on top of the lower bids to achieve technological parity, that is to bring the price up to the technological level of the bid supplied by the 'disadvantaged' seller. This might reverse the order of the bids. However, sometimes there are funding problems and the customer's hands are tied. This process is called 'loading' the bid, where the purpose is to bring the prices of the other bidders up. Being in the opposite situation of having the lowest priced bid, it is very important to avoid being loaded up. In this situation, it is of great importance to read the specifications closely, not adding extras above the specification for which the customer is unwilling to pay, but not being below the specifications either. It is vital to bid exactly according to the specifications. When followed exactly, the chance of being loaded up is reduced. Sometimes the company needs to take some risks by submitting a bid according to the specifications, although the MNC knows that the specifications cannot be fulfilled. Once the order is placed, the relationship and the convincing ability of the seller are used to persuade the customer that a 100 per cent fulfilment of the specifications is not necessary. Another reason for the customer not to pick the lowest bid is delivery time requirements. Perhaps the lowest bidder cannot deliver in the time required.

The post-tendering phase
After the tender has been submitted to the customer, it is followed up. This is a critical phase and real 'action time'. A close watch is held of what is happening with the bid, trying to find out how the evaluation is done, for example if consultants are used. The MNC is working through its friends at the buyer. This is the time when the real selling is going on. The bid is presented in a favourable way, highlighting the good parts and keeping a low profile on the less good parts. A bid not actively marketed at this stage will be forgotten, even if it is the best offer. One major reason is that the competitors are always active, highlighting the less good parts of the offer. Sometimes it is possible to make post-tender changes to the bid, that is to adjust the tender to the circumstances after it has already been submitted to the customer. The marketing process described applies to very large projects in the range of $100 million-$1 billion.

The Completion Cycle

After the contract is signed and the project has passed transition point 2, the marketing people hand over the execution of the project to the various business areas of the company, that is for manufacture, delivery and installation of the equipment. The regional sales office in Mumbai is not heavily involved in implementing the projects, which is handled by the business area in New Delhi. However, regional marketing keeps in touch with the customer because of being closer than the business area, thereby being the customers' channel to deal with problems and questions and customer service in general. This leading marketing unit is also responsible for the collection of money, document issues, etc.

The Follow-up Cycle

In case after-sales service is to be provided, it is already settled in the signed contract. Therefore this service is not sold after the contract has been signed. On the whole, long-term service contracts or after-sales services have so far been hard to sell in India, since there is no demand. But a change is probably under way. However, the relationship with the customer is kept alive through courtesy calls, since the seller wants to develop the relationship further by entering the long-term stage, or stay in it if there is already an established relationship. These calls are taken advantage of when a new project is coming up, in which case transition point 4 has been passed. Between projects, the contact frequency is low compared to the more frequent contacts with customers when tenders are influenced. In the new project, frequency increases a great deal again, reaching a peak during negotiations, after which the regional marketing unit in Mumbai, for example, has much less customer contact.

Rehabilitation projects
In other marketing situations, the follow-up cycle plays a more important role, for instance regarding sales of plants delivered by the MNC and the competitors. These sales are important to follow up, since they might generate future business. Sales in-between projects are important means to keep customer relationships alive. In Indpow's case, rehabilitation sales constitute a specific type of follow-up sales, which work as a bridge between projects. After being run for many years, plants might be in need of rehabilitation. If so, this business is often large enough to motivate a separate project. When such a rehabilitation project is set up, the regional sales office tries to influence the contents of the tender, where success partially depends on the competence of the buyers. Sometimes they will listen to several suppliers, trying to learn something from them. The process is much easier when good contacts are already established. If there is a need for help, most of it is received from the business area in New Delhi. For some plant projects much assistance is also received from foreign units, where most help is needed during negotiations.

To find new rehabilitation projects a list of suitable plants is kept, for example with their age, health condition, etc. The sales office in Mumbai uses the same list of plants as by other offices. Jobs and projects are also identified in the five-year plans and other official sources. For big projects there are usually two years from the first hints until the project really gets going. Informal sources are also used, as are industry houses, government officials, etc. When the appropriate time for rehabilitation has come, contacts are made with the owner of the plant or the owner makes contacts with the seller. If a suitable project is then spotted, the close contacts with the customer are used to discuss what needs to be done. The extent to which tender specifications for rehabilitation projects can be influenced depends on the competence of the buyers. If they know exactly what they want, the possibilities of influence are small. When assistance is sometimes required, summit meetings or hearings are held with the various possible suppliers.

ACTION NETWORKS

Following the network approach of this research, the organization of the project marketing process is viewed as an action network. Different marketing teams handle the marketing activities throughout the different stages of the project process. This team organization of project networks is a typical example of an action network. Flexibility is a major characteristic of the organization of these temporary lateral nets. They are accommodated to a number of factors, for instance the size of the project, the number of parties involved in the clusters, and the number of stages of the three sub-processes of the linking process: the product/service process, the relationship process and the marketing process. For large projects, for example, which take a long time to market and where many parties are involved throughout the linking process, the size and composition of the marketing team varies with the cycle of the marketing process. For smaller projects, on the other hand, more or less the same team handles the whole marketing process throughout the cycles. Another critical issue concerns the relation between this temporary action network and the more permanent organization network. People are taken from their permanent positions in the authority net to work for a shorter period in the lateral net, following which they return to their station in the organization network.

Action Networks in Indpow

Action networks are formed around project teams, which are organized differently depending on the type of project. The team organization is illustrated in Figure 4.1. For small projects, there is often the same action network (project organization) throughout most of the marketing process, for example a small team of up to three persons with a project leader responsible for forming the project, and for tendering and completing it. For large projects, the organization of the team varies with the evolvement of the marketing process, for example with separate screening, tracking, capturing and project management teams. The organization of marketing for medium-sized projects is a mix of these two extremes, where the screening activities, for example, might be organized separately, and where a few people belonging to a project management team will take care of all the other marketing activities.

Small and medium-sized projects
Marketing of electrical equipment and systems to industry, for example steel mills, consists of both turn key projects including complete installations and sales of pieces of equipment. When Indpow gets involved in a project, a project manager is assigned, who then picks a project team consisting of both technical and commercial people. The project manager is the single window to the customer. In the project teams there is normally an 'execution project manager' (with the team from the start), to whom the overreaching responsibilities are transferred upon execution of the project. If the product/service is supplied from abroad, a second (foreign) 'shadow' project manager is often assigned for that overseas part, but the Indian project manager is still the leading one. The Indian unit takes the initiatives in these matters as well as regarding the assistance needed from other group units. In general, India gets all the assistance required from the group. Information might also be received from principals in other parts of the world, for example from those who have contacts with the World Bank.

Large projects
The tracking during the scanning cycle is usually done locally in India by a *tracking team* consisting of a regional sales manager and representatives of the business area HQ, where the regional sales manager has the main responsibility. In some cases, when the customer is a partially foreign joint venture, persons from the group units outside India are used in evaluating the foreign partner. The information found is fed into both local and global databases, which, inter alia, help global units to see trends in different markets. Manufacturing units also uses these databases and technology centres found all over the world.

If an official announcement of a project is likely, meaning that the project is reasonably serious, a *screening team* is assembled. This follows from a decision by the tracking team to go on with the project, a decision mostly taken by consensus, since there is no point in overruling important participants like regional managers. Since business units abroad are usually involved in large projects, the decision to go on has to be approved by the lead centre to which the business area reports. At the lead centre it is considered what resources might be needed, if Indpow has the right technology to pursue the project, and the priority of the project. Overall, there is close interaction between business area and lead centre, since these units are seen as partners in this kind of business. The core technology resides at the lead centre. The global screening, which is sometimes preceded by less extensive local screening in India, is conducted by a screening team composed of people from the lead centre, people from the business area in India and people from other local business units abroad, which are involved in the project. At least a technician and a sales manager represent a business unit. If the project can be expected to include financing or investment by Indpow, people from these overseas functions also participate. If the local unit is well developed, there might be local leadership of the screening team, the advantage being that such a leader will be close to the customer. However, usually someone from the lead centre assumes leadership, which means frequent visits to India to get to know the customer. The leader is usually not formally assigned, but emerges more or less spontaneously during the process, as the competent person taking charge. Whoever the leader is, local units have a considerable influence on things, since they know the customer and the local conditions. Regarding the autonomy of the Indian segment, there are clear guidelines and specified frames within the group, which give a certain amount of freedom. There are also specific channels for finding information.

If the company decides to go on with the project, a *capture team* is set up to replace the screening team. This decision at the end of the scanning cycle about whether to enter the tendering cycle or not is a major decision at transition point 1. In the capture team persons are included who may contribute to a winning strategy. Some core members are always members of such an action network: a sales manager from the business area in India plus a technician. If Indpow in Europe is involved, they will contribute with a sales manager and a technician. Who takes the actual lead depends on the involvement of the parties in the project. If the core technology and the core equipment are from Sweden, then Sweden will lead. Usually there is a consensus regarding the lead roles, but one of the sales managers is always the leader of the process.

This core capture team has an initial brainstorming, where it is decided who else should be involved in the team or participate in team meetings. This depends to a large extent on which 'winning strategy' is preferred in the specific case, which in turn depends on the key drivers of the customer. To find out about this, a call is made to the regional sales manager, who knows the customer well. The team starts interacting with the customer, presenting images and products. For large projects within one business segment, these early visits are made by the leader of the BU, the group leader of the region, experts from BU and the project manager who also comes in early. But the members of the core capture team are still the drivers of the process in this 'think tank'. The activities of a capture team begin with a full-team meeting, where the drivers of the customer are discussed and competition is analysed, after which a 'game plan' is laid. Along with the strategy, an action plan is jointly developed by the team, consisting of the three 'Ws': who, what, when.

A major problem is that attention from top-level people, who often are very busy, is required more and more. This leads to a sort of internal competition for top-level attention between capture teams, where the more aggressive wins. It is no wonder that teams sometimes feel powerless and constrained. Some solutions to this problem have been discussed. One is to pick out a number of particularly important customers and assign some senior resources as 'key account managers' to them. Another problem with capture teams is their diverse composition. They usually consist of people from different cultures with different languages, backgrounds, professions, etc., often leading to misunderstandings and lack of communication. People from different cultures operate differently, where some are soft and some aggressive, reacting differently to things. Hence, it is very important to have managers with an international outlook, and who are experienced, cooperative, have a cultural understanding and know how the organization works. Actually a 'superman' is required, who is a leader and not a manager. To find such a person, there are training programmes for capture team members, especially for potential future 'key managers'. In order to determine where to put the resources in the most sensible way, there is a business development function at Indpow, making country plans and projections for different customers.

The *project management team* is formed later on in the marketing process to complete the project. Usually members from this team are not very active during the tendering cycle, except for resource allocation plans and completion schedules later on in the sales process. The reason is that there are penalties if delivery times are not kept. If project management has previously worked with the customer, this team might have an important role as an interface early on. The same is true if another business area has had business with the customer before and the Indian subsidiary has not. If members of these units know the customer well, they might be called into the capture team meetings.

To assist the action networks in the marketing process there is a combined *information, report, and support system* in the form of specific software used. This is global Indpow software, but adjusted to Indian conditions. It consists of formalized procedures for every step of the process on the way to a finished project. Data are fed into a set of form sheets corresponding to the following steps:

1. Sales Pursuit
2. Bid and Proposal
3. Plant Design
4. Project Management
5. Supply Chains
6. Install/Commissioning
7. Service/Support

Among the sales pursuit sheets, there is a forecast form containing the status and probabilities of a project. From this form, there are direct software links to other pages associated with the successive screening steps S1-S3, which makes it possible to follow the development of the project by comparing these pages. The software contains various parameters and questions, which result in opportunity analyses with scores helping to classify business, for example expected costs, customer opportunity profiles, the extent of customer contacts and the quality of these contacts (supporter, ally, etc.). There is also a feedback from the software with messages like 'customer contact is needed'. Another form gives information about the client's business. The data fed into these forms are seldom of an exact nature, so decision makers have to rely on judgments and guesses. For group contacts there is the PROMIS software, which reports on very large ongoing projects from all over the globe worth more than $3 million. Potentials and trends are found in this database, and also ongoing reference projects. Higher group management probably studies these reports, being of a rather short format. The priority and status of various local projects are determined in India and fed into the system. These software packages have newly been introduced, and have meant a major break-through for the Indian 'group'.

CONCLUSIONS

The influencing of the customer cluster takes place through a tri-part process consisting of the marketing process, the relationship process and the product/service process, together forming the business marketing process. This chapter is mainly about two processes, while the relationship process is taken up in Chapter 6 as part of the internationalization process of the firm. The international business marketing process usually begins before a specific project has been identified, that is before the project process is initiated during the formation period. The most critical marketing activities for getting first-mover advantages take place during this period and the bidding period, while the execution period is not so important from a marketing point of view, except towards the end, when the follow-up cycle starts close to the beginning of the termination period. The early start of business marketing activities for projects means that the pre-relationship stage is important. Careful preparations during the scanning cycle are critical for bringing the relationship process through the early stage via efficient handling of the tendering cycle to win the project. The relationship is further developed through the completion cycle in the development stage. Hopefully, satisfied members of the micro cluster will then set the relationship off to a prosperous future business through the relationship finally having reached the long-term stage.

During the scouting phase of the scanning cycle, the major organizational routine of the seller cluster concerns surveying different organizations in the broader network to identify upcoming projects. The main pre-relationship activities of this phase concern mapping the vertical, horizontal and diagonal dimensions of networks and scanning them through various information sources and intelligence networks. The outcome is increased focus on specific customers and projects, which is in line with trying to achieve first-mover advantages by obtaining information about a business opportunity as early as possible. Another major routine is about how to take the initiative at as early a stage as possible in order to create a project for a customer and then try to influence the latter to accept it. After having identified projects, their business potential is evaluated. First a preliminary evaluation is done in the tracking phase, followed by a more detailed assessment of a more limited number of projects in the screening phase. Based on the information and evaluations of the profit potential, it is decided at transition 1 if the MNC should go on with the project and submit a bid, or close it. A continuation means that the MNC commits itself to the project and starts to invest resources. The buyer is also engaged in investigating and evaluating the needs of the project and the suppliers that are able to fulfil them. A feasibility study is often done by the buyer, a consultant, or even sometimes by the seller.

The MNC mostly starts to influence specific parties of the macro and micro clusters already in the pre-tendering phase, which is mainly done through the linkage strategy. The seller now knows about different potential projects and project purchasers and begins trying to influence them. Based on various factors, the projects are evaluated further. At this phase, the different parties know too little about each other and therefore still experience high uncertainty. Even if the seller, for example, has enough knowledge about the customers and has a rather good idea about what own resources to use and capabilities to build on, the outcome is unknown, that is if there will be any business deal. The marketing activities during the pre-tendering phase begin in a general way and later become more specific, being grounded in the winning strategy and action plan developed. Two important parties of the macro cluster are often influenced, namely the end user and the consultant. A common marketing routine in the pre-tendering phase with the end user is to try to affect the tender specifications, where the aim is to recognize what products the firm could supply in terms of the specifications. The project has not yet been concretized in the pre-tendering phase, where marketing is largely a matter of selling ideas or project concepts. It is critical to create first-mover advantages already in this phase, since many competitors enter the business process in the next phase in connection with the publication of the tender. Thus, the aim is to pre-empt the business by coming in earlier than competitors in an effort to get the specification adjusted to the company's products.

In the tendering phase, which begins the bidding period, the seller is preparing the bid, which is then submitted to the buyer on a specific predetermined date. This phase starts with the buyer publishing the tender and ends with the seller supplying a bid. A critical decision concerns how much to invest in a bid, that is if the seller should become further involved in the relationship with a particular micro or macro cluster. The stakes are rather high, since it is expensive to produce bids, particularly for large projects. The chances of getting an order very much depend on how much the seller has managed to tie up the buyer in previous phases, that is how committed the buyer is. In the post-tendering phase, sealed bids are opened and evaluated by the buyer. This phase ends with the signing of the contract. Often it is possible to influence the buyer during this phase, meaning that the submitted tender is not final and the decision processes of the buyer cluster are not particularly strict. Negotiations are a critical part of this phase, especially if the bidding process is open, and if two or three sellers are selected for further bargaining. Bids are evaluated in both technical and economic terms.

Negotiations usually start with a preliminary bid followed by informal meetings to specify the final offer. After that, negotiations become more formalized, before the buyer finally decides on the supplier.

If the MNC wins the race and gets the order, the project process continues with implementing the deal. At this transition point 2, the relationship passes to the completion cycle, where the hardware and software contracted for are manufactured, delivered and installed. After the equipment has been tried out and proven to work, the completion cycle is over and the running of the project begins. Since the seller is usually not involved at this stage, the project is over as well. This is transition point 3, where the completion cycle shifts into the follow-up cycle.

It is important to distinguish between the process of the project and the marketing process and how they relate to the relationship process. Even if the project is over, the relationship developed can be used for follow-up sales and for getting future business, for example by using the project built as a reference object. A first-mover advantage has been achieved, which can be used to sell additional equipment and service. Information about new projects may also be obtained. Attempts are made to move the relationship into the long-term stage by social calls and other similar activities. Through this lengthy marketing process that has brought the relationship process from the pre-relationship stage, over the early stage and to the end of the development stage to the door-step of the long-term stage, the relationship with the customer is on the verge of being institutionalized. The development of the project has evolved to transition point 4, which connects the individual project processes and makes the buyer/seller relationship long-term.

Project marketing action networks are formed around project teams, through which the resources and capabilities are mobilized. The teams are organized differently depending on the type of project. For small projects, there is often the same project organization throughout the IBM process, for example a small team of up to three persons with a project leader responsible for establishing the project, tendering and completing the project. For large projects, the organization of the team varies with the business marketing process, for example with separate screening, tracking, capturing and project management teams. The organization of marketing for medium-sized projects is a mix of these two extremes, for example screening might be organized separately, but the number of people involved will be limited to one or two persons.

5. European, Chinese and Russian business networks

The inter-organizational approach to business marketing has been developed and is mainly valid in Western European markets. Its vocabulary, thought patterns and logic are mainly suitable to describe and explain the relationship behaviour of firms from these markets, especially the 15 mature European Union markets (Jansson, 1994a, 2006b). The basic ingredients of the inter-organization approach were outlined in Chapter 2 and adapted to the international business marketing strategy of European MNCs in emerging country markets. This aspect is developed in this chapter by looking closer at how the business marketing of MNCs belonging to the European business network is adapted to local market networks, in this case to business networks in the Chinese context as well as in the Russian context. To know how to deal with Chinese and Russian firms is of utmost importance in the era of the third wave of internationalization of firms. The Chinese business network dominates business in most Southeast Asian countries and in Greater China (Peoples Republic of China, Hongkong S.A.R. and the Republic of China – Taiwan). The Russian business network is found in Russia and many countries in Central and Eastern Europe as well as Central Asia. The Chinese business network is usually called the 'guanxi' network and the Russian business network the 'blat' network. First adaptations between the European and Chinese business networks are described followed by adaptations with the Russian business network. In this comparative process it is described how Chinese and Russian business networks function. Finally, these differences are discussed more deeply and local adaptations explained by viewing them as adaptations to institutional differences. The institutional network approach is thereby used, meaning that the institutional influence on network relationships is studied. The focus is on one major institution, namely country culture, which is one major informal rule system (Jansson, 2007).

THE CHINESE BUSINESS NETWORK IN SOUTHEAST ASIA

The differences and similarities between the European business network (EBN) and the Chinese business network (CBN) are illustrated by comparing two studies of the international business marketing of Swedish and Finnish

MNCs in three Southeast Asian countries: Malaysia, Singapore and Thailand. One study was conducted in 1984, 1985 and 1989 at 28 subsidiaries of 17 Swedish MNCs (Jansson, 1987, 1994a) and another study was made in 2003 with Finnish and Swedish managers at 26 Finnish and Swedish firms and subsidiaries (Ramström, 2005). A comparative analysis is made of how differences between networks take shape when firms from two very different network contexts meet: what does an adapted network between firms from two different contexts look like?

The inter-organizational approach to business marketing or the European business network is described in Chapter 2 and summarized in Figure 2.1. As found there, it originates from research on Swedish companies and has been extensively used to study the business marketing of industrial firms from Finland. These firms are therefore good representatives of the EBN and are hereafter called Nordic firms. They have evolved in a different network context compared to the overseas Chinese firms, and are therefore guided by different network principles and practices. According to the major strategic dilemma of local adaptation versus global integration, it is critical how much Finnish and Swedish MNCs adapt to the CBN when conducting business in Southeast Asia. Building on results from the two studies by Jansson and Ramström, summerized in Jansson and Ramström (2005), the conclusion is that as Finnish and Swedish firms develop relationships in the overseas Chinese context the resulting network is neither purely European nor purely overseas Chinese. Both types of firms deviate from their earlier behaviour. This part explores how each network (EBN and CBN) influences the mixed network, and is dedicated to describing the overall mixed network. Based on empirical findings, the purpose is to identify how the EBN has been influenced and modified by the Chinese business model while Swedish/Finnish firms are managing relationships in the ethnic Chinese context. The focus is on exploring how the mixed model takes shape using four aspects of high importance in international business marketing: (1) Purchasing; (2) business marketing; (3) 'genqing', 'guanxi', 'renqing' and 'face'; (4) gifts and kickbacks.

Purchasing

The purchasing of local Chinese customers is guided by intuition and business is based on feeling. While Nordic business people make decisions in a more rational way, the overseas Chinese decide more emotionally. Decision-making is characterized by spontaneity and seemingly little engagement in pre-planning. Overseas Chinese customer firms are therefore likely to seize unrelated opportunities as they present themselves. It does not mean that they do not engage in any planning, but their plans are not obvious or always visible to the Nordic firms. The influence of the hierarchical characteristic of the CBN on the mixed model is evident during purchasing. A contract is usually signed by several managers, who are responsible for the different departments involved in the purchase. Business is therefore tiresome and very bureaucratic. Although negotiations can be tiresome, lengthy negotiations are also considered a good way to get to know the other party, for instance learning whether the other person can be trusted or not. A rule of business is to never let the other party 'lose face'.

Price has a big impact on purchasing behaviour. There is a high degree of revenue orientation and price seems to matter most. One explanation is that the overseas Chinese are used to a sort of spot-mentality – 'going for the best possible deal', and minimizing risk. Another aspect of this price sensitiveness is haggling. Those who participate in the buying of a product are evaluated in terms of how much they contribute to reducing the price of the product. Consequently, most business deals are negotiated. This is particularly true for companies that sell equipment and projects. Even spare parts are sold through offers. Bargaining is very much a contribution to the mixed relationships by the CBN. A focus on price as a driver for perceived value also means that quality considerations are secondary. Since much of business is money driven, a contribution to a partner's cash flow is likely to result in a positive attitude towards the relationship. Even if customers are gradually becoming more quality conscious, it can still be difficult for Nordic companies to sell on the basis of quality, although this varies between different customer groups. However, Chinese salesmen employed by Nordic companies can still find the quality-oriented behaviour of these firms strange and difficult to handle. On the other hand, overseas Chinese purchasers seem to act differently when bargaining with Finns and Swedes than with other Chinese.

Chinese purchasers are deal-oriented, cash-prone and often have a rather low degree of technical knowledge. They have difficulties in defining their needs beforehand. Still the relationships seem to develop toward becoming more similar to the EBN. Even if still uneven, the level of capability of the purchasers in the engineering industry has improved over the years. Furthermore, despite advances in IT technology, decisions are still made face-to-face. Matters can be worked out over the telephone or Internet, but the final deals are always made face-to-face. Purchasing is often a slow process. For example, an overseas Chinese firm may require an offer within a couple of days, but may take several weeks or even months to reply with an order or inquiry. A lot of time is then spent with customers in specifying their needs, and offers are revised frequently.

Business Marketing

An influence of the overseas Chinese business network on the mixed network is identified through the high importance of personal relationships. In the Nordic context a social relationship is more an outcome of the business relationship. Business relationships between Nordic firms and overseas Chinese firms most often start with a good personal relationship; only thereafter does the business relationship start. This implies that the mixed network is largely influenced by the CBN, which stresses the importance of the social linkage or the social network. Accordingly, business decisions are based on a personal relationship to a higher degree than in the European context. Products and performance are basically secondary, and even when the product is superior it might not result in a deal if the personal relationship is not well managed.

While social interaction in the EBN has more of a supporting than a deterministic role for the business relationships, social interaction is more clearly and specifically expressed in the mixed relationship. The social linkage is mainly influenced by the CBN, where it is commonly believed that it is the person who creates the organization, not vice versa. Local business people therefore refer to a person (a business card) never to a company name.

Contact nets are characterized by a high degree of informality, underlining the exceptional importance of personal selling as the primary medium of transacting. Cultural influence is a major factor behind the critical role of the social linkage in the ethnic Chinese network. The Chinese display traditional ways of behaving in the business world, even in the mixed model. The high informality also means that business relationships between ethnic Chinese firms are usually paperless, in the sense that written formal contracts are just for looks. However, in the mixed model contracts may be part of business deals, mainly influenced by the EBN. In Thailand, for example, ethnic Chinese firms are aware that their partners' parent companies require written contracts, and therefore written contracts are also used.

The reliance on personal relationships makes it difficult to get direct access to new customers in the engineering industry. Many visits are required even before coming to the point of making an offer, in order to build a social relationship. Even more visits are required to get an order. Therefore Finnish and Swedish organizations visit their partners and customers more often than they would in their home context. In a few of the companies there are even some internal jokes that their sales personnel have their own office at their customer's or partner's organization. The length of the establishment period is mainly influenced by the value of the potential sale and the intricacy of the buying process, or how many decision levels have to be penetrated. It is also influenced by how strong an association the buyer has with other competitors. Ethnic Chinese typically draft broad contacts in many directions, which provide them with knowledge, which in turn allows them to plan better and to negotiate with many different customers.

In the EBN, performance or efficiency is mostly measured with financial criteria; the Nordic MNCs having financial rather than growth goals. At the end of the day what matters for these MNCs is the performance, and the business relationship can be broken if the performance is not satisfactory or if the parties feel that the relationship does not work to expectations. However, when these MNCs operate in Southeast Asia it works more according to the CBN, that is if two partners have started a relationship they live through it together. There is an expectation that one continues as a friend and a partner even if either party feels that the business relationship is not producing the desired outcomes.

Breaking a relationship can have severe consequences for the Nordic firm, because it will not only get a bad reputation with one firm, it will also most likely get a bad reputation in a much wider network of firms. Hence, it is sometimes required that a firm remains in the relationship even during times when it would make more sense economically to leave the market. If a business relationship is broken due to poor market conditions, then the firms breaking it might not be allowed to rebuild the business relationship since it earlier damaged its reputation.

Trust
In European firms, people are typically trusted until they have proven they cannot be trusted. In the overseas Chinese context, on the other hand, it is typically the other way around. People are distrusted until they have proven they can be trusted. In the mixed model overseas Chinese firms are adapting their behaviour by making extra efforts to earn trust. They respect the European firms' integrity, and appreciate that European managers openly inform them if something cannot be implemented. Denying or saying no would normally be avoided in a traditional overseas Chinese context because of the risk of causing loss of face. Although the Nordic managers are sometimes too blunt, the European firms' integrity instils a sense of trust and security in an atmosphere typically characterized by distrust.

'Heart', 'Genqing', 'Guanxi', 'Renqing' and Face

The strong influence on the IBM in Southeast Asia from the CBN is further seen in how relationships are established and maintained through the personal social linkage. Whether a salesman will get an order is largely determined by a combination of 'heart', 'genqing', 'guanxi', and 'renqing'. 'Buying your heart' illuminates an important aspect of the social network, namely the chemistry between persons in the overseas Chinese context. Social events therefore have a big role in business life. Dinners are often more important than lunches as meeting places. The function of social events is to learn about each other and develop trust, while meeting in a relaxed setting to cultivate the relationship. The setting is typically informal during these occasions, and many issues can be discussed more openly.

In addition to eating together, playing golf is important for developing social relationships or 'guanxi' (roughly meaning 'connections'), and virtually all local mangers play golf. Playing golf creates 'genqing', that is making it possible to create a relationship from a common background. Since continuity is important in social interaction, playing golf regularly gives the partners the opportunity to spend time with each other on a regular basis and hence develop strong social bonds. Gaining access to local personal networks does not seem to be a priority for the respondents in the second study. One respondent even claimed that access to social networks is not a requirement for strong relationships. Another claimed that good relationships with local employees are more important than access to local social networks. One negative expression of 'genqing' is that Nordic businesspersons often are considered out-group members. However, being foreign also means that Nordic firms receive differential treatment. The relationship mainly works through exchanging favours or 'renqing' in Chinese.

In the CBN there is no clear distinction between formal and informal relationships. Business letters can be formulated quite formally, but discussed in a rather informal fashion over lunch. The mixed model is different from the Chinese business model in the sense that the overseas Chinese are more formal and address more business issues than they would in a relationship with other Chinese firms. This is clearly a strong influence from the EBN, since Finnish/Swedish firms are accustomed to addressing business issues much earlier in the relationship.

Because of the importance of 'face', Finnish and Swedish firms often adopt a non-confrontational approach in SEA, and are more focused on achieving social harmony. 'Face' is important both internally within the Swedish/Finnish MNCs studied, and externally, in relations with other companies. Personal relations tend to be more restrained and harmonious than candid and conflict-oriented, particularly in selling to local Chinese firms. The firm's social behaviour is emphasized much more in the overseas Chinese context. This is clearly different from the Finnish and Swedish firms' behaviour in their home context, and this type of behaviour is, hence, strongly influenced by the CBN.

On the other hand, foreign firms are not expected to act correctly in all situations. They are treated differently and are forgiven for more things than local firms would be. Local businessmen are also more tolerant towards foreigners' mistakes, since they realize and accept that foreign firms cannot know all the customs and norms of local business.

Many of the respondents in the second study felt it is positive to be involved in a foreign firm. There is some added value and prestige for the local firms to have a foreign business partner, although this seems to vary a bit from country to country.

Gifts and Kickbacks

Another culturally determined aspect of networks in SEA is the closed network, where important parts of the network can be secret and hidden. It refers to the ability of performing some business deals that do not follow the rule of the law. While the terminology is changing, the system is not; what was earlier referred to as 'under the table' is currently referred to as 'under the carpet'. This aspect is seldom found in Finland or Sweden, which are two of the least corrupt countries in the world. However, it is a common element of many business transactions in Asia, often being a culturally determined unofficial underground part of the economy. In SEA it mostly goes under the name of 'crony capitalism'. In fact, the overseas Chinese view gift giving as a central ingredient of creating favours ('renqing') and building 'genqing'. Gifts need not be physical goods, they can also be for instance information, access to some resource, market knowledge and so on. The major challenge for Finnish and Swedish firms is that in their home environment, gift giving is viewed as illegal, and there are strict rules on what constitutes a legal business gift. The line between what is considered a legal or illegal gift is blurred in the overseas Chinese context. Often gift giving is a part of most transactions. The local businessmen typically do not see anything wrong in giving someone a little tip for a good service.

Another typical characteristic of purchasing behaviour for firms in SEA is the demand for kickbacks. This system seems to be more common in certain countries in SEA, for example Indonesia and the Philippines, and less in others, for example Malaysia and Thailand. Singapore is an exception, since there is little evidence of the kickback system. Usually the system works in one way in private industry and in another way in government. The kickback system also depends on how competitors act. If they give kickbacks, a company that does not finds itself at a competitive disadvantage. There are also differences depending on the type of product and the decision processes involved in purchasing. Governments almost always buy on the basis of tenders, where the major point of influence involves the writing of the tender specification. In private industry, building a continuous relation is critical. This allows the kickback system to thrive. In some industries, the long life-span of equipment, for instance, cannot be used as argument towards critical decision makers such as plant managers, who only reckon on having their job for a fairly brief period, tending to get it shortly before retirement. This provides a great opportunity to the person to collect a pension in this way.

The Nordic firms in the mixed model are considered transparent and open, and business is done in a respectable and straightforward way. This kind of transparency is sometimes quite surprising to the local businessmen, because they are used to a much more closed system, but very quickly start appreciating and liking it.

THE RUSSIAN BUSINESS NETWORK

Another approach to networking of relevance to international business marketing is found in Russia and some East European countries, for instance Poland and the Baltic States, namely the Russian business network (RBN). This type of social network developed in the Soviet Union and is mainly characterized as relationships based predominantly on personal features such as close friendship and trust (Agapitova, 2002). During the Soviet times it became an essential part of people's everyday life. A major feature of the RBN is 'blat'. In the centrally-planned era, it was a system of personal connections, which helped to overcome shortages of goods (Michailova and Worm, 2003). The second major characteristic of this system was the 'nomenklatura' or communist party elite network. According to Ledeneva (1998), 'blat' was a kind of barter system built on exchange of favours to get access during conditions of shortages and a state system of privileges, and where the favour of access was provided at public expense. It mainly served the needs of personal consumption and reorganized the official distribution of material welfare. How this system worked during the centrally-planned era is described in illustration A. The word 'blat' comes from Polish and means 'someone who provides an umbrella or cover'. It originates from Yiddish, where it means 'close/familiar', 'one of us' or 'one of our circles'.

Illustration A

Thanks to the good network of her mother, Kristine was employed as a stores manager in a well-known knitwear shop in 1977. She quickly learned the working strategies of her new job, mainly how to use the informal privileged position of disposing of the goods of the shop. The knitwear was in high demand, but the supply insufficient for the needs of the consumers. Only a few of these clothes were sold over the counter, while a large part was kept and exchanged for other goods. More and more exchange relationships were established. These were not based on exchange of goods per se but on access to public resources. By giving goods to favoured persons, Kristine got favours in return: access to other goods and services. Often she received gifts to put clothes aside.

> We could have sold 100 pieces of knitwear per day, if we would have had that many. But we only got about 100 per month. It was up to me to decide how many of these that should be put on the shelves in the shop – 20, or just 5. The rest we kept in the stores. People came with gifts and begged to buy our knitwear. Friends, officials' wives and famous actors came to the stores to try on the goods. One of the actors, who regularly got to buy our clothes, always brought with her tickets for the theatre. There was a butcher's shop 100 metres from our shop. The shop assistants from there came to us with fresh meat, which we could buy, and we let them buy our clothes. I had 'blat' with them, and they had 'blat' with me. (Barstad, 2004, my translation).

Other examples of using 'blat' were entry into popular universities, getting prestigious jobs and promotions, and obtaining apartments. The 'blat' social network included friends, family members, neighbours, co-workers and others. It was used to exchange goods, services, and favours. It did not have any monetary expression, and was basically an exchange of favours of access. 'Blat' was part of the centrally-planned economy. It was important to all people in the Soviet Union who wanted to have a decent life, where access to some goods was impossible without having 'blat'. There were three main characteristics of the social network of the RBN.

1. *Exchange of resources.* Through the own social network and its connections to other social networks, it was possible to get access to various types of resources, so called 'social resourcing'.
2. *Continuity.* The requirement for 'blat' is long-term and strong personal relationships.

3. *Trust and cooperation.* 'Blat' is based on social trustworthiness or emotional trust rather than professional trustworthiness.

To navigate in this system the right people must be known: those who have the power to open doors and help to overcome the obstacles imposed by the system. A special feature of the centrally-planned system was a kind of middlemen called pushers ('talchky'), who obtained scarce goods from other sources. These people used 'blat' or even bribery to get needed goods from government or from other sources (Agapitova, 2003). The 'nomenklatura' might be seen as a particular network within the 'blat' network. This network involved the elite from the Communist party, senior officials of the State, industrial organizations and research institutes. The network is more concentrated and central than the 'blat' network, representing the most powerful social structure and playing a significant role in all spheres of society.

During transition the 'nomenklatura' network benefited the most from privatization, and the network slowly decoupled with the rise of the new Russian business groups. Rather than being in power in the Soviet regime, they are now in power by owning enterprises and participating in the network of the same people from another perspective. Even if changed, the importance of 'blat' is still high. Personal contacts are very important, especially when dealing with the customs offices, the banking sector, regional administration and the health care sector. Here the old system characterized by shortages largely remains. In the highly bureaucratic state agencies, for example, 'blat' is the way to fix some matters faster. It is also useful for gathering information about how to deal in markets. Due to still being widely spread, this network serves as a linkage between business groups, regional networks and different 'blat' networks. However, it is also widely used for illegal actions. 'Blat', together with corruption, is often used to influence government authorities and other structures. It has become more related to economic interests and business compared to the communist period, when it was mainly associated with political consideration and private consumption. 'Blat' has become more and more materialistic, gradually losing its human face and becoming dominated by pragmatism and the rules of the market. It has transformed from being based on moral and ethical considerations to having an explicit financial expression. With transition the 'blat' system has changed from a positive 'favour-to-favour' system to a more corrupt system. It is now more materialistic and pragmatic than emotional and human. As discussed before, transition is characterized by a high level of uncertainty and ambiguity, typical when leaving an old and well-known society for a new and unknown society. This largely explains the staying power of the 'blat' system, since it helps to reduce this uncertainty. The social network is a main safe haven in times of great change.

INTERNATIONAL BUSINESS NETWORKS: A COMPARISON

The Impact of the Basic Rules

According to the institutional network approach introduced in Chapter 2, network behaviour is influenced by institutions, because they are excellent instruments to explain and predict business marketing behaviour. This implies that the differences and similarities between the European, Chinese and Russian business networks can be explained by relating these differences to the major institutional characteristics of the basic rules model. This is illustrated in Figure 5.1.

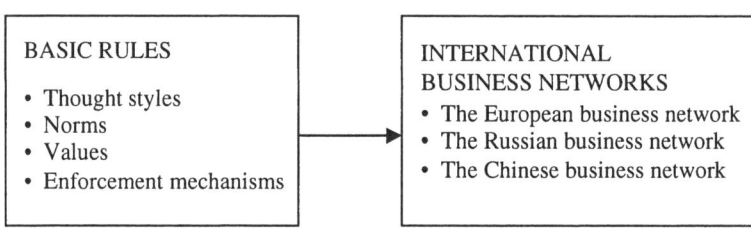

Figure 5.1   Impact of basic rules on international business networks

The most striking conclusion when comparing the results from the first study in the 1980s (Jansson, 1987, 1994a) and the second study in the 2000s (Ramström, 2005) is that relationships based on a mix of the European and Chinese networks in Southeast Asia have not changed much during this period. However, on a general level, ethnic Chinese network behaviour seems to be moving slowly towards the European network behaviour.

The external network of the MNC in markets and government is influenced by institutional structures ('macro rules'). The impact of these institutional structures determines what goes on inside the networks. Building on the major characteristic of emerging country markets being relationships societies, a basic networks model was developed in Chapter 2. The MNC, markets and society are described from a network perspective, with the linkages between the MNC network and some of its major external parties in product/service markets.

A key part of the institutional perspective of the INA is the basic rules model consisting of thought styles, values, norms and enforcement mechanisms. An MNC is, because of its multi-cultural basis, an institution consisting of many thought worlds, where cognitive systems tend to vary between its various units. Those employees sharing thoughts, making classifications and labelling reality in common have a unified thought style. Their common frame of reference works as guidelines for sense making and action. These established patterns of thinking therefore work as cognitive recipes for how people behave. Ideally, they produce a self-activated regular organizational behaviour. Norms and values also influence how people think and act. Values are the root of cultures and behaviour, defined as 'conceptions of the preferred' and as standards for comparison. They set the priorities and function as guiding principles. Norms, on the other hand, specify how things should be done. They work as guiding principles for how to act, a kind of decree about how one should act or how something should be constituted or organized. Organizational behaviour is also controlled by incentives and sanctions. Such enforcement mechanisms concern how to construct the sanction and incentive system in order to reward or punish individuals and groups within the MNC together with establishing surveillance and assessment systems to control enforcement.

Based on Figure 2.1, the main characteristics of the inter-organizational approach to business marketing used to characterize the European business network (EBN) are specified further in Table 5.1 from the institutional perspective, using the basic rules model from Jansson (2007). The EBN is directly contrasted to the major characteristics of the overseas Chinese business network (CBN) and the Russian business network (RBN). The comparison is grouped according to specific themes related to the basic rules model. The characteristic of the EBN is stated first followed by the comparable characteristic of the CBN and RBN according to the specific informal rule and type of basic rule. The traits of the CBN builds mainly on Jansson (1987, 1994a) and Ramström (2005) as well as on others' research on the overseas Chinese family business system since the 1970s (Redding, 1985, 1990, 1991, 1995a, 1995b; Redding and Richardson, 1986; Chu, 1991; Björkman, 1994; Hofstede, 1994; Chen, 1995; Lasserre and Schutte, 1995; 1999; Hamilton, 1996; Naisbit, 1996; Haley, 1997; Bjerke, 1999; Haley et al., 1999; Seligman, 1999; Tong and Bun, 1999; Yip, 2000; Backman, 1999; Tsui-Auch and Lee, 2003). The traits of the RBN mainly build on Trompenaars (1993); Hofstede (1994, 2001); Salmi (1995, 1996, 2000, 2004); Ledeneva (1998); Hampden-Turner and Trompenaars (2000); Johanson (2001, 2004a,b); Johanson et al., (2002) Michailova and Worm (2003); Hallén and Johanson (2004a,b); Jansson (2007); Jansson et al. (2007).

Thought Styles

The three business networks are compared along the following major thought styles: self, perception of time and causality.

Self

The first theme is 'self', which concerns how a person mentally relates to his social environment, for example if he looks upon himself as belonging to groups or not. This dimension is close to Hofstede's individualism/ collectivism dichotomy. Therefore, overseas Chinese do not join networks in the way westerners join organizations. Every individual has a social network built around him, consisting of family, relatives, colleagues and friends.

Table 5.1   Comparison of the international business networks according to the basic rules

Basic Rules	European business network	Russian business network	Chinese business network
Thought Styles			
Self	Firms in networks Individualistic	Networks Collective	Networks Collective
Perception of time	Mid/long term Changing/continuous	Short term Changing	Long term Lasting
Causality	Logical Brain	Logical Brain/heart	Logical Genqing/Heart
Norms			
Trust	Organizational/professional trustworthiness	Individual/social trustworthiness	Individual/social trustworthiness

Table 5.1   Continued

Basic Rules	European business network	Russian business network	Chinese business network
Values			
Achieved/ascribed status	Achieved mutuality	Blat (mix)	Guanxi (ascribed)
Inner/outer direction	Competitiveness	Legitimacy	Harmony: Ying-Yang
	Conflict	Conflict/harmony	Harmony
Universalism/	Profitability	Favours	Renqing
Particularism	Open	Closed	Closed
	Impersonal (formal)	Personal (informal)	Personal (informal)
Enforcement mechanism			
Authority	Hierarchical	Parental	Parental
	Decentralized	Centralized	Centralized
	Formal	Formal	Informal
Sanction Mechanism	Formal: Laws	Informal: Customs	Informal: Face
Type of sanction	Incentive	Punishment	Punishment

As a result of this interconnectedness between the networks of family members, the overseas Chinese business environment is explained as a series of interlocking networks, families and relatives. These inter-firm clusters have been referred to as 'business networks'. Consequently, networks have become the institutional medium of economic activity in the overseas Chinese community (Redding, 1990; Whitley, 1992b; Hamilton, 1996) and therefore it is not a question of becoming part of a certain type of network, but a question of becoming a trusted member in a networked society (Ramström, 2005).

The main focus of the EBN is centred on the individual firm of the network, forming a network around this firm. The focus of the Chinese business network, on the other hand, is on the network itself as an entity. This is a reflection of the collectivist world view of Chinese society in contrast to the more individualistic outlook of Western European societies in general (Hofstede, 1994). The situation is similar in Russia, where the informal social networks established during the period of the centrally planned economy are still important in business life. However, they are gradually changing with transition towards the West European 'firms in networks'. In the Western context as well as in Russia, it is mostly autonomous individuals in firms that are interconnected, and these relationships rest on rational and logical calculation and (voluntary) individual action. Chinese businessmen, on the other hand, tend to have a more holistic thinking. As a result of the network structure of society in China and Southeast Asia, the level of collectivism is high. Every individual has a social network built around him, consisting of family, relatives, colleagues and friends. In Russia, there is a collectivist world view, where people think that it is important to belong to groups, where they avoid standing out, and where they risk being punished for their own initiatives (Hofstede, 1994). Individualism is also a basic value of Russian culture. This group thinking seems more to be based on the working group than the family. In Western Europe, on the other hand, individualism is strong, and the rights of the individual are of the outmost importance (Halman, 1994).

The CBN is therefore understood to consist of loosely connected overseas Chinese firms, which are embedded in a larger context of extensive personal networks. Business groups are based on organizational alliances, and firms exist within networks involving suppliers, customers and other parties. But such prevailing relationships do not restrain the firm from seeking new markets and changing direction. Vertical integration is becoming less important, which also means that firms outsource many activities. However, networks of commitments do not normally connect across industrial sectors. Such inter-sector coordination in the overseas Chinese context is largely achieved by families establishing subsidiaries or joint ventures and partnerships with personally known and trusted entrepreneurs in business groups. This is well described by Backman (1999):

> What does it take to make a conglomerate in Asia? Take a bank, add some
> trading interests, some manufacturing interests, a stock broking firm, lots of
> real estate holdings, and perhaps a hotel, mix it all around to form a loose
> structure, but one in which lots of internal transactions take place and put the
> lot under the control of the family.

Thus, family firms are often interdependent with subcontractors and trading
agents. However, because most subcontractors are perceived as outsiders,
commitments are usually not long-term and therefore less extensive and long-
lasting (Whitley, 1991).

Perception of time
The following two aspects relate to the theme 'time', which explains how
people perceive time. Time can be perceived as linear, for example whether it
is possible to divide and measure time in a precise way, and whether time is
considered to be lost or not. A linear Western time perception is contrasted to
an Oriental circular time perception, which is found in many South and East
Asian religions. This is a major reason why overseas Chinese business
networks are relatively strong, last over the long term, and according to the
previous thought style represent a continuity of collective common interests
(families, communities and sets of friends and relatives). As shown above,
relationships between Swedish/Finnish firms are relatively weak and
generally represent short or mid-term economic interests, and have more
unstable and changing business networks. Russians have a short-term
orientation. There is little planning for the future, the focus is on the past and
the present, and managing is done on a day by day basis. There is high
uncertainty avoidance, where risk taking is discouraged and where people
avoid taking responsibility (Jansson, 2007).

Causality
Causality focuses on the thinking processes, for example, if it is abstract or
non-abstract, if logical connections are made between categories, and if
linear, sequential explanations are made. In the Western European country
markets it is mostly autonomous firms that are interconnected through
individuals, and these relationships rest on rational and logical calculation
and (voluntary) individual action. Chinese businessmen, on the other hand,
tend to have a more holistic thinking. Their business logic is guided by
intuition and business is based on feeling. While West European business
people make decisions rationally, the Chinese decide more emotionally, and
the way of thinking is not logical in the sense that westerners understand.
Business decisions are also perceived as emotional because the ethnic
Chinese take into consideration personal and mutual relationships. Chinese
firms are also seen to engage in rather little pre-planning, and it is not always
clear how the organization works. This could be interpreted as a result of the
local firms' tendencies not to have evolutionary strategies, that is they are
likely to seize unrelated opportunities as they present themselves. Related to
this aspect is the strong emotional theme of the Chinese. A common

metaphor for this strong emotional content of the relationships is the heart, while the brain is more symbolic of the less emotional western business relationships. There is a mix of 'genqing' and heart when the Chinese act as the buyer, with brain and logical thinking when acting as the seller.

'Heart' is an important part of the Russian business culture. Russians are seen as affectionate and are not afraid to show their feelings. They have a more Latin mentality, which expresses lots of emotions, physical contact, voice raising and immediate reactions, both verbally and non-verbally (Trompenaars, 1993).

Norms: Trustworthiness

Trust is a major norm prevailing in the social organization of the business network. Being a trustworthy seller, for example, creates expectations in the buyer that the seller will behave in a specific way, such as producing reliable goods. The fact that the seller can be trusted also makes the buyer act in a certain way toward the seller. Trust is mutual, since the trustworthiness of one party results in the other party trusting that party.

The CBN is characterized by the critical importance of individual and social trustworthiness as compared to organizational and professional trustworthiness in the European context (Jansson, 2007). 'Guanxi' behaviour goes deeper than professional friendship, and therefore the ethnic Chinese display traditional ways of behaving in the business world, even in the mixed model above.

Trust between firms in these markets is organizational and professionally based, and employees enter as buyers/sellers where the person is an official and has a professional role. Individuals in overseas Chinese organizations function as a person and the role is usually personal and private, and trust is individually based. Employees also enter as a person in business transactions. Related to this aspect is the strong emotional theme of the Chinese.

According to Johanson (2001), relationships and trust for individuals in the RBN are weighted higher than legal contracts, but relationship establishment usually starts from a situation of suspicion. The expectation, inherited from experience, is that one would be cheated. Decades of one-sided plan governance and centuries of an authoritative state have resulted in trust only being in place if the actors are extensively embedded and interlocked in the same network, that is, the consequences for cheating are perceived as more severe than the eventual rewards for behaving trustworthily, or through a long and iterative process that starts from suspicion. The result is an environment where different perspectives of reality exist and where friends stand up for one another regardless of past agreements. Close personal relationships are important as well as politeness and hospitality together with care for the weak

Thus, there are many similarities between the trust-based Chinese 'guanxi' network and the Russian 'blat' network, inclusive of the 'nomenklatura' network (Michailova and Worm, 2003). Both are social networks based on social trust, which is strongly related to favours and gifts as well as long-term and strong personal relationships. As discussed above, during the centrally-planned era, the 'blat' network was an informal barter system, where exchange of favours was built on favours of access to goods and services ('social resourcing'). With transition to a market economy, the 'blat' network has changed character from being based on friendship corruption to money corruption. The RBN has transformed from being based on moral and ethical considerations to having an explicit financial expression, being more materialistic and pragmatic than emotional and human.

Values

Some major values are found behind the thought styles and norms, namely achieved versus ascribed status, inner versus outer direction, and universalism versus particularism.

Achieved versus ascribed status

Ascribed versus achieved status concern what an actor's status in a network is based upon. An actor may for instance be ascribed a specific status based on factors such as common background. An example of ascribed status is when positions in networks are inherited based on family, clan or caste background. On the other hand, status may also be achieved based on the merits of the actor, for example the performance instead of the common background. A position based on seniority or sex is therefore more often ascribed than achieved compared with when it is based on skills and task performance.

While the EBN is built on mutual and common interests, the CBN is built on the persons having some kind of common background or 'genxing'. The main difference between 'blat' and 'guanxi' relationships is then that the Chinese business networks status is ascribed based more on family connections, while in the Russian networks status is achieved based more on secondary groups such as friends, neighbours, and co-workers in addition to the family. Personal relationships are also critical in business relationships because the state and governmental institutions are so weak. Thus, the RBN is found in-between the EBN and CBN along the achieved versus ascribed status dimension.

Inner direction versus outer direction

The inner-outer direction expresses whether values are located inside the individual or whether examples and influences are located outside. Morality or ethics, for example, deals with what is right or wrong, good or bad, and virtues. Regarding cultural differences between Westerns and Chinese, this dimension is further specified as the difference between a shame culture and a guilt culture. The former has an outer direction, while the latter has an inner direction. A major characteristic of relationships within the Chinese business network is face behaviour, which is the major expression of the shame culture. Values prevailing in the network here represent the dominant opinion among the actors. Individuals tend to follow the rules of the groups rather than their own conscience, for example often putting blame on the circumstances rather than themselves when something goes wrong. It contrasts with the more conflict-oriented relationships based on the Christian guilt culture of the European business network. A major value of the shame culture is harmony, which is created through the 'yin' and 'yang' balance between forces or ideas. In decision-making it is expressed as the 'both-and' principle of having a balance between major alternatives, which is contrasted with the Western 'either-or'/optimization principle of striving for the best alternative. The latter more conflict-oriented principle is classified as 'competitiveness' in Table 5.1.

In Russia, harmony or balance between alternatives prevailing in the CBN is not so important, and competitiveness is not as important as in the EBN. The value prevailing within the RBN is instead defined as 'legitimacy'. It is a question of creating a trade-off between harmony and competitiveness by being legitimate in the eyes of outside groups at the same time as business needs to be efficient to survive. According to Hampden-Turner and Trompenaars (2000), the Russian business culture is characterized by high outer direction, which conceives of virtue as outside the individual. For example, there is a tendency towards blaming others, discouraging risk taking, and following rules is rewarded. The outer-directed values lead to individuals using fate, chance and contingency with more skill than their opponents. Although business strategy is still focused on following external rules, competition is increasing with the development of the market economy.

Empathy referred to above is more inner directed. People have to be willing to acquire in-depth knowledge of their partners and to know what appeals to their needs. Since actors in the Chinese network are guided by 'heart', 'genqing' and 'face' it means that behaviour can be hard to interpret. Among other things, both empathy and face needs to be considered against the overall network of relationships between firms in order to not cause loss of face for anyone in the personal network.

Universalism versus particularism
The universal versus particularity dichotomy expresses how generally valid values are. For example if a rule is based on a universal value it is supposed to be valid for everybody and not only a particular group. Networks based on universal principles are more open than those based on particularistic principles. Relationship aspects related to this dichotomy are how open, formal, general and rational they are. Rationality concerns the goals or reasons behind relationships, whether they have a universal or particularistic orientation. This implies that there are specific reasons for how and why firms do business and how business people should relate to this. A relationship can be a result or outcome of universal or particularistic values, for instance that particular circumstances override the importance of abstract

rules in determining what is right and good. In such circumstances trust for individuals weighs higher than legal contracts. The degree of formality in a business network also has to do with how official and transparent activities should be.

The Western European network context is more based on universal principles, where firms are autonomous legal and financial entities facing largely anonymous and impersonal market pressures and both the networks and transactions are formal and to a degree impersonal (Whitley, 1992a; Lindell and Arvonen, 1996; Koopman 1991). Western European business networks are more organizational. Contractual and transactional relationships between the actors are often formed based on the general goals of the actors, which also may be individual, idiosyncratic and sometimes even opportunistic (Lasserre and Schutte, 1995). Business networks in the overseas Chinese context are more particularistic and family-oriented, resulting in the fact that relationships emerge from the person and are interpersonal or social.

The major rationality behind the EBN is efficiency, while the CBN is more governed by harmony. The former is also an outcome of universal values, while the latter is also a result of more particularistic values. While cooperation through relationships in the European business network largely evolves around profitability and efficiency issues, business cooperation in Southeast Asia evolves around harmony. Relationships in the overseas Chinese context build on reciprocal favours or 'renqing' between the individuals rather than on a common interest based on 'win-win' situation regarding profitability. Thus, relationships are personal, shared, confined and governed by sets of established social rules. 'Genqing' and 'renqing' often combine to make the business networks closed or secret rather than open and therefore hard to enter. These highly particularistic relationships with a low transparency are a major factor behind the corrupt practices typical of the 'crony capitalism' of Southeast Asia.

According to Trompenaars (1993) Russia is a highly particularistic society, where relationships and unique circumstances override the importance of abstract rules in determining what is right and good. Relationships and trust for individuals weigh higher than legal contracts. The result is an environment where different perspectives of reality exist and where friends stand up for one another regardless of past agreements. Close personal relationships are important as well as politeness and hospitality together with care for the weak.

While transparency is low in the Chinese and Russian context, it is high in the West European. The Chinese paradigm is much more informal, and characterized by affection, diffuseness, particularism, ascription and collectivism. The boundaries between formality and informality are quite clear in the West European context, while they are blurred in the Chinese and Russian contexts.

Enforcement Mechanisms

Values and norms expressed as priorities specify the actions that a set of individuals regards as correct or incorrect, according to which they are expected to decide and act. But such normative rules do not specify what happens if expectations based on them are not materialized, that is if behaviour supposed to be following from the norms do not take place. So, for behaviour to be effective in organizations, incentives and sanctions must also be present. The regulative aspect concerns how to construct the incentive system to best reward both the individual and the firm together with establishing a surveillance and assessment system to control the enforcement.

The regulatory aspect of an institution therefore reflects the existing law and rules of a particular environment that reward certain types of behaviour and punish others. Rules are enforced through diffuse informal mechanisms such as shaming activities, or may be highly formalized and assigned to specialized actors, such as the police or the courts. Hence, enforcement mechanisms produce economic and social control through regulations. Such regulatory processes involve the capacity to establish rules, inspect others' conformity to them and, as necessary, manipulate sanctions, such as rewards or punishments, in an attempt to influence future behaviour. These enforcement mechanisms can be either formal (for example wage reductions or increases) or informal (losing or gaining face).

Authority
Authority is a central aspect of the regulative dimension. For instance, powerful actors may either impose their will on others, provide inducements to secure compliance, or use authority in which coercive power is legitimized by a normative framework that both supports and constrains the exercise of power (Scott, 1995, 2001). Authority is related to Hofstede's dimension 'power distance'. For enforcement mechanisms to work they must be based on a suitable world view regarding power distance. Thus, the authority system is a major regulative factor of the organizations involved in networks, having a decisive effect on how relationships are organized. Authority is defined from a relationship perspective by Kakar (1971, p. 298) as 'a relationship between two individuals, one the superior and the other the subordinate, the relationship lying not in the individuals but in the positions they occupy in the formal hierarchy of the work organization'. Kakar (1971) distinguishes four basic ideal authority patterns or cultural forms.

In West European business networks, there is formal or hierarchical authority. Authority is legitimized by impersonal laws and rules, which are based on agreed principles of rationality. Authority is limited to areas of competence defined by these laws and based on integrity and fairness. The right to a competence field is determined by the capacity of a person and is not as in traditional societies, considered to be the property of a person's family or caste. In a Western organization with a professional ideology superiors legitimize their power and control of subordinates by their formal authority. The essence of civil-service involves acting in a stately, considered manner according to invariant, impersonal rules. The emotional affiliation and task control are both low in such a rule-determined organization. When the emotional affiliation is high, the ideology is characterized as fraternal. Authority is often delegated down, and it rests on formal rules and procedures. Autocratic behaviour is rarely seen in the organizations, and authority is linked to expertise and formally prescribed positions (Koopman, 1991; Whitley, 1992a).

According to parental authority social interaction is characterized by obedience and conformity and not by a personal power of initiative. Security for the subordinate is obtained by relying on the superior. The parental ideology is a relic from a traditional pre-industrial society. It is personal and the legalization is based on everyday routine and an unchanging past. People obey out of respect for the ruler's traditional status and decisions are limited by customs and traditions.

Overseas Chinese business networks are hierarchically structured, inter alia following the hierarchy of the family firm. Social position is important in the Chinese context because individuals do not feel comfortable unless they are in a hierarchical relationship with clearly defined roles (Kraar and Shapiro, 1994). Relationships in a person's network are therefore dyadic and hierarchical. This is in sharp contrast to Western Europe where business networks are more lateral and the social position of a business partner has no relevance to the initiation or performance of the business relationship. The authority system of Chinese business networks as well as organizations is highly paternalistic. The superiors have the right of decision, the emotional affiliation is low and task control by the superior of the subordinate high.

The Russian authority pattern also falls within this category. The regulative structure in the planned economy in the Soviet Union did not provide any incentives for firms to legally compete or to co-operate (Mattsson, 1993). The institutional structure did not promote relationships, which developed through a mutual exchange and adaptation process between the firms. Relationships were initiated and governed through the authority planning system (Johanson, 2004b). However, the official authority system is usually not trusted by business managers, who prefer to solve conflicts and disputes through their personal relations rather than by relying on the legal system (Hendley, 1997).

Sanctions
A vital aspect of the authority system is the sanction system. One major aspect relates to the type of sanction mechanism: laws or customs. Another aspect concerns the type of sanction: incentives or punishments. An important aspect of control mechanisms in the Chinese context is the concept of face. Face is an informal sanction mechanism or custom, which is difficult to define precisely. It involves issues such as a man's respect and status that fall within the regulative aspect. But it is also intimately related to the normative dimension through its moral base of shame. The fear of losing face

sets barriers to the Chinese people's behaviour and one's word and opinion are spoken with uttermost care.

Controlling and planning are, because of the avoidance of high uncertainty and the lack of trust, viewed as critical activities in the RBN, among other things reflecting the brain of the causality thought style. To control and to monitor employees and customers and suppliers is the way business is expected to be done in Russia.

In West Europe sanctions are mainly formal, in China informal and in Russia a mix of formal and informal depending on whether they relate to firms or the 'blat' network. Authority and responsibilities within the Western context are well defined and often law-like as they are formulated in text. These formal sanctions are based on a well developed legal system, where rules apply equally to all. The rights of the individual are best guaranteed through property rights, and there is a preference for written, rather than oral, contracts. The law is respected, contracts signed by individuals are legally binding, and breach of contract results in legal sanctions. Commercial organizations in both the public and private sector rest on strong legal institutions. Firms are typically derived from and share a common reliance on legal-rational norms and bases of legitimacy (Whitley, 1992a). Because of high confidence in legal institutions there is no need for sanctions working through personal relationships in order to guarantee contracts and commitments. However, legal institutions have not had a central importance in China and Russia and the legal framework is still weak. There are various degrees of legal uncertainties due to lack of credible enforcement of the rules that exist. The parental assertive authority does in the Chinese business system what law does in the West, and one reason why paternalism has evolved is that individual and corporate rights are only weakly protected by a legal infrastructure.

CONCLUSIONS

A major conclusion from the comparison of the results of the study in the 1980s and the one in the 2000s is that relationships based on a mix of the European and Chinese business networks in Southeast Asia has not changed much during this period. Most adaptations were made early and have prevailed during the years. Those changes that have occurred took place mainly in the Chinese business network, which has made the Chinese network approach resemble the European network more. The main reason seems to be a general Westernization of the East Asian societies, mainly taking place as a consequence of the financial crises in 1997. The network relationships have become more westernized in the overseas Chinese business network, which can be attributed to several factors. One is that more Chinese managers, especially younger generation managers, have a university degree from a western university or business school, foremost in the US, UK or Australia. Another is that more local firms are increasingly exposed to foreign business and are adapting some of their practices and, hence, becoming more experienced in doing business with foreign firms. There is also a growing number of local Chinese who are travelling to America and Europe to do business, and they are more comfortable with the Western way of managing business relationships.

The Nordic firms have adapted to network structures in the CBN, although they are purposefully maintaining a level of 'Finnishness' or 'Swedishness'. Findings also show that Nordic firms are not expected to comply with all the rules and regulations, norms and values of the ethnic Chinese context. They are at times even appreciated for and expected to show foreign behaviour.

Regarding the institutional influences on the differences between the international business networks, it is noted that in the overseas Chinese business network there is no distinguishing between business-related, family-related and socially-related networks. Most often business relationships are built on a strong personal relationship, making it difficult to distinguish between networks of social relationships and networks of business relationships. Social relationships are therefore an input to a business relationship, not an outcome of the relationship as in the Western European context. Moreover, a relationship in the overseas Chinese context also develops as a result of the individual being able to act in a respectful manner, and show respect for local traditions and other rules. Maintaining a good reputation is critically important in the ethnic Chinese context because the society as a whole has a network structure. Losing the support of even one local firm in such a networked society might have severe consequences for the continuing existence of the firm. Ethnic Chinese firms are unlikely to take another firm to court. Instead violations can lead to banishment from society as a whole. Becoming blacklisted is far worse than being sued since the entire network will refrain from doing business with the guilty party.

There are many similarities between the Chinese and Russian business networks. Both are very broad social networks involving close and long-term relationships, largely based on social trustworthiness. These personal connections are built into a hierarchical social structure. The ability to influence, pull strings and take care of friends when it is needed is seen as a status symbol, and the more rank and power one has. With the transition and change to a pecuniary market system, these systems have become more dissimilar. 'Blat' relationships have been corrupted into a more materialistic system. 'Guanxi' relationships are is still more emotional and human, and seem to be even more important in China now than under the centrally-planned period.

Business transactions in Western Europe are based on written and formal contracts. In the Chinese and Russian contexts they are less common, and social contracts in the form of verbal agreements and promises are often the basis for agreements and transactions. Individual trustworthiness is important because of a lack of a tradition of trust in organizations or formal laws. Thus, norms like trustworthiness could work as substitutes to regulations.

Punishments are not necessary if people follow the rules due to the fact that they trust one another to do so. Trustworthiness cannot be assumed and institutionalized law is inadequate for underpinning transactions. In order to guarantee reliability of economic transactions, trustworthiness from personal relationships is of prime importance. There is little need for lawyers if there is a great deal of reliance on personal obligation-bonding. So because of weak legal institutions 'guanxi' relations in China and 'blat' relations in Russia have become a substitute for the legal system.

The long-term orientation and high particularism combined with a weak formal, unpredictable and non-transparent institutional context, which characterize the environment of most Chinese business networks, means that actors have to make extensive investment in the network and demonstrate that they are committed before they can be accepted as legitimate business actors. They have to earn their trust, which means that demonstration of commitment is instrumental for development of trust. In the Russian network, short-term orientation is typical, which means that there is no patience. Firms do not have the time to wait. Firms are usually suspicious and assume that they will be cheated. As they are not willing to accept uncertainty, they prefer to control and monitor other actors. Demonstrating commitment and trusting others are risky procedures and are reserved for specific firms. In West Europe with its more developed legal base firms' trust and commitment evolve in an iterative process, uncertainty being gradually reduced as a result of satisfaction and positive outcomes from doing business in the past.

The findings about the mixed network in Southeast Asia should also be valid for doing business in mainland China, especially for Swedish and Finnish firms. First, as discussed above, the mix of the European business network and the Chinese business network in SEA has changed little during the past 25 years, indicating that these firms have tried out a working way of doing business with the Chinese. Secondly, numerous overseas Chinese business firms from SEA as well as from Taiwan and Hong Kong have moved back 'home' by investing in China. Thirdly, the private business sector in China has grown very rapidly during the last five years, inter alia due to these investments.

As found out in Chapter 1, one distinct characteristic of emerging country markets is that they are undergoing change. This market change is also a part of a general reformation of the whole society. There is a shift taking place, where relationships of business networks are changing from being mainly personal to impersonal. There is also a shift from price to quality orientation. The consequence of such a shift is that business practices in emerging country markets are becoming more similar to practices in Western markets. Because of this westernization Finnish and Swedish firms are able to identify familiar structures in these markets, and the dimensions of international business networks are becoming more similar as well.

6. Business marketing strategy in the internationalization process

This chapter develops one of the major aspects of international business marketing strategy introduced in Chapter 1, namely 'geographic spread'. From an international business marketing point of view two major strategic issues are involved:

1. *The entry strategy.* How firms get access to new customers in new geographic markets by marketing their products there, for example how the business marketing is initiated and built up in order to establish a strategic position in the local industry and how business marketing is done to maintain such a position.
2. *The internationalization strategy.* How business marketing is increasingly globalized by the expansion of the firm to growing number of countries.

How firms establish business marketing activities through the entry strategy is therefore an important part of the chapter. This aspect of the internationalization process mainly concerns international sellers and buyers. Four major strategic marketing issues are taken up in connection with entering networks in foreign markets. They are the entry modes of trade and FDI; the entry nodes of dyads and triads; the entry process of handling relationships during the various stages of their evolvement; and the entry roles of seller (exporter), buyer (importer) and producer. This entry strategy aspect is not much developed in the literature, especially when it comes to business marketing in emerging country markets and in relating these entry roles to each other.

The other business marketing strategy issue related to internationalization processes taken up is how marketing is influenced by the geographic expansion of the firm between different country markets. As indicated in Chapter 1, globalization issues today largely involve emerging markets, where Western firms face a very different context and the requirement of doing business in networks. Even if there are numerous studies on internationalization processes, the new situation of internationalizing to emerging markets has not been written about much, especially not about the critical role played by network relationships.

To start with, the relationship process dealt with earlier in Chapter 4 is merged with the internationalization process to establish a common background for international business marketing during the different stages of internationalization. This is done by blending the five stages of the relationship process with the stages of the internationalization process. When Western firms enter and expand between emerging country markets, they need to learn many new things. Therefore, knowledge and learning are key factors in internationalization, which are developed based on Jansson (2007). By defining learning as an organizational process and a way to make the resources and capabilities of the firm dynamic, the strategic aspect of IBM is stressed. IBM strategy is influenced by institutional differences between countries. Therefore it is necessary to adapt the concept psychic distance to the emerging markets' situation of larger distances and higher uncertainty. Institutional distance is thereby used as a more encompassing concept to cover the large cultural distance and other major institutional obstacles prevailing between different emerging country markets and towards mature markets.

The chapter builds on the basic research finding about internationalization processes, namely that how firms respond to changes in international markets largely depends on where in the internationalization process they are found, that is their degree of internationalization. From a business marketing perspective this means that international experience is gained by establishing and developing relationships with foreign business partners. It also implies that the more relationships that are established abroad the more internationally experienced the firm becomes. For example, for SMEs entering Eastern European markets, business networks are of extra high importance (Meyer and Skak, 2002).

INTERNATIONALIZATION IN NETWORKS

Internationalization processes take place in a stepwise manner (Jansson, 1989a, 1994b; Jansson and Sandberg, 2008). Companies commit themselves through a gradual learning process. This learning is incremental and takes place by doing business abroad, for example learning about the conditions in particular markets. Companies tend first to establish themselves in geographically and culturally proximate markets and increase their commitment more and more, starting with agents, and passing through sales companies to manufacturing companies (Johanson and Wiedersheim-Paul, 1975; Johanson and Vahlne, 1977). This has mainly been studied for MNCs but also for SMEs (Hohenthal, 2001). Research on the exporting of mainly North American small and large companies have reached similar conclusions (Bilkey, 1978; Cavusgil, 1980; Reid, 1981; Czinkota 1982). However, 'Born globals' or 'International new ventures' (that are international from inception) tend to follow another pattern (Oviatt and McDougall, 1994; McDougall and Oviatt, 2000; Cavusgil et al, 2002; Sharma and Blomstermo,

2003a; Zahra, 2005). The main difference concerns the 'leap-frogging' of small and high technology firms with a rapid, non-incremental internationalization process. Traditional stage models are claimed to be invalid for these 'leap-frogging' small companies (Knight and Cavusgil, 1996) and the network approach has been found to be more appropriate (Madsen and Servais, 1997; Coviello and McAuley, 1999; Andersson and Wictor, 2003).

A basic assumption in such internationalization process theory is that knowledge accumulation is continuous and dependent upon the duration of foreign operations (Forsgren, 2002; Sharma and Blomstermo, 2003b). The longer the firm has been involved in foreign operations, the more knowledge it accumulates about these operations. The more knowledge the firm has, the less uncertain it perceives the foreign market to be. Firms that lack knowledge about foreign markets even tend to overestimate risks. This corresponds to what Jansson (1989, 1994b) found about establishment processes in the regional emerging market context of Southeast Asia. The pace of investments between countries accelerated the more experienced the firms became, at the same time as the mode of establishment became slightly more direct for the later establishments.

Network theory is increasingly combined with classical internationalization process theory or stage theory in order to understand and explain the rapid internationalization of the firm, for example in Johanson and Vahlne (1990, 2003), Meyer and Skak (2002) and Bell et al. (2003). A major reason is that it is difficult to capture internationalization by using only one of these theoretical frameworks (Coviello and Munro, 1997; Björkman and Forsgren, 2000; Meyer and Skak, 2002; Bell et al., 2003).

Such integration is facilitated by the fact that traditional internationalization processes mainly concern marketing activities. However, this aspect is not very much developed, especially when it comes to business marketing in emerging markets, and the matter of building and handling network relationships. For SMEs entering Eastern European markets, for example, business networks are of extra high importance, since relationships are considered to be developed to provide bridges into foreign markets (Meyer and Skak, 2002: Meyer and Gelbuda, 2006).

The business network approach to internationalization has been developed by another branch of the Uppsala School, where relationships are viewed as constituting the core of the internationalization process (Håkansson, 1982; Hammarkvist et al., 1982; Jansson, 1989a, 1994a; Axelsson and Johanson, 1992; Håkansson and Snehota, 1995; Majkgård and Sharma, 1998; Johanson and Vahlne, 2003). Internationalization takes place through establishing and maintaining network relationships in foreign environments. An exporter/importer network is a temporary set of units, which has been formed out of different units in the organizations of the buyer and the seller. It is a value constellation established for the task of marketing/ purchasing a product/service package involving a certain combination of competences. A value constellation is a group of actors representing different units at the buyer and the seller that work together to create value for the customer (Normann and Ramirez, 1993). The international marketing and purchasing of products and know-how through this direct exporter/importer network means that a vertical network in the exporting region (for example a supplier's supplier network) is indirectly connected to another vertical network in the importing region (for example a buyer's buyer network). This larger vertical network, in its turn, is embedded in other regional and national networks, for example a financial network. The exporter/importer network is then part of a larger value constellation consisting of a supplying export network connected to a buying network in the emerging market. Such value constellations and international business marketing situations can be analysed by using network maps similar to those described in Chapter 3.

Internationalization of SMEs to the Baltic Sea Region

A study of the internationalization of small and medium-sized enterprises from Kalmar County to the Baltic States, Poland and Russia produced some interesting results about the character of the internationalization process to emerging country markets (Jansson and Sandberg, 2008). It is representative for firms in various stages of the internationalization process.

Relationships in networks
Relationships were found to be critical for doing business in the East Baltic countries: finding contacts and maintaining and developing them either directly or indirectly through own companies or middlemen. This confirmed earlier findings, for example by Salmi (2000). Those companies that had such relationships saw them as strengths, while companies that did not have them considered it a weakness. Other relationship-linked strengths on which the competitiveness rested were experience and reputation, market presence, a good assortment of unique high-quality products built on a high technical competence, and flexibility. Among the weaknesses noted are too high prices, and lack of resources, knowledge and time. The major opportunity involved growing markets and lower costs, while a major threat came from gradually rising local costs, which risked the area becoming uncompetitive in comparison with certain Asian countries. Another threat was increasing competition from domestic and foreign firms.

An unexpectedly large share of the regional trade took place through establishing two-party relationships or dyads between small customers and suppliers on either side of the Southern Baltic Sea. This was especially true for international purchasing or imports to the Kalmar County, while international selling or exporting was shared almost equally between dyads and three-party relationships. The higher importance of such triads or indirect relationships through distributors and agents compared to FDI fits with the general expectation based on earlier research that indirect trade accounts for a larger share of SMEs' international business activities in high-risk countries. However, the high importance of direct trade between customers and suppliers on either side of the Baltic Sea is more unexpected. One major reason is the geographical proximity of these markets. An indication of this is that triads dominate for the more remote Russia, especially for the export trade. The low importance of the entry mode FDI of SMEs is also demonstrated by the fact that the subsidiaries are spread out between the countries of the region with only one MNC having subsidiaries in most countries. The international activities almost entirely concern marketing aspects. Very little own production had been established abroad, as well as little outsourcing of production. Few examples of firms starting to shift their supplier base eastwards were detected. A follow up of some firms one year later showed that they had started to outsource, beginning with the most labour-intensive parts.

Regional and global internationalization processes

The more relationships that had been established in each East Baltic country, the higher the degree of internationalization of the SME was. In addition, the more countries with established relationships, the more internationally experienced was the firm. The internationalization process in the Baltic Sea region was limited to a few countries, usually one or two. Only for a small number of companies did the regional internationalization process cover most countries in the region. Still, about two-thirds of the number of firms was experienced in international business, since they were exporting to or importing from many other countries outside the Baltic Sea region. A comparison of such regional and global internationalization processes showed that the East Baltic markets were mostly of marginal importance, these having more similarities with far-off markets in other parts of central and eastern Europe and in Asia than with the closer and larger volume 'old' EU markets.

Institutional distance

Internationalization processes were influenced by the characteristics of the firms and the markets where they traded. Only a small part of the foreign trade turnover of these SMEs went to this region. Among the institutional factors in the local markets influencing internationalization processes, the economic and political environment was important as well as infrastructure, particularly communications across the Baltic Sea. Essential institutional distances existed due to culture (mainly language) and corruption. Internationalization processes tended to vary with the type of industry. The engineering industry was the dominating export industry. Still, compared to the Swedish trade with these countries certain key industries were missing, chiefly IT, telecommunications and service industries such as banking.

Although the short geographical distances prevailing in the Baltic Sea area would benefit trade, this potential seemed hard to take advantage of, especially by resource poor SMEs acting in a world characterized by large institutional distances between business environments. However, other studies of SMEs and larger firms from South Sweden (Småland) going abroad during 1999-2004 indicate that the importance of geographical distance had been diminished. China was the leading country for outsourcing, relocation of its own production, as well as for the establishment of new business ventures, far ahead of the Baltic countries and Poland in the former case and the Nordic countries in the latter case (Jansson et al., 2006; SIF, 2004). This also indicates that institutional distance is shorter than expected. The reason for this might be that these countries are perceived as equally risky, since most of them are transition countries, the large difference being between such countries and Western country markets. Another reason could be that the economic gains are of such a magnitude as to be worth the risk. A conclusion from the studies is that the SMEs' potential internationalization possibilities are prevented by the inability to change from domestic-like markets to foreign markets, particularly if there are large differences between these markets, making the business knowledge less relevant.

Major Factors of the Internationalization Process

Internationalization to emerging country markets takes place by establishing and maintaining business relationships in the foreign market networks. SMEs enter by establishing two-party or three-party relationships or entry nodes as they will be called here. Various entry modes such as subsidiaries, agents and distributors are used when building relationships. As was found in Chapter 4 for business marketing of projects the relationship process consists of five stages. In this chapter, this process is seen as an entry process. The establishment in a foreign market is part of a larger internationalization process where firms spread their activities between various foreign countries, first to a certain region and then further afield over the globe. This more overall internationalization process is also divided into five stages. The internationalization process model and the relationship process model are combined into a five plus five stages process for the internationalizing firm. It is influenced by the institutional distance between countries, and organizational learning is the key internal process behind these processes.

The integrated five relationship process stages and the five internationalization process stages are specified in Figure 6.1, as are the major factors influencing these processes: three major aspects of institutional distance and the three dimensions of the major internal driving force, namely organizational learning. This model is now described in more detail.

Stages of Internationalization

Based on the experiential knowledge process, internationalization processes are often divided into different degrees of internationalization or stages. According to Johanson and Mattsson (1991) inexperienced firms follow the traditional slow and gradual pattern (for instance the 'late starter'), while the internationalization of the more experienced company is less gradual and slow (for example the 'international among others').

Figure 6.1   Major factors of the internationalization process

A classical grouping of firms is made by Cavusgil (1980), which has been found to be valid also for exporting small and medium-sized enterprises (Gankema et al., 2000). According to their study, the internationalization of SMEs takes place in five stages (see Figure 6.2).

During the first stage, firms have a domestic market focus. Next follows the pre-export stage, when the firm evaluates the possibilities to start exporting. The third stage is experimental involvement, when exporting is a marginal activity. The fourth stage is active involvement, when international business is a normal activity, for example an important share of the turnover is exported. A suitable organizational structure is also in place for this activity. The fifth and last stage involves committed involvement in exporting. The firm can now be called international, since it is heavily involved in markets abroad.

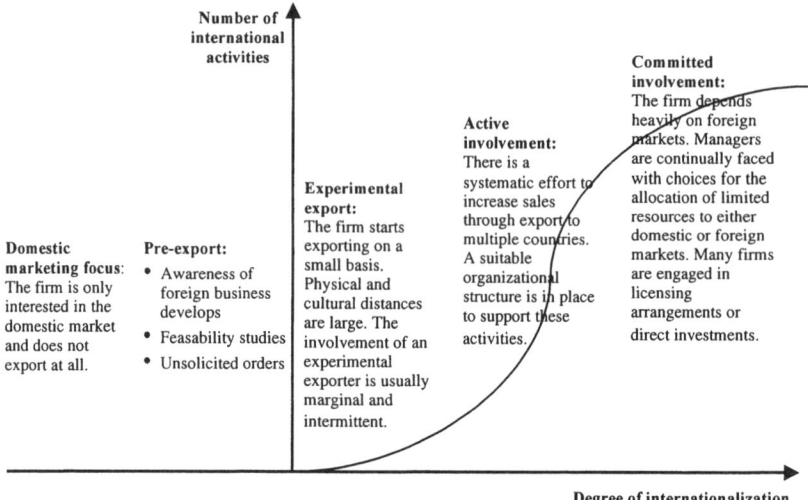

Figure 6.2   Stages of internationalization

Domestic marketing focus

The SME is operating in the domestic market and has no international business, and consequently no internationalization or foreign market knowledge. Still, this stage is important from the internationalization point of view, since the potential for being able to internationalize is developed here. This is especially relevant for firms from emerging country markets, which markets are in transition from an immature to a mature stage. Most firms need to first develop their sources of competitive advantage at home to be able to compete in foreign markets, especially in the more advanced mature markets.

Pre-export stage

At this stage, awareness is emerging within the firm about business opportunities in foreign markets or about threats from imports on the competitiveness of the firm in the home market, for instance due to off-shoring. 'Wake-up signals' could be that such international issues become 'hot' in the trade, press and politics, or that customers and competitors are internationalizing. During this stage, firms also start to passively react to unsolicited orders. Since the focus is still on the domestic market, the firm perceives export markets as very troublesome and risky. The firm might start to carry out research on foreign markets, but does not usually invest in export promotion campaigns and has little contact with foreign companies. It feels little real need to export and has no plans to do so in the future. There is no internationalization or foreign market knowledge.

Experimental export stage
The company is now actively reacting to the internationalization challenge through a trial and error process. It begins to develop a commitment to foreign customers and markets, first temporarily and irregularly on a small scale and then more permanently on a larger scale by:

- Carrying out research about foreign markets.
- Participating in export promotion campaigns.
- Feeling the need to export and planning to export.
- Actively reacting to unsolicited orders.
- Entering the foreign relationship process by developing relationships with firms abroad, normally as triads or three-part relationships using agents or distributors. Regular contacts are formed with key customers and alliances developed with export partners.
- Being prepared to make adaptations, for example of products.
- Starting to build up an export organization by appointing dedicated staff for this type of business.

At this stage the firm has a low internationalization knowledge, and highly focused market knowledge (network experiential and institutional knowledge).

Active involvement
International business is a regular feature. The company is focusing on key export markets and devotes substantial amounts of time and resources to entering and developing new markets. There are regular assessments of foreign markets, and marketing is adapted to them, for example promotion material in foreign languages. International business has been integrated into the organization of the firm, for instance senior management regularly visiting key partners to maintain relationships with them. Since exporting may account for up to 50 per cent of the turnover, opportunities on foreign markets are welcomed and seen as crucial to the business. More and more dyads are maintained in different countries and new customer relationships developed in present and new markets. Triads are developed in new markets, and are beginning to be replaced by dyads in 'old' markets. Adaptations are increasingly being made regularly to markets, customers and partners. There is medium internationalization knowledge, and medium diversified market knowledge.

Committed involvement
The majority of the turnover is generated through exports and significant amounts of time are spent on this activity, with senior and middle managers frequently visiting customers and foreign business partners. Exporting now accounts for more than 50 per cent of the turnover, and the domestic market is viewed as just another market. A large number of dyads are maintained in

different countries and new customer relationships are developed in 'old' and new markets. Triads are increasingly being replaced by dyads. Some triads are maintained and new triads developed in new markets. International business is an integral part of strategic management both in the shorter term and the longer term. Networks abroad provide critical information and quality assured partners deliver on time. Frequency of adaptations has slowed down. Internationalization knowledge is high and knowledge on foreign markets diversified.

Relationship Stages

From a business marketing point of view, the process of entering emerging country markets is a question of establishing relationships in networks. As found in Chapter 4, relationship processes tend to follow a certain pattern (Ford, 1980, 2002; Ford et al., 1998/2003), being separated into five stages (see Figure 6.3).

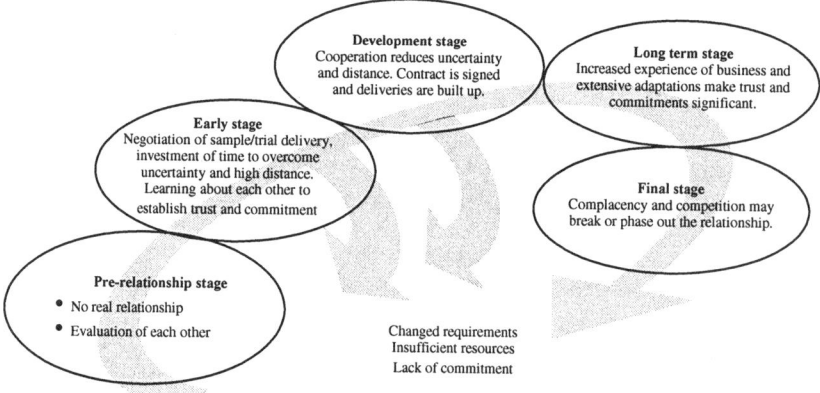

Figure 6.3   Relationship stages (Adapted from Ford, 1980 and Ford et al., 1998/2003)

The evolution of such dyadic (two-party) processes when establishing and developing buyer/seller relationships over time is valid for projects as well as for industrial products in general. The first stage takes up marketing activities before the relationship begins, for example network mapping in planning for taking over a customer from a competitor. To start this, the seller might be looking for factors in the networks that can spark a switch of suppliers by the customer. The next three stages show how direct buyer-seller relationships within networks are established. This development can be described according to a number of relationship factors and learning, for example how the experience, commitment and adaptations of the parties increase and how the distance and uncertainty between them are reduced. The variable experience indicates the amount of experience the respective parties have of each other. Both parties will judge their partner's commitment to the relationship. Commitment is to a large extent shown by the willingness to make adaptations. The variable distance is multifaceted and can be split into social, cultural, technological, time and geographical distance. Uncertainty deals with the fact that at the initial stages, it is difficult to assess the potential rewards and costs of the relationship. The major parts of the relationship process are summarized in Table 6.1. During the early stage and the development stage, the relationship is institutionalizing, while the long-term stage and the final stage represent the institutionalized relationship. The more experienced, the higher the commitment and trust, the lower the distance, the more adapted, and the lower the uncertainty, the higher is the degree of institutionalization.

The pre-relationship stage
This is where preparatory work takes place in order to evaluate new potential customers before networking starts. According to Chapter 3, network mapping is a major activity here. Concerning the relationship factors in Table 6.1, the experience of the customers in this stage is none or low, uncertainty high, distances large and commitment and adaptations zero.

The early stage
With networks mapped and relationships identified, the exploration of these start. Commitments are made to focus on specific customers, at most resulting in a sample delivery. Although still low, experience of customers is starting to build up. This is a mutual learning process, where the parties learn to know more and more about each other. Trust and commitment are being established and decisions are being made that also reflect personalities as opposed to the straight analytical decisions of the pre-relationship stage. The first adaptations are made, but are still few. Suppliers experience high uncertainty and high distances to the customers. Together these factors give a low degree of institutionalization of relationships.

The development stage
Business between the customer and the supplier starts to grow and resources are increasingly shared. Contracts are signed and there is a delivery build-up. Intensive mutual learning results in increased experience on both sides, as well as in reduced uncertainty and distances. Trust and commitments increase, which are signified by both formal and informal adaptations as well as cost savings. Relationships change character and become entirely focused on the dyad, in that way becoming deeper and broader. This means that the relationship is becoming institutionalized with common routines and habits starting to take form backed by shared norms and values. An important managerial task is to coordinate the development of new relationships with existing relationships.

Table 6.1   The relationship process (based on Ford, 1980)

Pre-relationship stage	Early stage	Development stage	Long-term stage	Final stage
Evaluation of new potential supplier	Negotiation of sample delivery	Contract signed, delivery build up	Routinized buying after several major purchases or large scale deliveries	Phasing out/interruption of relationship
Evaluation conditioned by: Experience with previous supplier	**Experience:** Low	**Experience:** Increasing	**Experience:** High	**Experience:** Very high
Uncertainty about relationships	**Uncertainty:** High	**Uncertainty:** Reduced	**Uncertainty:** Low	**Uncertainty:** Increasing
Distance from potential supplier	**Distance:** High	**Distance:** Reduced	**Distance:** Low	**Distance:** Increasing
Evaluation initiated by: Performance of existing supplier Efforts of non-supplier Overall policy decision	**Adaptation:** High investment management time	**Adaptation:** Increasingly formal and informal adaptations, cost savings increase	**Adaptation:** Extensive adaptations, cost savings are petering out	**Adaptation:** Extensive institutionalization
Commitment: Zero	**Commitment:** Low	**Commitment:** Increasing	**Commitment:** High	**Commitment:** Reducing

The long-term stage

After several major purchases or deliveries, the relationship is developed and now settles in a stable stage with continuous business going on between the parties. They have learnt to know and trust each other, which gives a high level of experience and the uncertainty is perceived as being low. Distances are small, commitment high and adaptations extensive. Relationships are now institutionalized by themselves and in relation to the network. They become more and more routine with established common thought styles, mutually acknowledged norms of conduct and standard operation procedures.

The main aim with building relationships is to reach the long-term stage, to get an ongoing long-term relationship with the buyer. If this is not accomplished, the relationship may retract to an earlier stage, even to the pre-relationship stage. In the latter case the relationship building may start all over again, perhaps this time with a new supplier.

The final stage

The deepening of the relationships in the long-term stage makes them extensively institutionalized and habitual with commitment even being taken for granted. There is even a risk that the relationships get stuck and become hard to adapt to ongoing environmental changes. A key issue in this mature stage is therefore to look for new possibilities to connect existing relationships. Otherwise the high trust, low distances and uncertainty might lead the parties to become complacent. The relationship is reaching a new stage where it could end: the final stage. So despite the high degree of institutionalization, this makes the relationship sensitive to being broken due to environmental changes and attacks by competitors. The relationship could be interrupted or phased out. However, as seen in Figure 6.3, relationships could be finalized already in earlier stages due to other such changed requirements, insufficient resources or lack of commitment.

The Five/Five Stages Models Combined

A more complete model of the internationalization of the firm is achieved when Ford's model is combined with Cavusgil's model. While the latter concerns how the international experience of the firm is developed, the former is a good approximation of how international experience is gained in a specific market or country. The more developed the customer relationships, the more experience the firm has of the particular foreign country market.

Based on Figure 6.3 the five stages of the relationship process are illustrated in Figure 6.4 as circles connected to each other. By establishing more and more customer relationships of this type abroad, the firm moves further and further along the internationalization process, starting in the experimental export stage. The larger the number of relationships established, the larger the part of the firm's resources and capabilities are dedicated to international business, which means that they are increasingly located abroad, among other things.

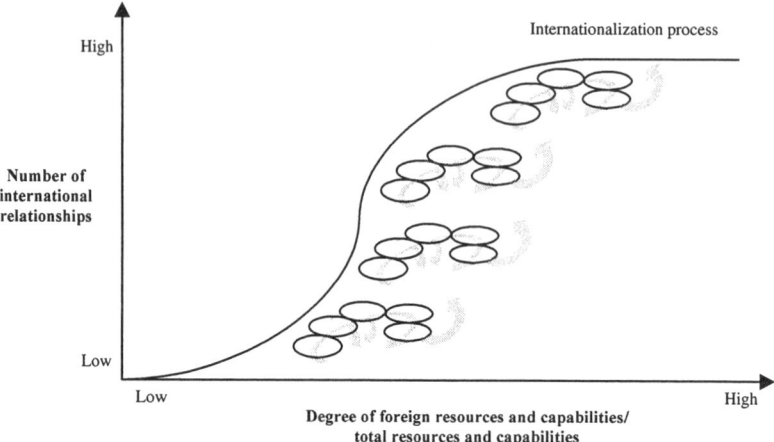

Figure 6.4   The five/five stages model (source: Jansson and Sandberg, 2008)

During the pre-relationship stage, the experience of the customers/ suppliers is none or very low, uncertainty high, distances large and commitment and adaptations zero. According to Cavusgil's five-stage model, for a firm that has a domestic market focus and starts to internationalize to a foreign country, the pre-relationship stage corresponds to the pre-export stage for the first foreign market (Gankema et al., 2000). The development of the relationships in the foreign country market starts in the early stage, when commitments and experience increase somewhat. According to Cavusgil's model, this is similar to the experimental export stage of an internationally inexperienced firm. This establishment of relationships in this stage and the other stages of the internationalization process is a mutual learning process, where the parties learn to know more and more about each other. High uncertainty is experienced and high distances prevail between the parties. The early stage is followed by the development stage, during which business between the customer and the supplier starts to grow and resources are increasingly shared. In this stage, there is a further development of the buyer/seller relationship signified by a delivery build-up and the signing of contracts. Intensive mutual learning results in increased experience on both sides, as well as in reduced uncertainty and distances. Trust and commitments increase, which are signified by both formal and informal adaptations as well as cost savings. Relationships become focused on the dyad. Next, after several major purchases or deliveries, the relationship is developed and settles in the long-term stage. The exporter and the importer have now learnt to know and trust each other, distances being small and commitment high. The main aim with building relationships is to reach the long-term stage, to get an ongoing long-term relationship. In the final stage, the relationship is phased out.

A limited number of relationships are developed, reach the long-term stage, and are finalized in the experimental export stage. In the active involvement and the committed involvement stages more and more customer relationships are established and terminated in more and more countries. Thus, relationships being at the core of the internationalization process follow a similar pattern as the internationalization process as a whole by showing how the gradual build up of international experience takes place. The more relationships in a foreign country that have reached later stages, the more internationally experienced and the higher the degree of internationalization of the firm. Further, the more countries with established relationships, the more internationally experienced the firm is.

Organizational Learning in Internationalization

As discussed above, acquiring experiential knowledge is the key factor of the internationalization process, being the major factor behind the stage character of such processes. This implies that organizational learning is a key issue. Firms gradually build up their knowledge about foreign operations through operating in foreign markets. They learn from past experience by transforming this experience to useful knowledge. This experiential knowledge about foreign markets is acquired in networks (Johanson and Vahlne, 2003; Blomstermo et al., 2004). Network experiential knowledge is gained by operating in local market networks, where also institutional knowledge is built up on the local market scene. Together these two types of knowledge about the individual markets add to the previous internationalization knowledge, setting the firm into a better position to internationalize further. These three types of experiential knowledge are path-dependent and unique for every firm, often being defined as a 'theory in use' (Eriksson et al., 1997). Hence, internationalization knowledge concerns general knowledge about how to operate in foreign markets, while network experiential knowledge and institutional knowledge are defined as knowledge about how to operate in specific markets.

The organizational learning of experiential knowledge is twofold: operational learning that occurs within an existing organizational process and conceptual learning that is more strategic or path breaking (Timlon, 2005), more similar to explorative learning (Forsgren, 2002). This division builds on Sharma and Blomstermo (2003b), who argue that the existing knowledge structure/state is rather restructured discontinuously or intermittently. The idea is further based on results from research on the internationalization of Western firms in emerging markets.

Viewed from the institutional network approach a thought style or 'thinking routine' is found behind a theory-in-use. This thought style is embedded in other institutional factors that make the organizational process be repeated, that is making it a routine. These other factors are mainly social norms and values. If the organizational process is a learning process, the thought style gives rise to a certain learning style. Such a style involves both basic attitudes towards learning as well as how learning takes place. Following a certain learning style, incremental learning or chiefly operational learning now takes place according to a specific thought style, where knowledge is accumulated following a theory-in-use. This type of learning process is broken when the learning style or the thought style behind it is changed, and the current experiential state of knowledge or theory-in-use is reformed. According to the learning style characterized by incremental learning new knowledge is interpreted and evaluated within the existing theory-in-use. Restructuring then takes place when this framework no longer is workable, this time through conceptual learning.

One possible instance of such change of the theory-in-use is when firms that have a domestic market focus start to export or import. According to Sharma and Blomstermo (2003a) firms with long domestic experience may have a rigid knowledge platform that takes time to change. Another instance is when the company moves from one type of market to another very different one, for example from mature markets in the West to emerging markets in the East. According to internationalization process theory, firms tend to internationalize to culturally similar markets, thereby building exports as much as possible on the experience from the domestic market. Cavusgil's (1980) stage theory is built on a similar idea, where internationalization is viewed as an innovation for the firm. Such an innovation is now possible to view as a reconceptualization of the current thought style, taking place through a learning process. The firm develops from a domestic market focus to active involvement through a learning process, thereby becoming more international. This learning takes place in the pre-export stage and the experimental export stage. Then, more learning in international markets brings the firm to the committed involvement stage. Behind such an organization innovation is a new learning style based on a new thought style together with new norms and possibly new values. New organizational processes for the international operations are discovered, learned through conceptual learning, and institutionalized into organizational routines based on a new knowledge platform. From this base, new operational learning and business process are set off. This fits with institutional theory, since organizational routines are so rigid that changes can be viewed as innovations (Jansson, 2007).

Institutional Distance

New stages of internationalization are established with the firm extending its business from one major type of market to another major type or from one type of foreign environment to another. These foreign country market environments or contexts are defined as institutional settings. The internationalization process is therefore determined by the institutional distance between country markets. This concept involves major differences between how societies are organized. It is a broader concept than psychic distance (Johanson and Wiedersheim-Paul, 1975) or cultural distance

(Majkgård, 1998). Rather, it improves cultural distance as a concept for international business research along the lines suggested by Shenkar (2001), Xu and Shenkar (2002) and Ionascu et al., (2004), being changed from a country-level characteristic to a country institutional profile based on institutional theory (Kostova, 1997). The institutional distance is assumed to be large when internationalization processes take place from old EU countries to new members as well to Asian countries. It is based on the institutional network approach.

According to the IBM strategy model (Figure 2.2), there is interplay between network relationships and institutions (for instance societal sectors) in the emerging country market, where institutions are seen as constituting the framework for different relationships. Institutions represent broad categories of conditions that influence how buyer/seller relationships are organized. This was developed in detail in Chapter 5 on how business relationships in and between Western European firms, Chinese and Russian firms are influenced by the institutional factors prevailing in the countries from where the firms originate.

As discussed earlier networks are influenced by institutional structures ('macro rules') of the societal sectors, for instance systems of property rights ('relationships rights') and other legal rules such as judicial and penal systems. Other examples of societal sectors of importance are cultural factors, as well as the political system in general, trade unions, business associations, business mores and conventions. The state participates both as a collective network actor, being in direct contact with the networking firm, and as an institutional structure outside the network, influencing relationships indirectly. The institutional context of the societal sectors and organizational fields of a specific emerging market might therefore facilitate or hinder internationalization moves to be implemented. Thus, internationalization concerns activities in network relationship processes with the purpose of bridging gaps or distances at three levels: between actors in networks, between organizational fields and between societal sectors.

BUSINESS MARKETING ENTRY STRATEGY

The business marketing strategy to enter a local market network consists of four major factors that need to be considered (they are shown in Figure 6.5):

1. *Entry mode.* Shall the MNC export, establish a company of its own or cooperate through forming a joint venture?
2. *Entry node.* How shall the MNC plug into the local market network? Either the MNC links up to the customers directly through forming dyads or indirectly through establishing triads, using an intermediary such as a distributor or an agent.
3. *Entry process.* How shall the MNC build relationships in the local market network?

4. *Entry role.* What commercial role is the MNC to perform in the local network – seller, buyer and/or manufacturer?

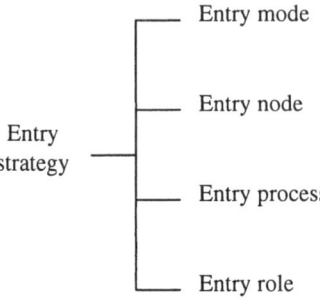

Figure 6.5   Entry strategy

Entry Mode

According to traditional research on the internationalization process, market entries either take place through intermediaries such as agents and distributors or through an own representative in the exporting/importing country, mainly a subsidiary. These represent various entry modes such as exporting, FDI, or joint ventures. Lu and Beamish (2001), for example, have found the SME choice of entry mode to highly affect the performance of companies. In its turn, the choice of entry mode is affected by the firm resources; larger firms tend to have larger economic and managerial resources for the investments demanded for own representation in the market of entry than smaller firms.

Nakos and Brouthers (2002) use Dunning's OLI framework to determine the entry mode strategy for SMEs. However, due to the limitations of this framework of only dealing with entry modes as structures, the authors were unable to investigate the importance of network relationships in the SME choice of entry mode for internationalization. The OLI framework, internalization theory, and other economic theories on the multinational firm have clear limitations regarding internationalization processes. Since they are static or structural, they are mainly useful for explaining entry modes as entry patterns and cannot be used to study processes.

Entry Node

The internationalization process is normally divided up into two parts: an external part dealing with the geographical spread to the international country markets and one internal part focusing on types of establishments or entry modes in a country. Strangely enough, the aspects of foreign markets are underrepresented in this theory, particularly since the international experience largely concerns such aspects. Two external factors are developed further in this book, namely the customer and the context. The first is developed by looking at how relationships are established with customers. Establishment points in networks are defined as entry nodes, for example directly with the customer or indirectly through an intermediary. In the latter case, the entry node is also an entry mode.

From a network perspective, entry modes may become an entry node, that is entry point into the network. Through the entry node, the seller network is connected to the local networks of the foreign market. A network map of the type illustrated in Figure 3.2 can be used to analyse the entry points. This kind of map fulfils the same function as the focal net as an analytical tool proposed by Salmi (2000) for investigating the network context when entering an emerging country market. As found in previous chapters, the key network for a seller is the buyer network. In principle, there are two major ways for a seller to connect to the buyer network in the foreign market or develop nodes through which to enter. Entries either take place directly with customers/suppliers or indirectly through intermediaries. Direct relationships, or dyads, are established between buyer and seller in the respective countries. The connection is either between a unit of the seller located in the buyer country or from the seller's location outside the buyer country. In the former case dyads are established through the entry mode FDI, that is a subsidiary in the exporting/importing country. In the latter case, the entry mode is trade or export. Indirect relationships, or triads, also concern trade as the entry mode and involve some outside party or other type of entry node, usually an intermediary of some kind, for instance an agent, dealer or distributor. Examples of factors influencing the entry node are the structure of the local market network (for instance loose or tight coupling), and the planned IBM strategy.

The entry node aspect of the entry strategy is elaborated on from a study made of the internationalization of firms from South Sweden to Poland during the 1990s and early 2000s (Blohm and Stojanovski, 2005).

Triads (third-party network)
A major issue of the network strategy in triads is to make an efficient trade-off between the linkage strategy to the third party and to the final customer. This is a typical strategic issue of the distributor network specialist. The linkage strategy of the exporter to the intermediary is dependent upon what kind of linkage strategy the intermediary is supposed to perform towards the customer, whether the intermediary effectuates its own strategy or a joint one together with the exporter. This decides how to allocate the marketing resources of the distributor network specialist between the relationships to the agent/distributor in comparison with the relationships to the customers. The Polish study involved the classical agency case, where the triad consists of a strong relationship with the agent and a very weak one with the buyers. It also included cases where the seller more equally balanced the relationships in the triad between the agent and customers. In such balanced triads there is

more of a sharing of the customer relationships with the agent. In the former unbalanced triads the seller is sometimes involved in the selling, but only when the agent wants. The agent sits on the customer relationships and the seller is mainly involved in solving certain technical problems and in delivery matters. The linkage strategy towards the agent is mainly supportive. Thus, the relationship with the agent provides the seller with a linkage to the market but which works differently depending upon the type of network strategy and the characteristics of the agent. The management of the information or communication linkage is done differently. It varies with how to get information about the market and how to communicate with customers and other parties in the foreign language belonging to another business culture. For example, much more hierarchical organizational structures in Poland resulted in a top-down communication through official channels both with customers and intermediaries. It was hard to develop a broad network of lateral relationships connecting buyers and sellers at different organizational levels. Such contacts were often necessary to fully succeed with the business marketing strategy, especially for technically complex products that require exchange of technical information. It also became harder to implement deals at operational levels and to follow them through after market operations. Communication channels also became very long and slow, where the main information linkage between the seller and the agent took place at the highest levels. This means that the control of the marketing process of the distributor/agent by the exporter is low.

This set up of relationships made the triad develop very slowly or not at all. The language/cultural barrier as well as the business cultural barrier were still present, hindering communication and the information linkage as well as the social linkage from developing further, setting definite limits to growth in the market. The exporter was continuously cut off from the customers, in particular since it was in the interest of the agent to keep the seller in the dark about market developments. Otherwise, the risk increased of being replaced by another agent or that the seller took over customer relationships by its own representation in the country. The remaining large social and cultural distances prevented the exporter from being involved in the market: to build up network experiential knowledge and institutional knowledge. Too little experiential learning took place by the seller, being mainly limited to the agent. This learning by the exporter was especially low when the relationship with the agent was weak, for example when the agent represented a number of companies when the seller had to compete with others about the agent's time and resources. Thus, a major conclusion from the study is that the agent often works badly as a mediator of information and knowledge. Another reason for the low learning of the seller is that experiential knowledge is mainly tacit, since it concerns experience, feelings and intuition. Such know-how is hard to transfer between parties and requires that the company is learning by operating in the market. Triads in emerging country markets are therefore paradoxical. Due to the high uncertainty experienced on these markets, low cost and flexible entry nodes are chosen such as triads. But, on the other hand, not operating in this foreign market hinders the seller from developing experiential knowledge about customers and the specific characteristics of the market. Uncertainty is not reduced or controlled for, which is necessary if the exporter were to be willing to expand business by investing more resources in the market.

This major problem of triads is not so severe in the case of more balanced relationships, since the seller also has a direct relationship with the customer. There is even an example of the Swedish seller dominating Polish customer relationships. The situation is the opposite of the one discussed above. The exporter mainly handles the linkage strategy towards the customers, while the agent works more as a support organization in the local market, assisting the seller with sales and service, and working as a language and cultural interpreter. Here, experiential learning takes places through the more active and broader engagement of the exporter in the triad, creating better circumstances for market expansion. However, communication problems related to language and organization culture of the type discussed above are also found for this type of agency relationship. These problems are hard to solve in any major way as long as the representative in the market is an independent firm, being hard to control by the seller.

Dyads (two-party network)
The more the seller is involved in the linkage strategy towards the customers, the more the triad resembles a dyad. This is also true for a buyer/importer involved in supplier relationships. The international supplier relationships studied were all well established and found in the long-term stage; many of them had been for many years. They both involved ordinary purchasing of components for the own production and outsourced products previously produced in Sweden, where the buyer took an active role in developing the quality of the supplier. Communication between the parties was the major problem, mainly due to language and cultural differences as well as ways to organize. The information linkage did not work so well and the social linkage became underdeveloped. For example, when a third person in the form of an interpreter is always present, it is hard to develop any deeper social relation built on trust. It was especially hard for the buyer to reach down to the operational levels through the tall hierarchy and to communicate with people at that level, for instance production planners, designers, foremen and workers. When representatives of the parties met only the upper echelons of the organizations were involved. This made it more difficult to check how the information given is perceived. In addition, cultural differences aggravated this situation further. However, due to better knowledge of English by the Polish suppliers, these problems were less than for exporter dyads at the same stage of relationship development. The main reason seems to be that the importer as a buyer has more power and can demand that key persons at the supplier speak English, which was not possible for the exporters. Still, the buyer had to visit the supplier more often to discuss the problems face-to-face, since communication by telephone or e-mail was difficult. At the end of

the day, the number of supplier relationships in the Polish market was limited, since it took so much time and resources to develop and maintain them. Even if one very experienced buyer firm had managed to standardize the relationships through well established organizational routines, they did not last long, since they continuously needed to be changed in the dynamic market.

Entry Process

As established above, entry processes in emerging country markets take place through establishing network relationships according to the IBM strategy followed.

Triads
The limitations of the entry node triad discussed earlier can be better understood by analysing the development of Polish customer relationships of the Swedish exporters according to the stage model in Figure 6.3 and Table 6.1. For the unbalanced triads, these relationships between manufacturer and customers had not moved beyond the early stage or the development stage. These stages were characterized by low commitment and few adaptations, since there were large social and cultural distances between the parties. The uncertainty perceived was high due to the fact that the parties had a low experiential knowledge about each other. Since the agent was responsible for the customer relationships, the direct buyer/seller relationships would not develop further. Even in balanced triads, when the seller jointly participated in customer relationships along with the agent, they were hard to develop further. The major reason was the language barrier, and the cultural barrier between organizations. As found above, the language barrier makes it hard to communicate with the right people and learn to know them. The communication takes place with those that know English, but who often do not know enough about the actual problem. The tall hierarchy and high power distance of Polish firms make lateral contacts almost impossible, which are necessary to succeed with the marketing of complex industrial products and projects. Communication is indirect to the seller from the top level of the buyer through the agent. The distances between the parties are not much reduced, which gives a low understanding of each other and few adaptations. Commitment grows slowly and the learning process is checked. Since trust is hard to increase, the uncertainty remains high. This makes the seller less prone to invest more in such relationships.

The question is whether the linkage strategy with the agent can compensate for this lack of development possibilities of the linkage strategy directly with the customers. The exporter could benefit from the agent taking care of developing more customer relationships in the market. As discussed before, this is only possible to a certain extent, mainly because the growth of experiential knowledge requires direct contact with the market and the customers.

Dyads

Direct producer/customer relationships or dyads do not suffer from this lack of direct contacts with customers. The international supplier relationships discussed previously in this chapter were all found in the long-term stage. They are characterized by high commitment and extensive adaptations. The experiential knowledge of the parties is high. The technological, time and geographical distances are low, while the social and cultural distances consisting of language and organization cultural barriers seem to be moderate and therefore possible to reduce further. The uncertainty is low to moderate. Through the adaptations made, the relationship had partly been standardized and made routine. The relationships studied developed mainly because the suppliers willingly adapted the production system and the logistic system to the demands of the buyers. To make it possible for the supplier to improve the quality of the products, the buyers shared their knowledge with them. Due to the knowledge gap between the parties, the way to handle this transfer of knowledge involved the most crucial adaptations behind how the relationship developed from the early stage to the long-term stage. This was especially true for relationships involving outsourced products, where the knowledge gap was large at the outset of the relationship. Communication through the information and know-how linkages played a critical role. Through these adaptations the technological, time and geographic distances had been more or less overcome. However, social and organizational barriers remained and were slowing down further developments of the relationship. Language problems and the very hierarchical organization of the seller prevented or rendered difficult communication with the operational levels in both organizations. Because of the great need to communicate, this was a large problem in subcontracting relationships, where products were designed in Sweden and produced in Poland. The social linkage was very important in these relationships, otherwise the communication would not work properly. The social linkage was closely related to the information and know-how linkages. When the parties trusted each other, the exchange of information became more open and reliable. However, as noted above, social relationships tend to become underdeveloped when barriers like these exist.

Entry Role

Firms enter foreign markets to perform three major commercial roles as international business operators: as seller, buyer or producer. The seller and buyer roles were illustrated above for the two major entry nodes. These roles will be developed further in this chapter, while the producer role is discussed in Chapter 7. The reason is that the first two roles are executed within the external network, while the third role is performed within the internal network.

Taking on the role as a buyer implies that the purchasing activities are internationalized. As found above, this buyer or importer role is not taken up much in the internationalization literature, nor in the international marketing literature. The increased international buying of inputs takes place through expansion to new supplier markets, either through replacing domestic production with imports or shifting from domestic suppliers to foreign suppliers. The first is the make or buy situation or the outsourcing issue. The second is a supplier selection situation or where to outsource, for example with the intention to shift the supplier base from high-cost to low-cost countries. This is the offshoring issue. This process is cost driven or market driven. In the latter case, the customer moves production abroad and the supplier follows. It could also happen that the customer faces cost pressures from customers abroad and to avoid being replaced by cheaper sources, the supplier moves production to keep the customer. Global sourcing is an example of highly internationalized purchasing.

The roles are linked to the entry nodes and entry modes in Figure 6.6. As illustrated in this chapter, for a buyer or seller, the relevant entry nodes are either dyads or triads, using the entry mode trade. The other modes such as FDI or joint ventures (JV) are taken up in Chapter 7.

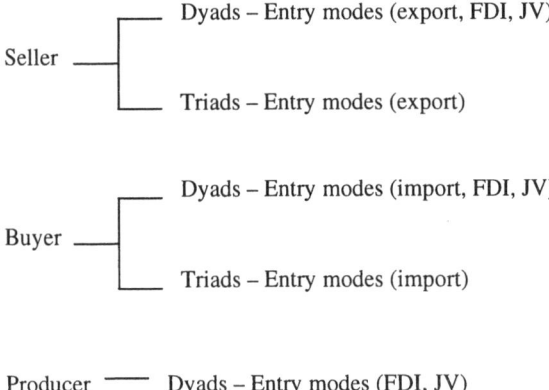

Figure 6.6   Entry roles related to entry nodes and entry modes

Since these entry nodes are related to the external network, they are not relevant for the producer role. However, if this role is combined with the buyer and seller roles, the entry nodes become relevant. If the producer is also a buyer, the products manufactured abroad are bought by the MNC for internal use, for example internal offshoring in the form of a component for the own production in the home country. The alternative is often to outsource the production to another foreign producer, when the role of the MNC is changed from being a producer to being a buyer. When the producer is also a seller, the manufactured products are either sold in the country where they are produced or exported to other foreign markets. In the former case, the establishment of a production unit could be a natural step in the internationalization process, starting with sales and later continuing with production in the foreign market. In the latter case, it could more be a question of taking advantage of shifting production costs in different parts of the world.

CONCLUSIONS

Network relationships are the core of the internationalization process. Internationalization of sales and purchasing or exporting/importing takes place through establishing and developing relationships in foreign market networks. A more complete model of the internationalization of the firm is achieved by combining this relationship process stage model with the relevant internationalization process model. While the latter concerns how the international experience of the firm is developed, the former is a good approximation of how international experience is gained in a specific market or country. For a firm that has a domestic market focus and starts to internationalize to a foreign country, the pre-relationship stage corresponds to the pre-export stage for the first market abroad. The development of the relationships in the foreign country market starts in the early stage, when commitments and experience increase somewhat. According to the internationalization process model, this is similar to the experimental export stage of an internationally inexperienced firm. More international experience is gained if the relationships come to the development stage, when business between the customer and the supplier starts to grow and resources are increasingly shared. The relationship is further developed and settles in the long-term stage. Relationships follow a similar pattern to the internationalization process as a whole by showing how the gradual build-up of international experience takes place. The more relationships in a foreign country that have reached later stages, the more internationally experienced and the higher the degree of internationalization of the firm. Further, the more countries with such established relationships, the more internationally experienced the firm is.

A vital part of the internationalization process is the entry strategy, which includes the entry mode, the entry node, the entry process and the entry role. The entry node was found to deal with the network strategy issue of establishing linkages directly to the final customers through dyads or having indirect linkages via distributors or agents by forming triads. Based on a study in Poland, it was discussed how to solve the major strategic issue in triads of the distributor network specialist about how to make the trade-off between and coordinate the linkage strategies to the third party and to the final customer. In unbalanced triads, the linkage strategy of the exporter to the intermediary is mainly supportive, since the agent/distributor is mainly the dominant party by handling the linkage strategy towards the customers. In balanced triads the situation is often the other way around. The exporter is leading the management of the relationships with the customers, while the role of the intermediary is more supportive. This also makes the exporter dominate the relationship with the agent or distributor. The more the seller is involved in the direct linkage strategy towards the customers, the more the triad resembles a dyad.

Regarding the entry process, the relationships of the exporter with customers are more developed in balanced than unbalanced triads. In the latter case, for example, they did not develop beyond a certain stage, either the early stage or the development stage. It was hard to compensate for this lack of customer contact with a strong relationship with the agent/distributor. A major reason was the low control of the intermediary, originating from the fact that not enough knowledge about the market is gained through this kind of arrangement. The best alternative seems to be to form dyads, that is to take over the customer relationships through changing the entry mode by setting up an own subsidiary. In general, the information or communication linkage as well as the social linkage were found to be critical for the development of the relationships.

For the entry roles of buyer or seller, the relevant entry nodes are either dyads or triads. Since these entry nodes are found in the external network, they are only relevant for the producer if this role is combined with either of the other two roles. If the producer is also a buyer, for example, the products manufactured abroad are bought by the MNC for internal use, for example internal offshoring of a component for own production in the home country. This producer role is expanded in the next chapter.

The network strategy and the linkage strategy in entering the emerging country market were influenced by two major types of institutional distance, namely the hierarchical organization of the firms in the respective country and the culture of each country, the latter aspect mainly manifesting itself as language problems. These distances affected all major aspects of the entry strategy. It did not matter whether the mode was an intermediary or a subsidiary; whether the entry mode was a dyad or a triad; how the entry process developed; and if the entry role was seller or purchaser. Internationalization varies with the degree of internationalization of the firm. The first internationalization step of an inexperienced firm is a difficult and critical strategic move, since it involves a transformation to a new theory-in-use or thought style based on a knowledge platform concerning international business instead of domestic business. The study of the internationalization processes to the emerging markets in the Baltic Sea region by small and medium-sized enterprises from Southeast Sweden confirms the picture of SMEs being bound to the home market or even to a specific region. Rather few firms took advantage of the gradual liberalization of these markets at close geographical distance by internationalizing their business. Almost all those that did already had an international experience.

The experiential organizational learning by the exporter was especially low in unbalanced triads, when the relationship with the agent was weak, for example when the agent represented a number of companies, and the exporter had to compete with others about the agent's time and resources. Another reason for the low learning of the seller is that experiential knowledge is mainly tacit. Such know-how is hard to transfer between parties and requires that the company is learning by operating in the market. From an organizational learning point of view, triads in emerging country markets are therefore paradoxical. Due to the high uncertainty experienced in these markets, low cost and flexible entry nodes are chosen such as triads. But, on the other hand, not operating in this foreign market hinders the seller to develop experiential knowledge about customers and the specific characteristics of the market. Uncertainty is not reduced or controlled for, which is necessary if the exporter were to be willing to expand business by investing more resources in the market.

7. Internal network organization of the internationalized firm

This chapter builds further on the internationalization processes of the previous chapter. The internationalization of the value chain is completed with the production activity. It was taken up briefly above in connection with the outsourcing of production or how the border line between the external and internal network has changed. But since production mainly belongs within the internal network, it is discussed in this chapter. Because relocation and restructuring of production play a key role in the third wave of internationalization, it is important to clarify and develop the role of this activity in the internationalization process.

This implies that the organization of the activities of the value chain is also internationalized, that is the infrastructure of the firm. With increasing shares of sales and resources devoted to international activities, the organization of the firm becomes more and more internationally oriented. Based on the internationalization of the activities of the value chain and growing internationalization of the organization, a distinction is made between two major types of internationally active firms, namely the internationalizing firm and the internationalized firm. Internationalization processes taken up in Chapter 6 mainly concern the internationalizing firm. Three forms of the fully internationalized firms are presented in this chapter, based on their degree of international experience and degree of international outlook. They are the Ethnocentric MNC, the Polycentric MNC and the Geocentric MNC. By relating these internationalized firms to domestic firms and internationalizing firms, more is known about the entire internationalization process, also its end. Illustrations are given of the internationalization processes of Ethnocentric MNCs to the new Eastern part of the EU and how production and other activities of the value chain are restructured on a global basis for Polycentric and Geocentric MNCs. Based on this further elaboration on the globalization processes of firms, the organization issue will be elaborated on further for the internationalized firm. The network aspect will be brought in to turn the organization of the internationalized firm into a hierarchical network. In that way, the internationalization of the organization of the MNC is elaborated on further at the same time as the chapter goes into how business marketing is controlled.

The network approach to international business marketing is developed further in the chapter as well as the next chapter by viewing the MNC organization as a network organization. The implications of a network approach to the organization of the MNC is developed, meaning that the MNC organization is translated into a network organization by specifying it as a hierarchical network and further developing various types of controls of the network relationships. According to the 'head office assignment' introduced in Chapter 1, MNC group networks constitute the overall conditions for local business marketing and organization. The local business marketing manager, who is normally sitting in the subsidiary looking out through the window at the local market site, is now instead looking out through the other window, the one facing the world or the group. What discretion or agency is there for local business marketing? Which are the basic internal network characteristics that constitute the constraints on adapting the IBM strategy to the external environment of the local emerging country market?

With the introduction of the network organization, the perspective of the book is changed from focusing on the analysis and formation of business strategy to concentrating on the implementation of strategy or the internal conditions for the realization of strategy and how it is controlled. This is done in accordance with the institutional network approach, which stresses the key role of organizational factors in connection with strategy. Resources and capabilities are organized through an internal network organization of the MNC, implying that competitive advantages are shaped by network structures, and governed by network controls. The last two chapters of the book are therefore about the role of the internal organizational network for IBM, mainly how this capacity platform brings about competitive advantages through effectuating IBM strategy. The purpose is to analyse how local/regional business marketing strategy is implemented through the local/regional organization of the MNC.

The chapter starts with the internationalization of production followed by the internationalization of organization. Based on these two sections and Chapter 6, five types of international firms are described, which directly leads to the specification of the internationalized firm as a hierarchical network. The major dimensions of this network organization come next, where the clustered group network is described and compared to some other types of group networks.

INTERNATIONALIZATION OF PRODUCTION

According to the internationalization process, production is moved abroad rather late, being the last establishment form in a country market. In today's global world this might still be true for the internationalizing firm, especially when entering the first foreign countries. But with the increasing possibilities to take advantage of global economies of scale and low labour costs, this simple idea is only part of the picture. For the internationalized firm, the situation is different and production mainly a matter of concentration /restructuring production on a global basis. According to Farrell (2004b, p. 88), the following five phases or stages can be found regarding internationalization of production:

1. Enter new markets. Companies use production models similar to the ones they deploy at home to enter new countries and expand their customer bases.

2. Move production abroad. Companies relocate their entire production processes to take advantage of cost differentials; they export finished goods globally.

3. Disaggregate the value chain. Companies' individual product components are manufactured in different locations or regions; countries may specialize in component manufacturing, assembly, or both.

4. Reengineer the value chain. Companies redesign their production processes, taking local factors into account, to maximize efficiencies and cost savings.

5. Create new markets. Given lower costs due to globalization, companies can offer new products at lower prices and can penetrate new market segments or geographies, or both.

These stages need not be sequential. At first, when being less global and entering markets the firm's domestic production is 'cloned' abroad. This fits with the internationalization process theory. At the second stage, being an internationalized firm beyond the internationalization process, whole production processes are relocated to take advantage of cost differentials worldwide. At the next stage, the value chain is disaggregated worldwide and individual product components manufactured in different locations or regions. At the fourth stage, companies reengineer the now global value chain by redesigning their production processes to maximize efficiencies and cost savings. At the last and now highly global stage, new markets are created due to the lower costs caused by globalization. Here, production is wholly integrated globally both geographically and with the other activities in the value chain.

The discussion so far concerns the internationalization of the major activities of the MNC: selling, purchasing and manufacturing. Built on this discussion of the various stages of internationalization for these major activities of the MNC, the internationalization of the organization is taken up. To put these processes into perspective, they are related to five types of international firms. A specific illustration is given here about what these processes look like within the internationalized firm. These parts, in their turn, are an input to the major part of the chapter: the major characteristics of the MNC when defined as a hierarchical network.

INTERNATIONALIZATION OF ORGANIZATION

The internationalization of the organization is now taken up to further illuminate the internationalization process. The multinational organization or the mother-daughter organization is an early type of worldwide organization for the MNC, which is typical of the first wave of internationalization of firms, especially for West-European companies. This type of organization promotes local responsiveness and has little global integration between various units throughout the world. The interwar period, for example, favoured a multi-domestic pattern of competition developed on a country-by-country basis, where little coordination and multinational control was required (Dunning, 1993). MNCs were not very diverse and were not divisionalized, for example along product lines, but functionally organized. Subsidiaries were loosely coupled and more controlled through informal means by 'the mother'.

The multi-divisional organization or international organization is a later form of worldwide organization structure. It was developed by big American corporations during the first wave of internationalization and was adopted by MNCs from West Europe during the second wave of internationalization of firms. This type of worldwide organization was more suitable, when the change to more global competition from multi-domestic competition affected the long-term competitive positions of MNCs and, as a consequence of that, their goals. The global integration of local market activities had become more essential for international competitiveness. With a rising international commitment and a growing interest to increase the control of international operations, an international division is sometimes created within the group. Later on, when international business has outgrown domestic business, the whole organizational infrastructure of the group changes to be based on the international operations, and a global divisional structure takes form (Stopford and Wells, 1972; Bartlett, 1986). This organization is centred on product/business divisions.

Later, in the 1970s, the global organization (Bartlett and Ghosal, 1989) appeared on the world scene represented by the Japanese keiretsus in connection with the second wave of internationalization of firms. This is a highly centralized way to organize, where the global value chain in the form of first mostly sales subsidiaries and later production units abroad are run from Japan, where key production, R&D, and the top of the pyramid are located. This global organization is traditionally not based on divisions but on functions. At that time, the world had become more integrated, which also made it possible to integrate on a world scale.

From the 1980s onwards, at the end of the second wave of internationalization of firms, Korean 'chaebols' and overseas Chinese family firms had also become active in international markets. This made the world market a much more competitive place. The global competitiveness originates more and more from such coordination of interrelated activities worldwide. With an established market position in most local markets of interest to the MNC and rising global competition, growth comes from an increased international involvement of the whole MNC than from initial entries in new geographic markets. It is vital to utilize synergistic advantages and to rationalize production and marketing, for instance. The competitive advantage achieved from integration through this organization is more sophisticated than is possible to achieve through the earlier types of global organization. Coordination is based on both the global interest and the local interest and not only on the global interest. This results in MNCs starting to change their organization into a 'glocalized' transnational or differentiated organization that is both global and local at the same time (Bartlett and Ghoshal, 1989; Jansson 1994b).

A most important aspect of the internationalization of the organization concerns the ownership structure. Due to the globalization of financial markets and the M&A wave of the 1990s the ownership structure of the MNCs has been internationalized. Together with the increasing 'cross-hauling' of FDI between countries during the third wave of internalization of firms, this has resulted in most economies today containing a mix of companies from many countries, representing different types of international firms and ways to organize the international activities.

TYPES OF INTERNATIONAL FIRMS

Based on the analysis of the internationalization processes above and in Chapter 6 related to the three waves of internationalization of firms, a distinction is made between three major types of firms: the domestic firm, the internationalizing firm and the internationalized firm. This grouping is mainly based on the degree of international experience of firms. To further distinguish between the internationalized firms, they are also grouped according to degree of internationally oriented thought style. This makes it possible divide up the internationalized firm into three types of MNCs: the Ethnocentric MNC, the Polycentric MNC and the Geocentric MNC. The six types of companies are related to each other in Figure 7.1.

Internationalization refers to the global spread of the firm. The foundational premise of research on internationalization processes is that the geographic spread takes place from the home country to foreign country markets, that is internationalization is the same as the passing of national borders. The degree of international outlook of the firm refers to the internationalization of the management philosophy or how the world view becomes increasingly global, the more national borders that are passed. Thus, it has to do with the internationalization of the collective mind of the company. This idea how management philosophy changes with internationalization is taken from Heenan and Perlmutter (1979), that is the orientation toward foreign people, ideas and resources in headquarters and subsidiaries, and in host and home countries. It mainly reflects specific country or national mind sets found within the MNC.

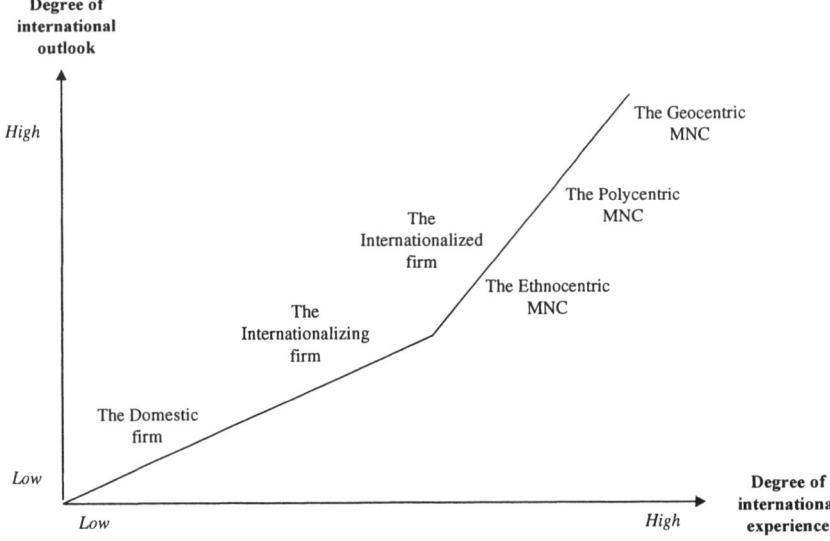

Figure 7.1   Types of international firms

This kind of management philosophy comes very close to express the collective world view of the multinational enterprise. This makes it possible to specify the management philosophy further according to the basic rules model (Jansson, 2007). This orientation of the MNC is therefore defined as the major thought style prevailing within the firm about its international operations, that is the internationalization of the thought styles of the firm. Based on this degree of international outlook and the degree of international experience of the firm, five types of international firms and one non-international firm are distinguished:

1. *The Domestic firm.* This is a company operating in the home market and has not yet started to internationalize and is therefore no MNC. There is no internationally oriented thought style and no international experience, since this company is entirely national.
2. *The Internationalizing firm.* This firm is internationalizing its activities in the value chain and is found somewhere in-between the home market and the fully internationalized firm, being an immature MNC. The degree of international experience and degree of international outlook vary with how much it has internationalized its operations. The entry strategy and internationalization process of Chapter 6 is mostly relevant for this type of firm, as it passes through its various stages. These strategies correspond to 'internationalization through ownership' and 'internationalization of the subsidiary's external business network' taken up for the 'Embedded Multinational' by Forsgren et al. (2005). In

Sweden today, internationalizing firms are mostly SMEs that either have potential to internationalize further or start to internationalize. The internationalizing firm was exemplified in the previous chapter, mainly SMEs going abroad from Southern Sweden to the emerging country markets of the East Baltic Sea region. Despite the fact that new international thought styles are being established in the firm, the dominating thought style stays national throughout this process.

3. *The Internationalized firm.* Regarding the geographic spread of the firm this type of MNC has reached the end of the internationalization process and is therefore considered to be a fully internationalized firm. Most activities of the value chain have been internationalized, and the firm has developed an organization suitable for its geographic spread of activities over the many international markets. Besides the two ways to internationalize referred to above by Forsgren et al. (2005), 'internationalization through the corporate business network' or 'internal internationalization' is most relevant for the internationalized firm. Depending upon the degree of international outlook and thereby type of internationally oriented thought style existing within its global organization, three major types of internationalized firms are distinguished, namely the Ethnocentric MNC, the Polycentric MNC and the Geocentric MNC. Each of these sub-forms of the internationalized firm is now elaborated on further.

The Ethnocentric MNC

The thought style of the Ethnocentric MNC is still dominated by the thought style set of the home country, which is also its major strategic base. Since most of its key activities are located in the home country there is a strong national bias within the MNC. The organizational infrastructure of this firm is characterized as a global organization or multinational organization. The multinational organization or the mother-daughter organization as being an early type of worldwide organization for the MNC is also found in the Ethnocentric MNC. Typical for both of them is that they are reminiscent of the internationalization period of the company or of the internationalizing firm.

Six of the smaller SMEs from Kalmar County included in the study referred to in Chapter 6 are typical examples of the ethnocentric MNC. Even if they are small (around 200-300 employees), they are resource rich, since they belong to a larger group, normally another MNC. These are highly specialized niche MNCs that are members of a larger group of companies, which will make final decisions on big strategic issues. The strategic base of these MNCs is in Southern Sweden, where the major strategic units, sales, production and main sub-suppliers are located. The foreign operations are mainly a sales organization which consists of a few sales centres (for example local engineering offices) and sales subsidiaries but mostly of agents and distributors (indirect relationships or triads). A few of them have a small part of their production abroad. An exception is a company that already outsourced production to Eastern Europe at the beginning of the 1990s and now has a value added structure that makes present and future adaptations easier to the increasing specialization of the production chain in the Baltic Sea area. Despite a main foreign supplier base, one firm in the electronics industry was struggling with a biased cost structure for some years. It has been closed down and moved to another Nordic country. These MNCs are becoming more global by growing in present markets and expanding to new country markets. However, as discussed above, only a small but growing part of their business is done in emerging country markets, where there are good expansion possibilities. Their strategic production base is more or less intact in the region and is not undergoing any major shift to Eastern Europe or China.

Most other MNCs studied from Southern Sweden are small highly specialized production centres within a multinational group, for instance Scania or sub-suppliers in an internationally specialized value-added chain within the vehicle industry. They produce for all three types of internationalized firms, defined above.

The Polycentric MNC

A number of different thought styles co-exist within the MNC. The thought style related to the home market still remains, but does not dominate as in the Ethnocentric MNC. So even if the strategic bases of the polycentric MNC are spread over the globe, one major centre remains in the home country. The firm may still have many activities in the home country: production, R&D activities and Group HQ. But most business areas are located in other parts of the world. The international organization of the MNC described above approximates the organizational infrastructure of this firm. Actually, this type of organization epitomizes the Polycentric MNC, since it is based on the organization being centred on product/business divisions. For this type of internationalized firm, the value chain is often disaggregated and reengineered on a global basis. Usually the home country is still important, but there are also other centres located in host countries.

Volvo and Scania, or other big MNCs in the vehicle industry, are good examples of this kind of firm. The Volvo group has its HQ and most business areas located in Sweden, but there are also vital centres in other European countries, in the Americas (USA and Brazil) and others coming up in Asia, for example in South Korea, Japan, China and India. The case of how General Motors in 2005 located the production of its new standard car model between Opel in Russelheim, Germany and Saab Automobile in Trollhättan, Sweden is a good example of a location problem on an EU basis within a polycentric MNC. Here, one established production centre (originally an acquired company) was competing with another established centre (originally also acquired). The HQ of this US corporation set the rules and made the final decision, which to a large extent was determined by the global situation in the industry, for instance over-capacity and increased ongoing concentration in an oligopolistic world market structure. The decision was of high strategic significance for the countries involved, since the outcome could result in a close down of either of these factories. A major condition for these Western European sites to compete for this production was a considerable reduction of their relatively very high labour costs and other costs, which could not be achieved without government involvement.

The Geocentric MNC

A company having a transnational organization is closest to the Geocentric MNC. It is a kind of uninational firm, where the world is seen as one entity in the same way as a nation is. The company meets different demands in the world market, even having global customers. It employs the best people for a certain job irrespective of their nationality. The best location is found for the different units depending upon actual worldwide needs and not because of the origin of the company. For instance, where a product company, that represents the global interest, is located depends on the worldwide interest of the company. However, few MNCs have reached this ideal state of the true transnational firm. They are still bound by historically and geographically based institutional ties like the differentiated group organization. The main point is that its organization is globally based and does not have one dominating regional strategic base, for example in Europe, Asia, or North America. Rather, it is equally big in each of these continents, having a multi-centred organization based on all three continents.

The Geocentric MNC therefore has a global outlook. The thought style is global in the true meaning of the word. It has opened up to the world. It takes advantage of outside opportunities no matter where they arise, uses the cheapest resources no matter where they are produced, hires the best people no matter where they were born, and faces any competitor no matter where it comes from. There might not be any strategic base left in the home country. It is not traditionally bound to any particular place, rather looking at the world as one big market, and therefore being located in the most suitable place in relation to its activities, inclusive of its headquarters. This type of firm can be said to represent the end of the globalization process according to traditional internationalization process theory. Home is everywhere or in no particular place. It operates on a global basis for all business activities and has a global firm infrastructure. It is best characterized to follow the principles of the transnational organization, sometimes operating a 'regioncentric' organization. There is either a continentally based headquarters or one virtual global headquarters for the world-scale operations.

Case illustration: Relocation of production within the Geocentric MNC
Some major characteristics of the Geocentric MNC are now illustrated from within an MNC that has moved production from a factory in a small town in

Central Sweden to other parts of Europe. The example comes from Mineikytë and Steponavièiûtë (2005). It well illustrates the last two stages of the internationalization of production taken up above. This relocation took place within a company belonging to a large US company, and which had been bought from a big Swedish MNC a few years earlier. After being acquired, this company has gradually been disinvested in Sweden and integrated with other group businesses in the world, mainly in Europe. In a couple of years, it was changed from a company with most of its strategic base in Sweden to having left the country. This relocation process is depicted in Figure 7.2.

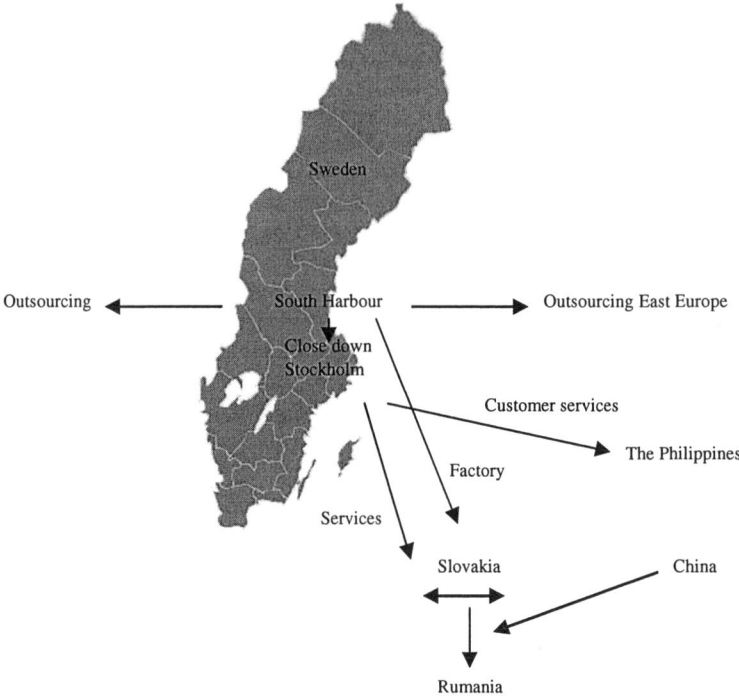

Figure 7.2   Relocation of the Geocentric MNC

The main reason for this disappearing act was lower labour costs, in this case in Slovakia, where they amount to about 10 per cent of the costs in Sweden. Overhead costs are also lower, roughly by 20 per cent. In addition, material costs are being reduced by continuously shifting the supplier base out of Western Europe to Eastern Europe. This is a good illustration of how a Geocentric MNC responds to global developments, in this case a region-centred MNC. It shows that restructuring in the geocentric firm is much more complex than closing down a factory in one country and setting it up in another. The case demonstrates that it was only the most modern part of the factory that was moved abroad (to Slovakia). Production of parts that were at the end of their product life cycle were kept in Sweden, either being outsourced in Sweden or abroad to Eastern Europe. Some products were finished. The close down of the factory was part of the continuous disaggregating and reengineering of the value chain on primarily an EU basis. It involved a larger part of the production system and was a response to the geographical spread of the customer structure within the EU as well as increasing price pressures in this highly competitive and dynamic global industry.

Production was moved closer to the now major customers in Central and Southern Europe as well as in the Middle East and North Africa. Close relationships with large customers are a key strategic factor in the industry. In addition, products are heavy and expensive to transport. Thus, the location disadvantage of Swedish production in relation to the customers plus price pressures were increasing to a certain point, which made changes necessary. Some customer related operations were also jointly moved out of another unit (in Stockholm) to Slovakia, namely equipment and knowledge that are required to customize and service products. The part of production kept in Sweden was mainly related to the main customer and former owner there. A major reason for moving production to another EU country and not to China was that the company has a region-centric organization in Europe as well in other parts of the world. Still, these relocations were influenced by the production situation in China, since some parts for the product moved were already made there. There are also plans to outsource call centre activities for customer service to the Philippines, which is an important centre for the group in Asia.

Due to an ongoing reorganization of the group, the production moved was integrated with another product division in Slovakia, enlarging the country as a centre for production in Europe for the MNC. This was not planned in advance but an adaptation to the evolving competitive situation in this hi-tech and dynamic industry. For the same reason, there was not only a transfer of knowledge from Sweden to Slovakia but also an upgrading of it at the same time. Due to increasing costs, labour turnover and high inflation in Slovakia, studies were already ongoing within the MNC about moving some production from Slovakia to Romania to take advantage of even lower labour costs.

This relocation of these various activities of the value chain between different places in the world is hard to describe as a traditional internationalization process. It is more the already internationalized firm that reorganizes on a global basis to increase its competitiveness in world markets. The restructuring is based on a global outlook and where national interests are considered together with other major decision factors according to the geocentric thought style of the MNC. There is an obvious difference to the situation for the General Motors case referred to above as an example of the Polycentric MNC, where the national interests were much stronger and a more important part of the strategic decision process.

SPECIFYING THE MULTINATIONAL CORPORATION AS A HIERARCHICAL NETWORK

In this and the previous chapter, three forms of internationalized firms have been discussed based on the internationalization of the major activities of the value chain, and how these gradually increasing international activities are organized over time. The organization issue will now be elaborated on further for the three forms of internationalized firms. A major observation from studies on the internationalization of the organization of MNCs is that it has become more and more network like. For example, the current major recommended way to organize – the transnational organization – is also called the integrated network (Bartlett and Ghoshal, 1989). The internationalized firm will therefore now be described from a network perspective as a hierarchical network. The focus will be on the Polycentric MNC, since it seems to be the most common type of internationalized firm, at least for the European MNCs that are mainly dealt with in the book. When specified from a network perspective, it is defined as the clustered group network. The focus on this group network is also motivated by the fact that most MNCs, for which the local and regional network organization are taken up in the next chapter, belongs within this type of group network.

But before the clustered group network is presented, the major factors of the network organization of the internationalized firm will be developed. Unlike the market networks analysed in previous chapters, the network organization pattern of this MNC is characterized as a hierarchical network. The main issue for the international organization of this hierarchical network concerns solving the basic strategic dilemma between global integration and local differentiation: to organize this trade-off to achieve sustainable competitive advantages. When interpreted from a network perspective, this dilemma becomes whether to organize the trade-off between tight and loose coupling on one hand, or strong and weak linkages on the other. It is a well-known fact from organizational network studies that networks with a tight network organization structure based on a dense linkage pattern are vulnerable to external disturbances. Changes travel fast through networks organized in this way, which could create an information overload and too many conflicts. Loosely coupled networks and networks with a low density have the opposite characteristics. Since independent individual units do not have much contact, information and resource exchange is low. Disturbances are confined to parts of the network, which reduce the number of overall conflicts. The solution of the strategic dilemma lies in finding the right trade-off between these extremes for various tasks for the network as a whole. A high degree of local adaptation denotes loose couplings between subsidiaries and headquarters, while a high degree of global integration takes place through tightly coupled networks consisting of strong linkages between units. In this latter type of network, the strong ties in the form of intersections or 'bridges' can be organized through teams, task forces, committees, integrators and integrative units like regional headquarters.

Following Ghoshal and Bartlett (1990), internal and external networks are combined and this entire network defined to consist of organization sets. The sets are divided up into two categories: internal networks consist of organization sets, while external networks consist of organization clusters, where each set and cluster is coordinated through linkages within itself as well as across themselves. The term density is used to characterize the linkage pattern of the network. Density is defined as the percentage of actual to potential ties among members within organization sets and clusters as well as between them. As a consequence, the term 'within density' is used to describe the density of linkages within one set or cluster, while the term 'across density' signifies the density of relationships within the whole network. In accordance with the marketing perspective of the book, the focus is on the across-density, that is how the focal organization of the local organization set (for example the subsidiary) is coupled to the group network.

The directions dimensions from network mapping in Chapter 3 is also used to describe the linkage pattern of the hierarchical network, that is the vertical, horizontal and diagonal dimensions. The dominant structure of authority nets (see below) is vertical, while lateral nets concern horizontal and diagonal dimensions. All three dimensions are relevant for the social nets.

In addition to the linkage patterns and network organization structures of the hierarchical network of the MNC discussed above, controls of the units within the network play a vital role for how to solve the strategic dilemma between local adaptation and global integration. The more a subsidiary is controlled by the group, for instance, the less is its autonomy, the more its strategies are constrained, and the fewer possibilities it has to adapt to the local external environment. Three main types of network controls are found for the relationships: process (behaviour) control, output (performance) control and input (conditional) control.

Major Network Organization Sub-forms

The linkage patterns and network organization structures are used as a basis for establishing three major subforms of the hierarchical network, through which business marketing is implemented: the authority net, the lateral net and the social net. Together with the network controls and the main interests found within the MNC, these network organization subforms constitute a major head form, the MNC hierarchical network of the internationalized firm, which is summarized in Table 7.1. The three nets are also illustrated in Figure 7.3.

The authority net follows the formal and impersonal authority structure of the company determining how the organization is segmented, for example the centralization/decentralization of decision-making. This prescribed network is mainly a vertically organized net and forms the official communication channels of the organization.

Table 7.1   Major dimensions of the hierarchical network

NETS (ORGANIZATION SUBFORMS)

The Authority Net
- Segmentation and linking (grouping) of organizational units, shaping the formal structure, for example by function, product, area, matrix
- Centralization or decentralization of decision making through the hierarchy of formal authority
- Ownership pattern

The Lateral Net
Cross-departmental/divisional/company relations, for example direct managerial contact, temporary or permanent teams, task forces, committees, integrators, and integrative departments

The Social Net
- The social side of coalitions (task-oriented unexpected linkages between units)
- Non-task-oriented social linkages (cliques)

MAIN INTERESTS

- **Group interest**
- **Global (product/functional) interest**
- **Local interest**

NETWORK CONTROLS

Process control
- Direct (behaviour control): Orders, advice, dialogue
- Indirect (rules): Information stored in texts (formalization and standardization): written policies, rules, job descriptions, and standard procedures, through instruments such as manuals, charts etc. They are used in the planning and budget system

Output (performance) control
- Financial performance, technical reports, sales and marketing data, mainly organized through a planning and budget system
- Market control: Prices. Transfer prices stored in numbers

Input control
- Socialization, building on organizational culture of known and shared strategic objectives and values by training, transfer of managers, career path management, measurement and reward systems, informal communication (see above)

Source: Based on Jansson et al. (1995).

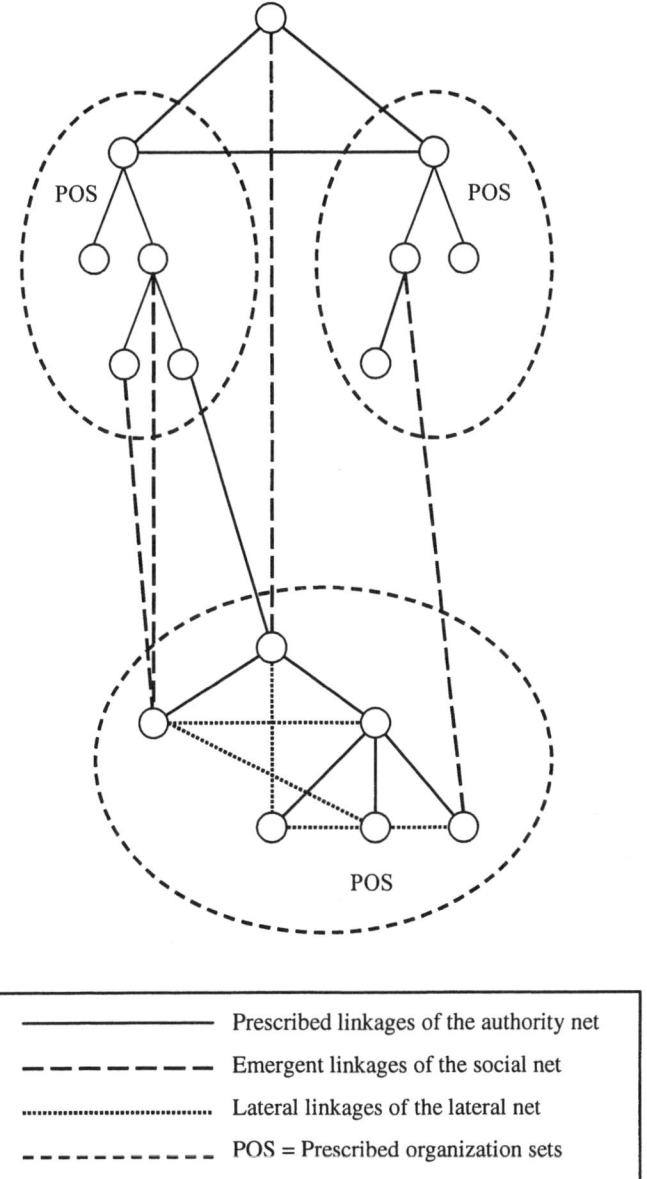

Figure 7.3   Authority, social and lateral nets

The lateral net includes both horizontal and diagonal relations between units, for example cross-departmental relations through project groups, committees, etc. This net is both prescribed and emergent. The communication network, for example, is quasi-official, where some linkages are prescribed from above, while others emerge from below. An example of a lateral net is an action network, for example a cross-departmental project group, where the departments involved are prescribed by rule or order, while the persons representing the departments are determined from time to time by the actual task. The social net consists of social linkages and is established from below in the organization due to unexpected and spontaneous reasons or for social reasons. These are the unofficial linkages of the organization, which could take place in any direction: vertical, horizontal or diagonal. Emergent social nets are created for certain tasks or due to purely social reasons. This means that the social part of a lateral net is defined as a social net.

A vital basis for the authority net is legal construction of the units of the MNC. Whether units within the group are wholly or partly owned by the group is one important factor behind the structure of the prescribed net. For example, if the local unit is a subsidiary (that is owned) rather than being a subordinated administrative unit gives the local unit a more independent standing (autonomy) and the MNC a more decentralized organization structure. Control of the authority, lateral and social nets comprising the hierarchical network takes place through three main types of control: process control, output control and input control, which are now elaborated on further.

Types of Network Control

There are three main types of control within the hierarchical network of the implementation of business marketing (see Table 7.1). These controls work as guiding principles to be followed by organizational members and mechanisms for ensuring that rules are followed.

Output control

Output control is based on the planning and budget system that is mainly seen as an incentive- and sanction-oriented system. Marketing, production and financial performance, for instance, are surveyed through the reporting system. This performance control is normally based on an internal transfer price system in an organization consisting of fully incorporated units or sometimes of profit centres. Price works as a market control, being based on viewing the organization as an internal market. Internal units are left to operate on their own in competition with each other and with firms in the external market, implying that intra-organizational relationships are market-oriented and price driven. Competition in markets controls the unit rather than the hierarchy. Such market control of subsidiaries seems to be more practiced for small market companies in far-off countries than for large market companies in main markets (Jansson, 1994b). Price could thus be a main information carrier in output control that is chiefly achieved through a type of prescribed network: the planning and budget system.

Process control

Process control is based on incentives and punishments. It involves direct personal surveillance (behaviour control), mainly executed in the authority net. Examples of corrective mechanisms used in this case are personal instruments such as orders, advice and dialogue. Career path management, transfer of managers, measurement and reward systems, and informal communication are other examples of instruments for process control, which are part of the MNC's reward/punishment system. Process control also involves norms manifested through formalization and standardization of information, for example written policies, job descriptions, manuals and charts. These rules work more as guiding principles than enforcers of behaviour.

Input control

Many of the controls mentioned above are also important in input control, since they contribute to socializing people into the values and thought styles of the organization. Socialization is one way of globally integrating autonomous units through the use of normative rules and thought styles, that is to indoctrinate managers into group values, norms and ways of thinking, for example to identify with the whole group and not only with the local subsidiary. In such cases, the values and norms of managers become closely aligned to those of the group as a whole. This can be achieved through a transfer of information, influence and people among various group units according to a management development and transfer programme. The budget system is also usually an important mode for socialization, not only being a process control. It is also based on certain values and thought styles at the same time as it constitutes a number of norms to be followed by the employees. In addition, it works as a channel for the communication of norms, values and thought styles.

The values and norms of the individuals as well as know-how and decision-making are influenced by exchange through the networks, for instance informal communication through lateral and social nets such as personal contacts among managers, attendance at conferences and transfers of managers. Communication through these nets is only broadly prescribed, within which emergent networks are allowed to develop. Lateral or cross-divisional relations are encouraged, for example direct managerial contacts and temporary teams. The formation of such relations is dependent upon actual needs. Similarly, more prescribed means such as courses, conferences, etc. are arranged to give knowledge about how the organization works and should work. But these means also give employees opportunity to meet to develop relationships. Therefore, how they are organized varies with subject and participants.

Direct controls such as traditional process controls of subordinates through the authority net and indirect controls through norms established through formal network rules, procedures and manuals are usually less important in the highly decentralized multi-level, multi-hierarchical and multi-national MNC. Rather, indirect controls of behaviour such as output controls are more important. These controls manifested through the planning and budget system intend to control the results of organizational behaviour. Another vital indirect control of behaviour finally takes place through input controls, for instance norms for how people are selected and socialized into corporate values and beliefs. In a divisionalized company such as the Polycentric MNC, indirect input and output controls are supposed to be more critical controls for achieving competitive advantage than the traditional hierarchical enforcement mechanisms through the authority net more characteristic of functional organization. As noted above, controls in the modern MNC take different rationalities of the organization into consideration, for example local responsiveness and global integration. Direct intervention is thus selective in such an organization, where control is mostly of this indirect type.

Main Interests

Certain major interests tend to dominate the MNC organization. Behind these interests are found the basic rules in the form of specific values, norms and thought styles that work as guiding principles for decisions and actions as well as enforcement mechanisms behind their implementation. The degree of international outlook is thus a major manifestation of such an interest. Divisionalized network structures dominate among MNCs today. They consist of incorporated units, which are segmented according to some basic principles: the products, the location (geography), or a combination of both these bases. Three main interests are distinguished behind how networks are organized and controlled within such a decentralized structure. These interests create different authorities or broad standpoints with ensuing political processes within the MNC. They assume that legitimacy is important also within the MNC network (Jansson, 2007). Conflicts between these interests may block the implementation of strategy and hamper the MNC to achieve competitive advantages. Since these interests are all economical in nature, they are mainly based on an efficiency orientation as the basic value or guiding principle. These are basic interests within the group that represent different authorities based on different efficiency rationalities.

Global interest
Two interests have to do with the spatial aspect (that distinguishes MNCs from uninational corporations): the global and local interests. These interests express the strategic intents behind global integration and local adaptation. The main purpose of some units within the MNC is to work with the global aspect of an activity, for example a product or project. The global product interest, or the principle of global integration, is represented by the management of the product divisions, the product companies, the business areas, or whatever these representatives of the global product interest may be

called within the individual MNCs. Such units have a worldwide responsibility for their products.

Bartlett and Ghoshal (1991) have developed three main types of international management role found within the multinational corporation, which largely correspond with the three sets of interests in Table 7.1. The strategic role of integrating activities worldwide is normally delegated to the divisional level by group management and is divided up among several divisions, which could be product-based or based on the geographic dimension. The main function to be performed here is maintenance of global efficiency and competitiveness, for example scale economies, synergies and competitive advantages on a worldwide scale, by transnational integration of activities. Bartlett and Ghoshal (1991) identify three main strategic roles for product division management, namely those of being:

1. A global business strategist.
2. An architect of asset configuration, being responsible for the coordination of key assets and locating them in a manner that support the strategic objectives.
3. A transnational coordinator, for example in implementing marketing strategy.

Local interest

The primary task of other units is to operate locally, for example a sales subsidiary. The management of the individual market company must respond to local demands and opportunities founded on local values, norms and thought styles. Such managers possess strong national interests and function as spokesmen for this rationality of national responsiveness within the MNC.

According to Bartlett and Ghoshal (1992a), there are three main roles for the manager of a subsidiary in a given country, those being:

1. A bicultural interpreter. The main task here is to integrate local company perspective with group perspective.
2. A defender and representative of the country in question.
3. A front-line implementor of group strategies and policies.

Group interest

The third interest refers to the entirety of the company as such and is found in all companies. It is here called the group interest or the company-wide interest. While the global and local interests are parochial, the group interest represents the common interest of the firm. The task of Group Management (GM) at the headquarters is to look after the interests of the group as a whole, for example by establishing the standards and norms valid for the group as a whole and controlling these by working as a controller, a coordinator or a mediator. These roles can be performed in such ways as solving conflicts between local interests and global product interests within a matrix organization. The GM gets its mandate from the board or ultimately from the shareholders and other stakeholders, for instance home government. This task is accomplished by having a network organization structure and types of network controls that ultimately favour this interest. A primary task is then to control the parochial interests so they do not get out of hand and conflict too much with each other and the company-wide interest.

According to Bartlett and Ghoshal (1992a), the overall corporate interests are:

1. To create a diverse set of business, functional and geographic management groups, assigning them specific roles and responsibilities, and presenting in an adequate way the strategic focus and vision.
2. To give each unit organizational legitimacy.
3. To balance and to integrate.

Besides competition for the internal resources of the MNC between these three separate interests, there is also competition among the various global interests and local interests. Following from the part above on the internationalization of the organization of the firm, the importance of the global and local interests within an MNC varies with how internationalized the firm is. At earlier stages of internationalization, the global interest is weak or even non-existent. An international division within an otherwise functionally organized company more likely looks after the local interest than the global interest, where the main conflicts will be with the functional departments. It also varies with the organization of the MNC. This is the case in the later stages, when the firm is operating more on a world scale. The global interest dominates in a worldwide product organization, since the whole firm is organized according to it. Most MNCs classified as having an international organization seem to be organized in that way (Bartlett and Ghoshal, 1989). As a whole, it is a partly centralized, partly decentralized organization, where focus is on middle management. In an area organization it is the other way around. It is dominated by the local interest. This is also typical of the multinational organization form. The international matrix organization formally considers both these interests at the same time. The main organizational task is then to bridge these interests, from the company-wide interest.

The Clustered Group Network

It can now be concluded that the multi-divisional organization is the most common way for the internationalized firm to organize. Therefore, it is fruitful to penetrate this organization more by viewing it from a network perspective. The key subform of this hierarchical group network is the authority net. This prescribed organization structure, which comes close to the formal organization, is the backbone of the organization structure of the Western MNC. Dependent upon the degree of coupling between different units within the group network as a result of density, a distinction can be made between different types of hierarchical network forms, for example dependent on how the trade-off between local differentiation and global integration in the group is organized.

The authority net of this group network is based on either products or geography, and how this structure is divisionalized and departmentalized. This means that the group network is decentralized. Such MNCs have a divisionalized network structure with a high capability for internal control of strategic decision-making. It is based on segmentation of various units and of strategic and operative decisions as well as having advanced incentive systems (Jansson, 1994a). From a network perspective this is a highly prescribed network that is tightly coupled across organization sets vertically but loosely coupled horizontally (Jansson et al., 1995). The dense vertical clusters are usually based on an authority net following the product dimension but they could also be organized according to function. If this clustered group network is based on a functional organization, it is usually of a more top-down and centralized kind than if the organization is based on products. This type of international group network is illustrated in Figure 7.4.

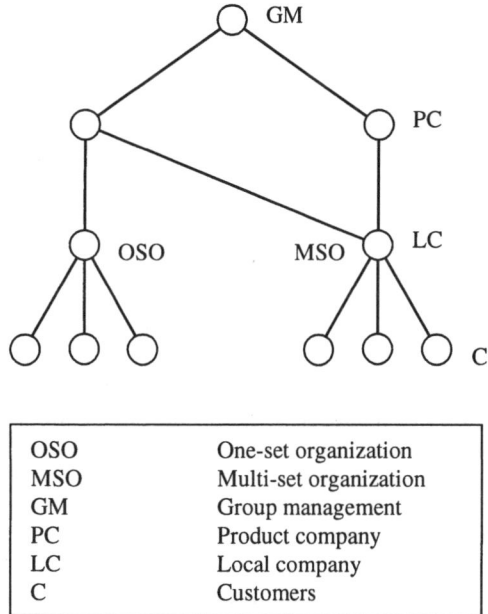

OSO	One-set organization
MSO	Multi-set organization
GM	Group management
PC	Product company
LC	Local company
C	Customers

Figure 7.4   The clustered group network

Global integration on product basis is the most common feature found among MNCs. In such cases, activities throughout the globe are divided up according to product type and the prescribed hierarchical network is clustered around the product companies/divisions. Such a product cluster is tightly coupled within itself (the vertical dimension) but loosely coupled to other clusters (the horizontal dimension). The local market dimension is subordinated to the global product dimension. An efficient coordination of global product interests and local interests increases the competitiveness of the corporation, particularly if competition is global. The global product organization is one example of this type of hierarchical network (Jansson, 1987, 1994b). International organization is another example. The authority of the product companies over the local subsidiaries is meant to control local decision-making and implementation. But this rationality of favouring global interests in decision making or conflict resolution through the authority net could be achieved at the expense of adaptability of local networks, for example low product adaptation to local conditions and less possibilities to customize market networks. Product companies do not accept decisions by their subsidiaries that do not conform to the global objectives. Such an unbalanced situation could lead to sub-optimization as seen from the company-wide interest. This risk of having too little local responsiveness increases the higher the overall density is within the local organization set.

In a clustered group network based on the product dimension (a global product organization) the market company reports directly to the management of the product company, which reports to group management (GM). With this organization, the control of the market companies becomes more formalized and they are more closely connected to the product companies, which often mean that their independence is low. Ideally, if this vertically segmented network should be fully developed, every one of the concern's market companies should be linked to only one of the product companies. When the local market clusters are all joined to one global product set through the local company, the local market organization is defined as a one-set organization (OSO). In that way, direct and strong vertical linkages are created between these units. This is, however, many times not possible, particularly for companies operating in small markets. There is not enough ground to completely segment the organization vertically all the way from the factory to the customer. The across density of such a mixed market company is higher, since it represents more than one product company. This authority problem of having pure vertical clusters and not opaque mixed varieties can be solved in various ways. One alternative is to slice up the market company's organization according to the structure of the group's product companies. In such a mixed company each 'slice' has a subordinated direct linkage to its product company. This is defined as a multi-sets organization (MSO), and means that local market clusters are through the local subsidiary connected to two or more global product sets. Another possibility is to hierarchically tie up the market company to its most important product company and link it loosely to the other product companies, for example through a market solution such as an agent contract rather than an authority relationship.

Lateral and social nets are anchored in the authority net, implying that the latter net creates different conditions for these other nets. Different constraints are therefore created for other nets. As discussed above, the authority net is the backbone of the hierarchical network form. The clustered group network has a typical structure of the authority net, which was described above. From a coordination point of view, a large disadvantage of the authority net of this group network is the discrimination of lateral nets. The strong vertical authority hierarchy makes it very difficult to establish quasi-official linkages in the horizontal and diagonal directions, for example between the separate sales units in a country. Similarly, social nets in these directions are not favoured either and are therefore mostly of a vertical kind. But, on the other hand, certain environmental developments make lateral unofficial contacts necessary, for example drastic markets changes, converging technologies and growing needs to coordinate marketing to large global customers.

However, this discrimination of lateral nets in the global network organization does not seem to take place for the international marketing of large projects. As found in the section on action networks in Chapter 4, a critical issue concerns the relation between the temporary project (action) network and the more permanent organization network, for example how people are taken from their permanent positions in the authority net to work for a shorter period in the lateral project net, and later return to their station in the organization network. Flexibility is a major characteristic of such temporary lateral nets, as its organization varies between different phases of the marketing process of the project. Different teams are engaged throughout the process. One team is often doing the scanning and the screening of different business opportunities, another team handles the bidding, and still another team is responsible for the build-up and start-up of the project.

Other Types of Group Networks

Lateral nets are more favoured within a matrix organization, which can be classified as a tightly coupled group network. Here, the importance of the lateral net is according to the authority net accepted and parts of the lateral net formalized as one of the matrix dimensions. This combined vertical and lateral authority structure even favours social nets through the many conflicts created, for example through the classical problem of having two bosses at the same time. There might even be problems in having too many such networks and the information overload they create.

These two major types of global network organization differ from a common third type of global organization structure often taken up in international business literature, namely the transnational organization or the integrated network (Bartlett, 1986; Bartlett and Ghoshal, 1989). From a network perspective, this organization can be classified as a differentiated group network. Judging from the literature, it is supposed to be more neutral in relation to the various types of nets discussed in this section. In addition, it does not seem to suffer from any specific bias toward a certain network configuration as shown by the clustered group network. The differentiated group network will have the mix of networks suitable to the international environment and its coordination needs. To be able to achieve this, authority nets, especially the vertical levels, are restricted to basic core operations of a more mechanistic nature, for example production, logistics and finance. The now flat organization is opened up for quasi-official lateral nets and non-official social nets. These latter networks are often customer-based rather than product-based. Due to this stronger emphasis on lateral and social nets, this type of configuration of the entire hierarchical network has been named as an integrated network. But perhaps a more suitable name is the opaque network model.

CONCLUSIONS

The focus is shifted from organization as a capability for implementing international business marketing to its actual implementation. The organization of strategy is analysed in accordance with the network approach, which means that the basic characteristics of the network organization constitute constraints on adaptations to the external environments of various emerging country markets. Resources are organized through an internal network organization, implying that competitive advantages are shaped by managerial processes within network organization structures, governed by network controls and based on main interests.

Ways to internationalize mainly vary with how much experience firms have in operating in foreign markets. Internationalized firms are in a better position to take advantage of these business opportunities, both to sell more, relocate production and shift the supplier base eastwards. Another major issue is how traditional MNC organizations can be kept in a more globalized world. Is it possible to sustain the competitive advantage that originates from its present regional base, for example when production costs are only fraction of those in adjacent countries and when the supplier base in general seems to be moving to the new EU countries in Eastern Europe or to China/India? As illustrated in this chapter, such a reorganization of internationalized activities takes place within the Geocentric MNC as combined and complex processes of relocation, outsourcing and shifting of the supplier base. The internationalization of production today is often part of the disaggregation and reengineering of the value chain on a global basis. It takes place both internally when products are made within the firm abroad instead of at home, or externally when production is outsourced or the supplier base restructured.

The internal environment of the MNC is viewed to consist of networks. Responses to different events are organized within an internal network, which consists of the group network organization as well as the local and regional organization. Thus, the internal framework of the MNC also consists of networks. Since the book focuses on international business marketing activities in emerging country markets, it is concentrated on the MNCs' operations in these markets, that is to the subsidiaries there. This aspect is developed further in the next chapter.

Internationalization of the organization of firms has taken place in different forms over the years, where the transnational organization is the latest form, being a major characteristic of the Geocentric MNC. Its organization is region centric in contrast to the Polycentric MNC, which is typified by the international organization. This organization is centred on product divisions rather than geographical centres. The Geocentric MNC is signified by the globalization of the headquarters, either having continentally based headquarters or one virtual global headquarters for the world-scale operations. This MNC operates on the global basis for all business activities and has a global firm infrastructure.

The organization issue is elaborated on further for these three forms of internationalized firms at the same time as the chapter goes into how business marketing is controlled. The hierarchical network is specified to consist of network controls, main interests and three subforms: the authority net, the lateral net and the social net. Lateral and social nets are anchored in the authority net, creating different constraints for other nets. Through these dimensions one major type of hierarchical network common in emerging country markets is identified, namely the clustered group network. It consists of global product sets and local market clusters, which are subordinated to the product sets.

Ideally, if this vertically segmented network should be fully developed, every one of the concern's market companies should be linked to only one of the product sets. In that way, direct and strong vertical linkages are created between these units. This is, however, often not possible, particularly for companies operating in the often smaller emerging country markets. There is not enough ground to completely segment the organization vertically all the way from the factory to the customer. The clustered group network is compared to two other common types of global network organization structures: the tightly coupled group network and the differentiated group network.

How global products sets and local market clusters are linked to each other within the clustered group network is developed further in the next chapter. The perspective is shifted by looking at the network organization from below. The local network organization is analysed as local and regional hubs that connect external local market networks with the internal group network.

8. Local and regional network organization for dyads and triads

This chapter is mainly about how the MNC implements international business marketing in emerging country markets through the local and regional network organization set up within the global MNC network. It discusses the major strategic dilemma of local adaptation and global integration from the perspective of the units in these markets. By taking such a bottom-up view, the MNC is turned upside down. It is discussed how MNCs are organized at the local and regional levels, mainly the subsidiary and regional headquarters organization. Issues are taken up such as: what possibilities does the organization of the MNC offer for implementing strategies that need to be adapted to the specific external environment of the emerging country markets at the same time as it is integrated with marketing strategy at the corporate level?

In accordance with the network approach to MNC organization developed in the previous chapter, local units markets are looked upon as nodes in a large network, which connect actors in the local external network and actors inside the MNC in other countries. The main linkage between the local network and the internal MNC network outside the emerging country market is defined as a local hub, for example organized as a subsidiary. Such a subsidiary is therefore not seen as the end of an internal network but as a local hub interlinking the internal MNC network to local external networks. MNC networks differ in local responsiveness and worldwide integration of relationships and therefore set different limits for how local national networks work, thereby constraining local business marketing. Hence, the local units are seen as critical intersections in the global network of the MNC, joining external local networks with the internal worldwide network. Through these network junctions incoming relationships and outgoing relationships are matched to each other. The organization of local business marketing activities is also influenced by the internationalization process, for example how internationalized the firm is. This means that the local organization changes continuously. The local organization is also influenced by the entry strategy of the firm, for example the MNC could establish through forming three-party dealer networks. Such an entry node is different from having a local hub to establish direct contacts with customers. This is rather a question of organizing dyads through building subsidiaries, that is rather entering through having another entry mode.

The chapter therefore focuses on the local network organization for managing triads as well as for managing dyads. Two major ways of organizing local MNC networks in emerging country markets are thereby taken up, namely:

1. The network organization of local hubs or the local network organization within one country.
2. The network organization of regional hubs or the regional network organization at an intermediary level between this local organization and the network of the entire MNC group. Regional network organization is of special relevance in emerging country markets, since these markets are often located far away from the headquarters of the Western MNC, which are usually found in Europe or North America.

Since the organization of the local and regional hubs is highly influenced by how the whole network of the MNC group is organized, this local and regional organization is analysed in relation to the network organization of the group throughout the chapter. The linkage between local network organization and group network organization is analysed by looking at the position of the networks in relation to each other. This internal network position is defined as the degree of coupling between the local hub (for example a subsidiary) and the group network. The coupling varies with how much coordination there is of organizational processes for solving various marketing issues. It also varies with how much control there is of these processes, namely the control of local networks by other group units. The chapter is mainly devoted to relations between local product/service market networks and the group network. But local networks with government are also briefly taken up. In the final section, network organization at the regional level is described and analysed.

Seen from the standpoint of the research on the MNC subsidiary, the 'subsidiary choice' perspective is developed further (Birkinshaw et al., 1998). But this focus is related to the other two perspectives: 'head office assignment' and 'environmental determinism'. So, while concentrating on one perspective, subsidiary strategy is also viewed as being influenced by factors representing the other two perspectives.

The first part of the chapter is devoted to the local organization of triads by illustrating how a network organization is gradually built up to manage such three-party networks. This part continues the internationalization process of the MNC organization from Chapters 6 and 7 by taking up how the local network organization is established and expanded. This process section is followed by a structural section on the organization of dyads in local emerging country markets, mainly as a local hub organization within the clustered group network. Finally, the organization of dyads and triads is penetrated further by going deeper into the regional network organization.

ESTABLISHING LOCAL NETWORK ORGANIZATION FOR TRIADS

The organization of business marketing activities on a local basis develops gradually within the MNC. The entry strategy of the MNC could be to establish itself in emerging country markets through forming three-party dealer networks. This entry node is different from establishing local hubs to get direct contacts with customers, which is a question of organizing dyads through building subsidiaries, that is entering through another entry mode. The organization of dyads in local emerging country markets is taken up later in the chapter. The first part is devoted to the local organization of triads. As discussed in Chapter 6, some major problems with triads are that the supplier becomes too distant from the market by having too few contacts with final customers. The intermediary is often an inefficient mediator of information and knowledge. The learning of the seller is insufficient, since tacit experiential knowledge is hard to transfer between parties and requires that the company is learning by operating in the market. Triads in emerging country markets are therefore paradoxical. Due to the high uncertainty experienced in these markets, low cost and flexible entry nodes are chosen such as triads. But, on the other hand, not operating in this foreign market hinders the seller from developing experiential knowledge about customers and the specific characteristics of the market. Uncertainty is not reduced or controlled for, which is necessary if the firm were willing to expand business by investing more resources in the market. This major problem of triads is not so severe in the latter case of more balanced relationships, since the seller also has a direct relationship with the customer.

This growth process is illustrated in this section for an MNC building a marketing organization in the Middle East and North African (MENA) region. The competencies are established to operate as a distributor network specialist, which is a competence mainly suited to managing triads. The MNC is Volvo Construction Equipment (VCE), which is the fourth largest in the world in the construction industry after Caterpillar, Komatsu and CNH (Case-New Holland). VCE has been active many years in different countries in the MENA region selling construction equipment, mainly haulers, loaders and excavators (for further information on this MNC, see www.volvo.com). Since this region from a marketing point of view is heterogeneous, and has a special competitive climate, a regional perspective was taken at the end of the 1990s in order to gather market intelligence, mobilize forces and put more focus on the region. To be flexible, only a few people, who could be moved relatively easily, were employed during the initial establishment phase. Two centrally located cities in the region were selected as hubs: Dubai as the centre for the Middle East and Cairo as the centre for North Africa. These cities have a relatively well-developed infrastructure, the working schedules of the two cities complement each other, and their proximity to business is good. While Cairo is less expensive to stay in, Dubai is one of the most expensive cities in the whole MENA region.

The regional hubs are very small business marketing organizations and are controlled directly from the marketing company 'International' in Sweden. These organizations are limited to business marketing activities, mostly dealer development and sales and product support functions. As a distributor network specialist, the major functions of the regional hubs are to provide the local dealers with marketing, sales and product support. Pushing dealer focus and development programmes are other important tasks, as well as collecting and reporting marketing information. Thus, the local external network relations (the spokes) focus on the dealers. However, the staff at the regional hubs conduct more tasks than their assigned responsibilities require, mainly by being directly involved in customer relationships. In that way the relationships in the triad become more balanced. First, the regional hubs address customer concerns through frequent visits to new as well as old customers. Second, the regional hubs tend to play an important role in the dealers' negotiations with customers, the downside being to make some dealers more passive in the negotiation process. After the establishment of the regional hubs, some dealers have in fact been supported by the regional VCE staff in every deal. Contrary to VCE's aims of less involvement in direct sales, both customers and dealers appreciated this larger than planned activity.

By the relocation of VCE marketing staff to the region, the customers enjoy more attention through the company's increased national responsiveness. By having 'Westerners' assisting in making the deals, the customers appear to feel more important and appreciated, being taken more seriously than earlier. The customers tend to see VCE as a more serious player, since the company put efforts into increasing its presence. Consequently, the customers' trust in VCE and the dealers seems to have increased. The customers also appear to enjoy the closer contact with regional representatives of the company. The customers seem to feel that the company better understands their problems. Furthermore, quicker deals are sealed and the customers get quicker responses in the negotiation process. By assisting the dealer negotiating with the customer, most deals are sealed without the dealers having to contact the marketing company in Sweden for a price or a guarantee settlement. All these factors explain the customers' positive reaction to the regional hubs and in several of the MENA markets there has been a noted sales increase. The downside of the VCE's regional staff participating in direct customer relationships is the double work performed and the obvious risk that the dealers get used to VCE's engagement. Even if it benefits business in the short run, the long-run effect may be negative depending on how the relationships to the dealers are affected. *In toto*, the interests of the dealers and customers are given more weight by VCE.

A reason for establishing the regional hubs was the need to control the dealers to a larger extent in order to get more attention on the VCE franchise, inter alia to increase VCE's share of mind at the dealers. Conflicts between VCE and the local dealers are more easily solved through the intermediary role of the hubs. The information flow has also improved significantly. The vertical control has been extended. All dealers controlled by the regional hubs in MENA have agreed to perform standardized reporting of sales, orders and inventory to the marketing company in Sweden, something that was more or less impossible to attain before the regional hubs were set up. The regional staffs have also put pressure on the dealers by forcing them to reorganize in order to reach a higher focus on the VCE franchise. The dealers assigned salesmen and managers dedicated solely to this franchise. The implementation of a dealer development programme also improved the vertical control of the dealers. The goal was to help dealers to achieve higher standards of service to the customers, create consistent product support, build closer relationships between the dealer and VCE, and create better understanding of dealer- and market needs and requirements. However, since the programme was originally developed for the mature markets of Western Europe and North America, there was a risk that the programme would be implemented in the wrong way. The dealers could be wrongly or unfairly evaluated and the dealers might not appreciate being compared with others. If that happens, the programme does not act as a stimulus for the dealers but instead could deject them.

In fact, controlling dealers is a delicate affair. Since VCE wants to have independent dealers, controls cannot be overstretched. The establishment of the regional hubs led to divergent reactions among the dealers in the MENA region. For instance, weaker and less developed dealers were mostly positive to the establishment, since they benefited the most from the support and directions given by VCE. The most developed dealers in the larger markets in the region, however, were negative initially, mainly because their independence was reduced. The main reason for this reaction seems to be that the establishment decision was not anchored at the top management of the dealers. However, with time these dealers have accepted the presence of regional staff, and suspicion has turned into appreciation, most likely due to the better understanding, communication and noted sales increase.

Still, the goals between VCE and the dealers differ. While VCE strives for maximum profits in the long run, the dealers are short sighted in this respect. There was also a gap between VCE's ambitions and the dealers' possibilities. VCE has far reaching plans to develop the dealers, but the dealers lack many of the resources and capabilities for meeting VCE's demands. So, having a strong regional presence in MENA seems necessary to get the dealers to focus on VCE's franchise. VCE also has problems with the dealer's spare parts policy, mainly high spare parts pricing and low spare parts inventory.

Developing the Network Organization on a Regional Basis

By increasing its presence through the establishment of the regional hubs, VCE has started to further exploit local opportunities in selected markets of MENA. The company is forcing the dealers to refocus and restructure, capturing VCE's intentions, making them understand that they share common goals. The operations of the regional hubs are however still relatively limited, mostly focusing on various dealer support activities. Moreover, the regional hubs' operations are more or less directed from the central sales company in Sweden. Even if the commitment of this sales company to the MENA region has increased, the commitment of the VCE group is rather low, since this region is still considered as marginal. However, markets will continue to grow and competition increase, to a larger extent utilizing their big potential. The reasons behind establishing the regional hubs then become even stronger in future, perhaps even leading to a need to develop the regional hubs further. The two regional hubs established so far only cover five markets, although the region encompasses more than twenty. For instance, one traveling salesman based in Sweden handles the markets of Iran, Iraq, Libya and Algeria, although the demand for construction equipment within these markets occasionally explodes. The risks of missing opportunities are obvious. Fast changes in their politically unstable environment are common, which requires VCE to be able to react quickly in order to grasp new opportunities. A prerequisite is to have correct and up to date information, which is difficult to attain when the sales force is located in Sweden. Moreover, VCE has dealers in several other markets in the MENA region, which are not covered by the existing regional hubs. The central marketing company in Sweden handles contacts with these dealers and visits them about once a year. The majority of these dealers are undeveloped when it comes to the VCE franchise, and there appears to be a great need for developing and controlling them. There are at least three different options for VCE to develop the regional hubs and by that increase its presence in the MENA region. These are:

1. More regional hubs could be established in the markets with the greatest potential.
2. More markets could be added to the responsibilities of the existing regional hubs.
3. A subregion could be developed, through building up a regional marketing and sales company.

These alternatives are evaluated in Table 8.1. As observed there, the advantages of establishing more regional hubs are the same as those discussed above for the two hubs already established.

This is a question of reducing the distance to more markets in the MENA region having more than two regional hubs of the same type as already established. However, there are some drawbacks connected to the expansion of regional hubs. There could be difficulties in finding competent expatriates, who also are willing to move to the markets. Although these regional hubs are small and flexible, the risk increases for this uncertain and complex region as a whole with the enlarged investment there.

Table 8.1   Pros and cons of different options of regional organization development

	+	−
Keep the present structure	Low Costs High flexibility Easy to control the hubs Key markets covered	Hard to have a strategy for the whole region Not all markets covered Low customer focus Risk to be bypassed by competitors
More regional hubs	Closer distance to markets Very high customer focus Very high control of dealers Develop new dealers High flexibility	Few appropriate locations for regional hubs High establishment costs Ineffective duplication of competence
More markets covered from existing regional hubs	Easy to reach more markets High customer focus High control of dealers Low establishment cost	Requires more staff Reduces flexibility
RHQ	Better regional strategy Low transaction costs High overall control of all dealers Low enforcement costs Low information costs The region gains more attention from HQ	Higher costs requires larger sales Low flexibility Shifts power away from HQ

Source: Engström and Johansson (2000).

Establishing more regional hubs would not be an optimal solution for developing and implementing a common regional business marketing strategy, since the regional presence would be spread out instead of concentrated in the MENA region.

Another possibility would be to enlarge the existing regional hubs in MENA to cover more markets, since the region is rather limited and concentrated. The greatest advantage with this option is that the staff at the current regional hubs could relatively easily and with very short notice reach the markets in the region which now are covered from Sweden. The reasons for enlarging the presence in this way are similar to those discussed for the previous alternative and for establishing the current two regional hubs. If the capacity of the present hubs could be used, the establishment costs would be marginal and definitely lower than in the previous alternative. However, since this is not the case, additional staff would be needed, which would not make this alternative that much cheaper than the previous one. The larger organization will also decrease the flexibility of the existing regional hubs.

Both alternatives discussed above mean that the business marketing activities of VCE increase in the MENA region. With increasing business, the volume of sales may rise to a level that justifies the integration of the regional hubs into an incorporated regional hub, being a profit centre and having total responsibility for the company's business in the region. The authority of the regional centre is augmented. The MENA region is geographically concentrated with relatively good communications linking the countries together, and similarities in institutional backgrounds. Culture, language, religion and business mores, for example, make the countries a naturally secluded region for an RHQ. The establishment of an incorporated regional hub would more easily accomplish regional IBM development and implementation. It would make it possible to implement the marketing activities discussed above. The potential to give specific support to business development within the region would increase, facilitating the development of dealers. More dealers could be controlled. Sales could be controlled and coordinated better for the whole region. Local markets could get more attention from VCE, and accessibility to regional market information could increase significantly. As part of the reorganization of business marketing, more functions would have to be relocated or built up in the region, for example administrative functions such as accounting, finance and shipping, as well as co-ordination of orders, product and marketing support. The possibilities to control dealers would be enhanced and inefficiencies in decision making and implementation of decisions reduced. Conflicts within the triad between customers, dealers and VCE would be more easily solved. However, the more the dealers are developed, the more independent they will be and the more the need for vertical control will decline. The flexibility of this type of regional hub would be lower compared to the other options discussed above. An incorporated regional hub improves the possibilities for being nationally responsive. It also increases the possibilities for integrating activities within the region and with group units outside the region. Because of the relatively limited product portfolio of the complex construction equipment produced, it is essential to standardize products to take advantage of economies of scale on a global basis. An incorporated regional hub could therefore offer the best possibilities for an efficient trade-off between local adaptation and global integration. These regional hubs were mainly set up to improve on local responsiveness.

LOCAL NETWORK ORGANIZATION FOR DYADS

Dyads are either managed directly from the home country or by establishing an own representative in the foreign market, usually a subsidiary. In the distant emerging country markets the latter alternative is the most common and is therefore analysed here. From a network perspective the subsidiary is seen as a hub that connects the internal relationships coming from group units outside the emerging country market and the external relationships coming from customers in the local market networks. An efficient trade-off between global integration and local responsiveness requires some kind of linking mechanism between these networks. This linking mechanism of the local hub, for example the entry node, is illustrated as a network linking grid in Figure 8.1.

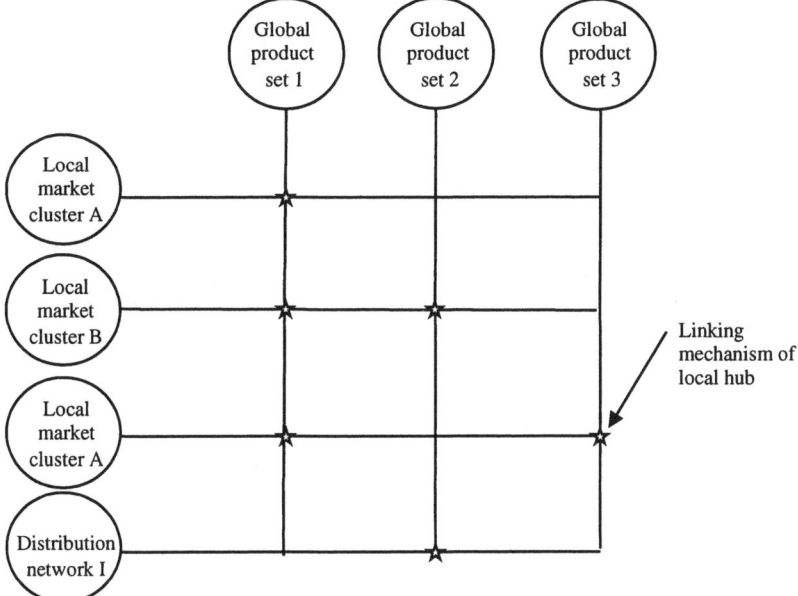

Figure 8.1   Network linking grid at the local hub

The local hub links up three local market clusters consisting of dyads to three global product sets. A cluster of triads in the form of a distribution network has also been added to show how the management of dyads can be combined with management of triads. Thus, the organization of this local hub mainly concerns marketing management of dyads. The organization of this hub influences the possibilities of achieving sustainable competitive advantages in local emerging country markets by its critical influence on local responsiveness. But the organization of this major intersection is also critical for getting competitive advantages in other markets, for example the co-ordination of the organizational capabilities through the internal network with the group's other resources and capabilities. In fact, it is a question of achieving a trade-off between the specialization of the organizational capabilities to the local country market environment at the same time as getting a beneficial leverage effect of these organizational capabilities at the global group level, that is the familiar trade-off between global integration and local responsiveness.

Local Hub Organization within the Clustered Group Network Organization

Because of the dominance of the clustered hierarchical network organization among MNCs, the local hub organization of such a group structure for managing dyads is mainly analysed. As discussed in Chapter 7, a main characteristic of the clustered group network is to extend the authority net based on vertical value chains to all relevant markets in the world throughout the entire organization. This means that the trade-off between local responsiveness and global integrations is solved by reproducing the existing network organization of the MNC, for example by extending the main types of linkages from the global product sets (product companies) out into the market to the customers of the local market clusters. The principle is to connect a local market cluster to one major type set of vertical relationships coming down from a product company, that is a global product set. This vertical authority net consists of a number of 'straight pipelines' from the product companies through the local intersections to the local customers. This network is controlled by the product company interest, which could, however, severely constrain adaptation possibilities of the local market cluster.

Another way is to develop the local hub into a transformation mechanism between the internal global network and local external network. To be able to adapt to local conditions, for example, there is a need to organize local linkages according to specific market conditions, and global linkages according to supply sources. Particularly, when all products sold are bought from the group, it is essential to reflect the group's product company organization on the input side. The critical local organization issue concerns this linking mechanism between the specific conditions in the local market clusters and the generally oriented global product sets, for example how to adapt a sales budget based on local customer needs to the group's budget system based on products. Depending on how this transformation problem is solved, the degree of coupling between in- and outgoing relationships will vary. For example, a more organic or emergent local network organization that is continuously adapted to shifting customer needs is more loosely coupled to the more tightly structured relationships of the global product sets.

One-set and multi-set organizations

The development of a more market-adjusted organization of the intersection over time was found at subsidiaries of Swedish MNCs in Southeast Asia (Jansson, 1994b). At the beginning local networks were left to themselves, inter alia, because it was believed that local responsiveness should be high. For example, it was a common belief that Chinese salesmen, mostly because of their high entrepreneurial spirit, should be given a large degree of freedom to build and run local customer relationships based on specific group-oriented bonus systems. But this adaptation of the sales organization to local conditions went too far in some companies, particularly in direct selling of technically complex industrial products. One drawback, for instance, was that individual salesmen could not observe all vital market movements and therefore needed central guidance.

MNCs in Southeast Asia organized linking mechanisms between the product dimension and the local geographic dimension in different ways and with mixed results. Local organization was usually a compromise between the existing group structure and local conditions. The global authority net was segmented along the vertical dimension, where a trade-off was made between the global product authority and the local market authority, implying a loose coupling or low horizontal coordination between the vertical clusters. The efficiency of this global product organization was therefore determined by how well one managed to establish and maintain a mechanism in this local hub for translating local demands into 'supplies' from the group. The smaller the subsidiary was, the more unbalanced this vertical relation was and the more difficult it was to make such a trade-off efficient. At the beginning of the operations in Southeast Asia, the organizational principles of the clustered group network was usually reproduced as far as possible and a clear priority given to efficiency as looked upon from the global product company, giving a low responsiveness to local conditions. This strategic misfit between the product company and the market company made the total organization of the MNC inefficient, which could result in sub-optimal strategy and organization in the local market.

When the local market clusters are all joined to one global product set, the local market organization is defined as an one-set organization (OSO). This was taken up in the previous chapter and illustrated for the clustered group network in Figure 7.4. A multi-set organization (MSO), on the other hand, was defined as when the local market clusters are connected to two or more global product sets. In this situation, a larger number of different types of market clusters are joined together through the local hub with more internal sets. This is the case when product companies share a sales subsidiary, which is divided into 'slices', each 'slice' consisting of a one-to-one relation between cluster and set. Such a multi-sets organization was common in the small markets of Southeast Asia in the 1990s, when a fully-fledged global product organization was not economical because of high establishment costs of one-set organizations (Jansson, 1994b). Since it was inefficient to organize major vertical sets separately, they were integrated into one common organization. This MSO is different from the collection of 'pure' one-set organizations found in large EU markets. Here, due to larger market size, each market company can be assigned to one specific product company, which brings about a group with several market companies in a country, each representing a product company.

A major advantage of sharing a subsidiary is that local customers meet one representative of the group and not several as in large EU markets. Furthermore, frequency of contacts can be reduced. In the MSO, a market company represents the whole group, where the mix of internal global product sets represented varies between market companies. Because of changing types of connections to the group, this internal multi-set is hierarchically organized in different ways. In one case the organization of the local hub is 'sliced' among the product companies, where each global product set is organized in the same way. In another case, the market company is hierarchically subordinated to the largest product company, while the market company is an agent for the other product companies. This means a mixed organization of the local market clusters with one vertical set being a hierarchical authority net and the others being more similar to a market net. In a third case, the company representing the local market clusters is formally subordinated to general management, meaning that the relationships to the product companies are lateral or even market-like.

For some MNCs, the group network tended to segregate into two main parts, one with one-set subsidiaries and another with multi-set subsidiaries. The former part is a clustered group network, while the latter is a geographic form. Such a mix of the local network organization becomes arbitrary, for example the control of such multi-set intersections or their role within the group. The borders between these organization types are often opaque and fluid, largely because management is not aware of the main differences created between subsidiaries organized according two different principles. The main difference is between few and homogeneous relationships in the former case and many heterogeneous relationships in the latter case. One solution to this problem would be to clearly separate these types of intersections from one another into two tightly coupled group networks with a very loose coupling in-between, for example separating the product-based organization from the geographically-based one. One result would be a better demarcation of these borders, for instance the authority over different types of market companies between group management and product division management.

Internal Network Position

The internal network position expresses the trade-off between local adaptation and global integration, and is specified as the degree of coupling of the local country market network to the internal network of the MNC. This means that the more loosely coupled the local network is to the group network, the more autonomous the local hub is, and the lower its integration with the group is. As discussed above, this also implies that the higher the local adaptation of business marketing becomes. The degree of autonomy varies with how much coordination there is of decision-making between the local network and the group network regarding certain international marketing issues.

First two internal network positions of this type are discussed, namely whether the local network and group network are loosely or tightly coupled. Local networks in Southeast Asia usually were loosely coupled to the group network within the clustered group network. One major reason was the stronger need for local responsiveness in these specific and distant markets. Authority and lateral nets as well as network controls developed for marketing activities, for example in Western Europe, were unsuitable or worked in another way for the minor markets in Asia. The local competitive situation was specific in Southeast Asia and India for the European MNCs studied, which, among other things, resulted in a dominance of the entry mode subsidiaries over cooperation like joint ventures. However, in Southeast Asia these MNCs had a tighter coupling of the local network organization to the group than their international competitors. This was a consequence of their high-technological profile, which manifested itself in a dominance of the global product interest. Accordingly, their competitive strength was mainly founded on high product quality, training and service. Such a business marketing strategy in an environment characterized by stiff price competition, low technical levels and a lack of long-term investment thinking demanded an extensive transfer of technology and localization of technical expertise, which was best organized internally.

Another reason for the loose coupling of activities in Southeast Asia and India was the need for a high degree of responsiveness to the local environment. This followed from the many tie-ups to various parties in the local market network. However, the outcome of this need for a high adaptability to the circumstances of these emerging country markets marked a strong conflict between the global product interests and local interests, which, as was found above, was solved at the expense of the local interest in the clustered group network.

Since units in emerging country markets in Southeast Asia during the 1980s and 1990s were loosely coupled to the group and of marginal importance to it, the impact on the hierarchical network of the group was insignificant. Such constraints may cause misfits within the group. The MNC organization was mainly based on the companies' business in the industrialized countries in Western Europe and North America, the local network organizations in Southeast Asia being less integrated into this group network. Misfits can be caused by the following constraints:

1. A small market volume in the emerging country market constitutes too limited a foundation for decomposing the organization into separate units such as product companies or distribution and production units.
2. A high degree of adaptation of IBM inclusive of production to the specific local market made the local company unfit for the global group structure. The commitment of the group towards local units situated in a country, where majority ownership sometimes is disallowed, is many times less compared to other countries. It is considered as an affiliated company instead of a subsidiary, being more loosely coupled to the group.
3. The group structure is unfit for the structure of the market company, which was discussed at length above. The international organization of the group is too constrained, for example too home-market determined.

The degree of coupling also seems to change over time. When business in markets such as those in Southeast Asia became more essential for the group, the local market interest grew in importance and became more pronounced within the group, reducing the dominance of the global product interest. As a consequence, local business marketing strategy and organization became more tightly coupled to the group outside the emerging country market, mainly with the product companies. The local subsidiaries were taken more seriously. First, their businesses became more important to the group. Second, due to the specific problems found in emerging country markets, the group devoted comparatively more time to these operations in order to come to terms with them and integrate them into the international business marketing strategies. For a few MNCs studied, the Asian markets were already at the beginning of the 1990s of vital importance to the groups and the subsidiaries in the area were therefore well integrated into the group organization. For two of these MNCs, the local organization even had a critical impact on the global network organization of these groups. The organization or the group became more decentralized in order to have a higher degree of local adaptation of business marketing strategies.

Studies in India (Jansson, 1982, 2007; Jansson et al., 1995) of local MNC-government networks (MGN) found that the IBM was mainly locally decided, with the subsidiaries of the European MNCs as the acting party. The groups and subsidiaries were loosely coupled with regard to government matters. No direct linkages were found between government units in India and group units outside the country, meaning that the MGNs were local and indirectly coupled to the group through the local hub. Thus, there was no direct participation in decisions regarding local networks by other group units. The MGN was the responsibility of the Indian company, for which there was no direct control by other group units. For the network and linkage strategies toward governments, the subsidiary could be labelled an autonomous subsidiary. The degree of integration of these strategies with the group was low and the degree of localization high.

Direct or indirect control of local external networks
Tight or loose coupling only gives a general idea about the internal network position of the local hub. It is possible to specify the degree of coupling more by looking at the control of the subsidiary network by the group (Jansson et al., 1995). The more local networks are controlled by the group, the higher the integration of business marketing with the group. Viewed from the perspective of the local external network, through which sustainable competitive advantages are achieved, the control by the group is divided up accordingly:

1. A direct control of decisions regarding the business marketing issues relevant for a specific local market network. This is done by looking at whether such issues are included in the normal reporting routines, or whether there are special control routines, for example requiring marketing investments to be approved by the group before being implemented.
2. An indirect control where there are no such direct controls of the local business marketing, only being included in the general control of the local hub as a whole.

The analysis of the internal network position of the subsidiary and the local external network can be improved by using these two dimensions. A separation is then made between controls of business marketing issues relevant for a specific external network and general controls valid for all local external networks. Examples of issues in this case are those relating to marketing and technology transfer. When there are only indirect controls of the subsidiary's activities in external networks, the control of business marketing is at the low end of the scale, resulting in loose coupling and a strong internal network position. This autonomy of the local subsidiary does not only vary with how its external networks are controlled by the group but also by how much they are controlled. The more intense each control is applied or the heavier the control becomes, the less the autonomy is. Hence, autonomy increases with less direct and less intensive use of controls, implying that the integration of the local external network with the subsidiary-group network varies with these two dimensions of the degree of coupling variable. The more local networks are controlled, either directly or indirectly, the higher the coupling and the lower the autonomy of the subsidiary and the local external network.

The study of internal network positions in MNC-government networks in India based on such variables showed that a critical question is how to make the right trade-off between the main types of external networks and controls. Subsidiaries in far-off and institutionally distant markets such as India seem to have a low degree of coupling and control with a high degree of local adaptation of business marketing. The environment is so specific that it does not matter what basic type of global network structure the group has or how large its business in India is. From the standpoint of the local network organization, the positive side of this position is autonomy, while the negative side is low influence within the group network. However, the network position is a relative measure, and does not mean that the unit is completely autonomous, only that it is comparatively less integrated than many other units within the network, thereby having a larger degree of local adaptation of business marketing. For instance, it is still vital to ensure that the operations do not lead to sub-optimization in the way that they conflict with the major interests within the MNC such as the global product interest or the group interest. Functions at lower group levels are separated to operate on their own, for example relationships with government usually belong to this category. Although there was some variation, the coupling of the MGN into the MNC network was generally found to be low. However, the general management of the subsidiary was not separated from the MNC as a whole and was integrated into the group through the different types of network controls discussed in Chapter 7 (see Table 7.1). The main problem is rather to differentiate between the controls within the group, since a standardized global type of control could reduce the profitability of a local unit. However, this did not seem to be the case for the groups studied, where controls were differentiated among subsidiaries, and where the lesser control of the Indian subsidiaries was a case in point. In addition, controls were used differently. Yet, other controls are unsuitable due to specific market conditions prevailing in the country.

REGIONAL NETWORK ORGANIZATION

With increasing business and number of customer relationships and local hubs in various emerging country markets, the need increases for intermediary nodes between local networks and group units in Europe, for example. The need for an additional level of internal nodes between local and global network levels develops. The more business has grown in Asian emerging country markets for European MNCs, for example, the more the contact between units in local markets and the group has increased and the more the need has been felt to reduce the rising number of contacts and relationships between units in Europe and Asia. In addition, the need for integration of local activities increased both within the region as well as with central group units, for example to leverage strategies to take advantage of economies of scale and to learn about local conditions in the region. As business was growing in a region, it was also felt more important to develop local strategies and to have a better control of local external networks. As local business in this part of the world has become more important to the group, the strategic situation has changed and so has the IBM. The basic strategic dilemma is changes of global integration versus local adaptation.

A new solution to this dilemma was found through establishing an organizational unit in the network at the intermediary regional level between the local and global levels. For example, regional hubs have been established by many MNCs in Southeast Asia to take care of intermediate or regional functions such as marketing, administration, manufacturing, purchasing, finance and various types of support. Most MNCs had some kind of regional network organization in this area (Jansson, 1991, 1994b). The main issues involved in this kind of organization are illustrated in Figure 8.2. The regional organization concerns the coordination of relationships between different national emerging country markets as well as developing businesses further in these markets. This kind of international regional organization is important to distinguish from a national regional organization found within one country, for example in large emerging country markets such as India, China or Russia.

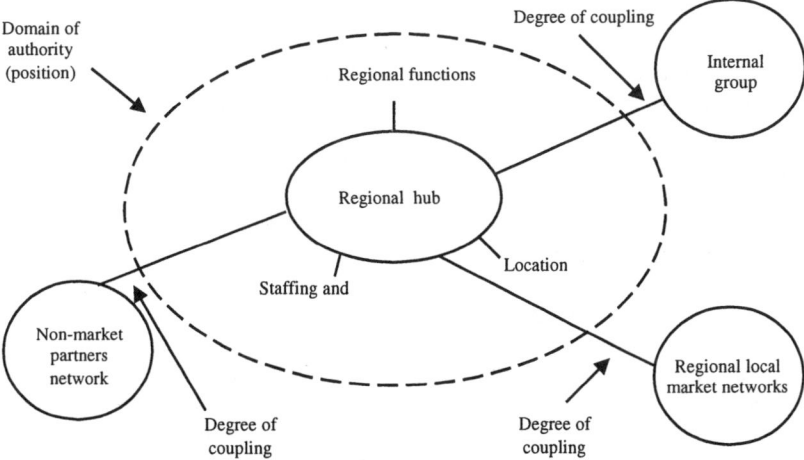

Figure 8.2   Organization of the regional hub

Integration of business marketing can be improved by establishing such a regional hub. The possibilities to control local networks are better from a regional hub in the area than from Europe. Decisions on business marketing are improved because of shorter communication channels, leading to a quicker response to market demand. It is also easier to start new local business ventures, if knowledge and authority are located in the area close to the markets. This was shown to be important in the fast growing Southeast Asian markets of the 1980s and 1990s. The establishment of a regional hub increased national responsiveness and the coordination on a regional basis of such adaptations to different emerging country market environments. By developing regional marketing strategies and having qualified people to implement these strategies, customer demands could be satisfied more efficiently, for example demands regarding local presence and continuous contacts together with quick responses to questions. A regional hub reduces both marketing and administrative distances. The regional unit may also be an important hub in the group's intelligence network by being well updated on developments in the area, for example political, economic and technological developments. Low costs for well-educated personnel are a vital localization factor for the office.

Regional Functions

Regional hubs take form gradually with regional activities reaching a certain momentum. More and more business marketing activities are located at the regional hub, usually starting with sales and then adding administrative functions. Most local relationships of the MNCs studied in Southeast Asia were sales oriented (Jansson, 1991, 1994b). Three main business marketing management functions were located at the regional level:

1. Control and coordination of sales in the region. Control takes place of the dyads of the market companies in the region or of triads, when there are dealers.
2. Participation in marketing and market intelligence activities.
3. Marketing support.

A critical organization issue for the technologically advanced industrial MNCs concerned how to organize the connection between basic R&D, product development and customer needs in local markets. Certain engineering functions were located at the regional level, for example technical expertise brought closer to the local scene from Europe to assist in the marketing of technologically complex products in local networks. The few established engineering capacities in Southeast Asia were found at the regional level, and were mainly used by customer specialists to adapt or develop products to local needs.

   Another vital regional marketing function is to build up local contact nets with high government officials and to participate in various stages of negotiation, taking place when the marketing of projects to government is important. The country manager of the local subsidiary often has too low an authority to represent the MNC for such large business deals.

Types of Regional Network Organization

Based on degree of authority given to the regional hub, three major types of regional hub are distinguished, namely the incorporated regional hub, the administrative regional hub and the diffuse regional hub (see Figure 8.3). Depending upon how the first hub is organized in relation to its spokes, three major types of regional network are distinguished: the multi-set regional network, the one-set regional network and the multi-country regional hub.

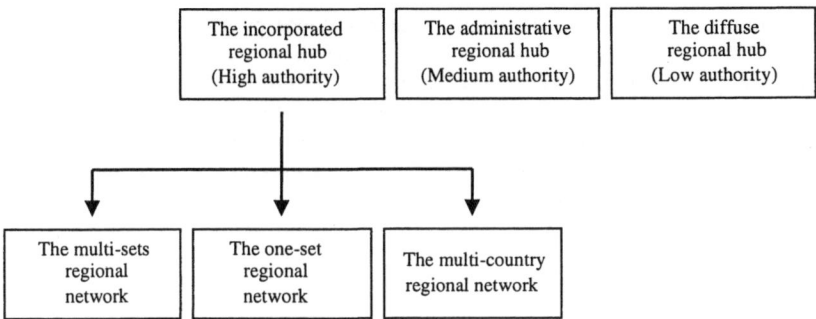

Figure 8.3   Types of regional network organization

1. The incorporated regional hub

When the regional hub is incorporated, it gets a legally legitimized authority over the other internal units (usually local market companies) in the region. This internal part of the regional network is classified as a separate regional authority net or mini group. It is the same as the vertical regional headquarters (RHQ) model, where the relationship between RHQ and local units is strictly hierarchical and where there are no links between national units and group headquarters (Lasserre and Schutte, 1995/1999). Depending upon how this type of hub is organized in relation to its spokes, three major types of regional networks are distinguished.

a. The multi-set regional network. In this type of regional organization, the hub represents a number of businesses in the group, usually those in demand in the region. It becomes the hub of a certain number of global product sets, for example, where each such spoke or regional set consists of a number of local market clusters. This means that a number of local market clusters and regional product sets are controlled from this position as head of the spokes in the region. One can say that the control span at the regional headquarters of such sets and clusters varies from low to high. Depending on how different interests within the group are favoured by the solution to the global integration and local responsiveness dilemma, there are different network organization patterns. When the regional network organization is oriented towards local interests and local adaptation issues dominate over global integration issues, there is a multi-domestic regional organization pattern. This is a decentralized regional organization with a stronger authority of the local hubs. In the opposite situation global interests dominate over local interests, which implies a strong authority of the regional hub representing the global interests, and the network pattern is defined as a global structure. When there is a balance between local and global interests, the regional organization is characterized as a transnational structure. A detailed discussion of these major types of RHQ organizational structures is found in Lasserre and Schutte (1995/1999).

b. The one-set regional network. This hub only represents one global product set. There is one spoke, through which a number of local market clusters is controlled. This makes the control span of regional sets and market clusters low. Since the global product interest dominates this type of network organization, it falls within the clustered group network organization

c. The multi-country regional network. A special case is when a group's business in the region is so small that only one company is established to cover the whole region, or when a small MNC establishes itself in a central location in a region with the purpose of covering the whole region from there. The MNC now has only one incorporated company in the region, which then in a natural way represents the whole group and has the responsibility for the whole region. This is a kind of local subsidiary, but which covers several countries in a region instead of one country. With only one company in the region there is no regional internal network (no internal spokes), which makes this organization very similar to the multi-set organization of local hubs discussed at the beginning of the chapter. The major difference is that the external local networks are not located in one country but in several countries, forming a regional hub organizing a number of multi-country market clusters.

Regarding the balance between local and global interests, the first two forms (except 1c) above are typical for large MNCs with several market companies in a region representing several product companies (vertical global product sets). Through regional functions the local interests are included and given extra weight as far as the product companies are concerned. Through the regional organization the local interest is strengthened within the group, being strongest for the multi-set regional network (1a). Here, a central unit has the authority to negotiate on behalf of the whole regional internal network and therefore has a higher bargaining power than when each subsidiary negotiates for itself. However, the formal authority position of this type of regional hub within the group network varies. In some groups it is strong and on a par with the product companies, forming a two-dimensional horizontal network based on product and geography. Here, there is a balance between local and global interests. Sometimes, the organization of a group network is also formalized into a prescribed matrix organization. When it is not, local hubs are only connected to one of these two organizational dimensions, either a regional hub or to a global product set. When they are connected to the regional hub, the relationships of the local hubs to the global product companies are often of an arm's-length nature, products being exchanged internally through a network of buyer/seller relationships. This two-dimensional organization blends formal relationships with a regional hub and informal relationships with the global product sets. The balance between local and global interests is organized differently: less importance for the authority net and more importance for the social and lateral nets. The local interest has the least strength in the group as a whole when the organization of the regional hub favours global integration, for example for the global structure above: an incorporated hub within the clustered group network, mostly organized as one-set regional networks. Such regional organization is more oriented towards global integration than local responsiveness.

2. The administrative regional hub

The administrative regional hub consists of a separate regional office with a managing director for the region. This office only has administrative and support functions, while business operations are done by the local subsidiaries. The regional hub has no monopoly right on the relationships to the group, for example to the global product sets. Rather, the local subsidiaries have their own internal business relations with group units outside the region. Therefore, the control of the regional hub over the regional network is normally weaker than when there is an incorporated regional hub. Still, the authority of the administrative office over regional business operations varies. It is higher when the regional vertical relationships of the internal network are tightly coupled, meaning that this network is subordinated to the office.   In such cases, the regional organization comes closest to resembling the authority net found in the multi-set network organization discussed above. However, the network organization pattern built on an administrative office is normally weaker and more horizontally coupled. In that way, it is more like the horizontal RHQ model than the vertical RHQ model (Lasserre and Schutte, 1995/1999). The network operates on a consensus basis, with the authority of the regional hub to some degree dependent on the local hubs. The more dependent the regional hub is on its spokes, the more tightly coupled horizontally is the internal regional network. In this case the authority of the regional hub is low and its dependence on local units high. The vertical authority net is loosely coupled, whereas the horizontal lateral and social nets are tightly coupled. In case the units are also loosely coupled horizontally, the rationale for the regional organization is gone, and it can be dismantled (or not established). The weaker the authorities of a regional hub like this, the lower its centrality within the group network. If the position is too weak within a clustered group network, for example, with its strong vertical product sets, the regional hub could easily get into an intermediate position between the product and market companies. In cases where there are strong and independent local subsidiaries, they could also bypass the regional hub through using lateral and social nets.

3. The diffuse regional hub

The organization of this regional hub is diffuse, since regional responsibilities and coordination are either commonly organized in one of the market companies or spread out among them. Lasserre and Schutte (1995/1999) call this type of regional organization the virtual RHQ, since there is no separate RHQ with its own office and staff. Although there is a need for regional functions, regional turnover is too low to allow a separate regional office. The regional network organization of this type is even more variable than when the regional hub is organized as an administrative office. The organization of this type of regional hub varies. When a subsidiary manager is appointed regional manager, there is certain strength of the vertical coupling of an authority net. When the responsibility is only to coordinate, the regional network is entirely consensus based with a horizontal organization consisting of lateral and social nets. Usually the regional organization as a whole is a mix of various hierarchical and arm's-length networks like these, meaning that the degree of vertical and horizontal couplings varies a lot. These regional hubs could be located in the region or sometimes even in the home office.

CONCLUSIONS

Local organization within the clustered group network is usually a compromise between the existing group structure and local conditions. If there is to be an efficient trade-off between global integration and local responsiveness, it is critical to develop a linking mechanism in the local hub between the main relationships coming from the group network (for example global product sets) and the relationships coming from the external market clusters. From the point of view of the IBM, it is a question of achieving a trade-off between the specialization of the resources and organizational capabilities to the local market environment at the same time as getting a beneficial leverage effect from these capabilities at the global group level. The organization of the local hub within the clustered group organization is either defined as a one-set organization or a multi-set organization. This latter type of organization is often found in emerging country markets since it is inefficient to organize major vertical global product sets separately, they are assembled in one local hub.

A way to express the trade-off between local adaptation and global integration is the internal network position. It is defined as the degree of coupling, which expresses where the position is found along a continuum between autonomy and integration. The more loosely coupled or autonomous the local network, the higher the local adaptation of business marketing and the lower the integration of marketing with the group. Local networks in emerging country markets are usually loosely coupled to the group network within the clustered group network. One major reason is the stronger need for local adaptation to these distant markets with their specific characteristics.

The position along the degree of coupling continuum is specified further based on the control of the local network by the group network. The more local networks are controlled by the group, the higher the integration of business marketing with the group. Viewed from the perspective of the local hub, a separation is made between direct controls of strategic issues relevant for a specific external network and indirect general controls valid for all local external networks. The autonomy of the local hub does not only vary with how its external networks are controlled by the group but also by how much they are controlled. Local hubs in far-off and institutionally distant emerging country markets seem to have a low degree of coupling and control with a high degree of local adaptation of business marketing. The local networks are integrated into the group network through the different types of controls. Seen on a relative basis, they are less integrated than many other local units within the group network, thereby having a larger degree of local adaptation of business. The advantage of this position is autonomy, while the downside is low influence within the group network.

With an increasing business and number of customer relationships and local hubs in various emerging country markets, the need increases for intermediary hubs between group companies in Europe, for example, and local hubs in emerging country markets. This intersection is seen as a regional network consisting of a hub with spokes linked to it. More integration of local marketing activities is required, for example leveraging strategies to take advantage of economies of scale and to learn about local conditions in the region. Such a regional network organization usually takes form gradually and is institutionalized when the regional activities reach a certain momentum. More and more functions are located at the regional hub, usually starting with sales and then adding administrative functions. As demonstrated by the VCE example, the regional hub becomes an important platform in the further internationalization of the firm. After the initial phase, different options were contemplated by VCE to develop the regional hubs for controlling triads and to increase its presence in the region.

Based on the degree of authority given to the regional hub, three major types of regional network organization are distinguished. The first one is the incorporated regional hub, which is a separate regional authority net or mini group. Depending upon how this type of hub is organized in relation to its spokes, three major types of regional network are distinguished: the multi-set regional network, the one-set regional hub and the multi-country regional hub. The second type of regional network organization is the administrative regional network, which consists of a separate regional office with a managing director for the region. This office only has administrative and support functions, while business operations are done by the local subsidiaries. The third type of regional organization is the diffuse regional hub, where regional responsibilities and coordination are either commonly organized in one of the market companies or spread out among them. The first two forms of regional network organization are typical for large MNCs with several market companies in a region representing several product companies, and having the tightly coupled group network. Through regional functions local interests are included and given extra weight as far as the product companies are concerned. Through a regional organization the local interest is strengthened within the group.

Bibliography

Agapitova, N. (2003) 'The Impact of Social Networks on Innovation and Industrial Development: Social Dimensions of Industrial Dynamics in Russia', *DRUID Summer Conference*, Copenhagen, June 12-14.

Aldrich, H. and Whetten, D.A. (1981) 'Organization-sets, Action-sets, and Networks: Making the Most of Simplicity', in P. Nyström and W.H. Starbuck (eds), *Handbook of Organizational Design*, vol. 1, New York: Oxford University Press.

Ames, C.B. and Hlavacek, J.D. (1984) *Managerial Marketing for Industrial Firms*, New York: Random House.

Anderson, J.C., Håkansson, H. and Johanson, J. (1994) 'Dyadic Business Relationships within a Business Network Context', *Journal of Marketing*, vol. 58, no. 4, pp. 1-15.

Anderson, J.C. and Naurus, J.A. (2004) *Business Market Management*, Upper Saddle River, NJ: Pearson/Prentice Hall.

Andersson, S. and Wiktor, I. (2003) 'Innovative International Strategies in New Firms: Born Globals – the Swedish Case' *Journal of International Entrepreneurship*, vol. 1, pp. 249-76.

Axelsson, B. (1992). 'Corporate Strategy Models and Networks – Diverging Perspectives', in B. Axelsson and G. Easton (eds), *Industrial Networks. A New Reality*, London: Routledge.

Axelsson, B. and Easton, G. (1992) *Industrial Networks. A New Reality*, London: Routledge.

Axelsson, B. and Johanson, J. (1992) 'Foreign Market Entry – the Textbook vs. The Network View', in B. Axelsson and E. Easton (eds), *A New View of Reality*, London: Routledge.

Backman, M. (1999) *Asian Eclipse, Exposing the Dark Side of Business in Asia,* Singapore and New York: John Wiley.

Bansard, D., Bernard, C. and Salle, R. (1993) 'Project Marketing: Beyond Competitive Bidding Strategies', *International Business Review*, vol. 2, no. 2, pp. 125-41.

Bartlett, C.A. (1986) 'Building and Managing the Transnational: The New Organizational Challenge', in M. Porter (ed.), *Competition in Global Industries*, Cambridge, MA: Harvard Business School Press, pp. 367-401.

Bartlett, C.A. and Ghoshal, S. (1989) *Managing Across Borders: The Transnational Solution*, Boston, MA: Free Press.

Bartlett, C.A. and Ghoshal, S. (1992a) 'What is a Global Manager', Harvard Business Review, September-October, pp. 124-32.

Bartlett, C.A. and Ghoshal, S. (1992b) *Transnational Management. Text, Cases, and Readings in Cross-border Management*, Homewood, IL: Irwin.
Barstad, A. (2004) 'Årsaker til Korrupsjonsvekst i det Postsovjetiske Europa – et Antropologisk Perspektiv', *Nordisk Øst-Forum*, vol. 18, nr. 4, pp. 473-89.
Bell, J., McNaughton, R., Young, S. and Crick, D. (2003) 'Towards an Integrative Model of Small Firm Internationalization', *Journal of International Entrepreneurship*, vol. 1, pp. 339-62.
Berliner, J.S. (1952) 'The Informal Organization of the Soviet Firm', *Quarterly Journal of Economics*, vol. 66, no. 3, pp. 342-65.
Bharadway, V.T., Swaroop, G.M. and Vittal, I. (2005) 'Winning the Indian Consumer', *McKinsey Quarterly*, special edition, pp. 43-51.
Bilkey, W.J. (1978) 'An Attempted Integration of the Literature on the Export Behaviour of Firms', *Journal of International Business Studies*, vol. 9, no. 1, pp. 33-46.
Birkinshaw, J. (2001) 'Strategy and Management in MNE Subsidiaries', in A.M. Rugman and T.L. Brewer (eds), *The Oxford Handbook of International Business*, Oxford: Oxford University Press, pp. 380-401.
Birkinshaw, J., Hood, N. and Jonsson, S. (1998) 'Building Firm-Specific Advantages in Multinational Corporations: The Role of Subsidiary Initiative', *Strategic Management Journal*, vol. 19, pp. 221-41.
Bjerke, B. (1999) *Business Leadership and Culture. National Management Styles in the Global Economy*, Cheltenham, UK and Northampton, MA, USA: Edward Elgar Publishing.
Björkman, I. (1994) *Doing Business in China*, Helsinki: Swedish School of Economics.
Björkman, I. and Forsgren, M. (2000) 'Nordic International Business Research – A Review of Its Development', *International Studies of Management and Organization*, vol. 30, no. 1, pp. 6-25.
Blankenburg, D. and Johanson, J. (1992) 'Managing Network Connections in International Business', *Scandinavian International Business Review*, vol. 1, no. I, pp. 5-19.
Blau, P. (1964) *Exchange and Power in Social Life*, New York: Wiley.
Blau, P. (1987) 'Microprocess and Macrostructure', in K.S. Cook (ed.), *Social Exchange Theory*, Beverly Hills: Sage, pp. 83-100.
Blohm, K. and Stojanovski, S. (2005) *Språket som bro och barriär – En studie hur svenska SMF begränsas av språkliga kommunikationsbarriärer på den polska marknaden*, Masters Thesis, Baltic Business School, University of Kalmar.
Blomstermo, A., Eriksson, K., Lindstrand, A. and Sharma, D.D. (2004) 'The Perceived Usefulness of Network Experiential Knowledge in the Internationalizing Firm', *Journal of International Management*, vol. 10, pp. 355-73.
Boye, P., Jansson, H. and Sandberg, S. (2004) *Transnationell Affärssamverkan i Östersjöregionen*, BBRI Rapport 2004:1.

Campbell, J. and Lindberg, L. (1990) 'Property Rights and the Organization of Economic Activity by the State', *American Sociological Review*, vol. 55, pp. 634-47.

Cavusgil, S.T. (1980) 'On the Internationalization Process of Firms', *European Research*, vol. 8, no. 6, pp. 273-81.

Cavusgil, S.T., Ghauri, P.N. and Agarwal, M.R. (2002) *Entry Strategies for Emerging Markets – Entry and Negotiation Strategies*, London: Sage Publications.

Chen, M. (1995) *Asian Management Systems: Chinese, Japanese and Korean Styles of Business*, London: Routledge.

Chisnall, P.M. (1989) *Strategic Industrial Marketing*, London: Prentice Hall.

Chu, C. (1991) The *Asian Mind as a Game: Unlocking the Hidden Agenda of the Asian Business Culture – a Westerner's Survival Manual*, New York: Rawson Associates.

Cook, K.S. and Emerson, R.M. (1984) 'Exchange Networks and the Analysis of Complex Organizations', *Research in the Sociology of Organizations*, vol. 3, pp. 1-30.

Cova, B. and Hoskins, S. (1997) 'A Twin-track Networking Approach to Project Marketing', *European Management Journal*, vol. 15, no. 5, pp. 546-56.

Coviello, N. and McAuley, A. (1999) 'Internationalisation and the Smaller Firm: A Review of Contemporary Empirical Research', *Management International Review*, vol. 39, no. 3, pp. 223-56.

Coviello, N. and Munro, H. (1997) 'Network Relationships and the Internationalization Process of Small Software Firms', *International Business Review*, vol. 6, no. 4, pp. 361-86.

Czinkota, M.R. (1982) *Export Development Strategies*, New York: Praeger.

Day, G. (1994). 'The Capabilities of Market-Driven Organization', *Journal of Marketing*, vol. 58, October, pp. 37-52.

Douglas, M. (1986) *How Institutions Think*, Syracuse University Press.

Dunning, J.H. (1988) *Explaining International Production*, London: Unwin and Hyman.

Dunning, J.H. (1993) *Multinational Enterprises and the Global Economy*, Wokingham: Addison-Wesley.

Dwyer, F.R., Schurr, P.H. and Oh, S. (1987) 'Developing Buyer-Seller Relationships', *Journal of Marketing*, vol. 51, pp. 11-27.

Easton, G. (1992) 'Industrial Networks: a Review' in B. Axelsson and G. Easton, (eds), *Industrial Networks. A New Reality*, London: Routledge.

Ehn, B. and Löfgren, O. (1982) *Kulturanalys*, Stockholm: Liber Förlag.

El-Ansary, A. (1983) 'The General Theory of Marketing: Revisited', in S.D. Hunt (ed.), *Marketing Theory. The Philosophy of Marketing Science*, Homewood, IL: Irwin, pp. 271-76.

El-Ansary, A. (1997) 'Relationship Marketing – A Marketing Channel Context', in Sheth, J.N. and Parvatiyar, A. (eds), *Research in Marketing*, Greenwich, CT: JAI Press, vol. 13, pp. 33-46.

El-Ansary, A. (2004) *Relationship Marketing – A School of Thought in Historical Perspective*, Draft, Coggin College of Business, University of North Florida, Jacksonville.

Emerson, R.M. (1962) 'Power-Dependence Relations', *American Sociological Review*, vol. 27, pp. 31-400.

Engström, J. and Johansson, A. (2000) *Regional Organisations in Emerging Markets – The Case of Volvo CE in the Middle East and North Africa*, Master Thesis, Graduate Business School, School of Economics and Commercial Law, Göteborg University.

Eriksson, K., Johanson, J., Majkgård, A. and Sharma, D.D. (1997) 'Experiential Knowledge and Cost in the Internationalization Process', *Journal of International Business Studies*, vol. 28, no. 2, pp. 337-60.

Farrell, D. (2004a) 'Sector by Sector', *McKinsey Quarterly*, 2004 special edition, pp. 117-19.

Farrell, D. (2004b) 'Beyond Offshoring: Assess Your Company's Global Potential', *Harvard Business Review*, December, pp. 82-90.

Ford, D. (1980) 'The Development of Buyer-seller Relationships in Industrial Markets', *European Journal of Marketing*, vol. 14, no. 5/6, pp. 339-53.

Ford, D. (2002) *Understanding Business Marketing and Purchasing*, London: Thomson.

Ford, D., Gadde, L.E., Håkansson, H. and Snehota, I. (1998/2003) *Managing Business Relationships*, Chichester: John Wiley & Sons, Ltd.

Ford, D., Gadde, L.E., Håkansson, H. and Snehota, I. (2006) *The Business Marketing Course – Managing in Complex Networks*, Second Edition, Chichester: John Wiley & Sons, Ltd.

Forsgren, M. (2002) 'The Concept of Learning in the Uppsala Internationalization Process Model: A Critical Review', *International Business Review*, vol. 11, pp. 257-77.

Forsgren, M. and Pahlberg, C. (1991) *Managing International Networks*, IMP Conference Paper, Department of Business Studies, Uppsala University.

Forsgren, M., Holm, U. and Johansson, J. (2005) *Managing the Embedded Multinational – a Business Network View*, Cheltenham, UK and Northampton, MA, USA: Edward Elgar Publishing.

Friman, M., Gärling, T., Millet, B., Mattsson, J. and Johnston, R. (2002) 'An Analysis of International Business-to-Business Relationships Based on the Commitment-Trust Theory', *Industrial Marketing Management*, vol. 31, no. 5, pp. 403-9.

Gankema, H.G., Snuif, H.R. and Zwart, P.S. (2000) 'The Internationalization Process of Small and Medium-sized Enterprises: An Evaluation of Stage Theory', *Journal of Small Business Management*, vol. 38, no. 4, pp. 15-27.

Ghauri, P. (1983) *Negotiating International Package Deals. Swedish Firms and Developing Countries*, Acta Universitatis Upsaliensis, Uppsala (dissertation).

Ghoshal, S. and Bartlett, C. (1990) 'The Multinational Corporation as an Interorganizational Network', *Academy of Management Review*, vol. 15, no. 4, pp. 603-25.

Gordon, I.H. (1998) *Relationship Marketing*, Toronto: John Wiley and Sons.

Granovetter, M. (1985) 'Action and Social Structure: The Problem of Embeddedness', *American Journal of Sociology*, vol. 91, no. 3.

Granovetter, M. (1992) 'The Sociological and Economic Approaches to Labor Market Analysis: A Social Structure View', in M. Granovetter and R. Swedberg (eds), *The Sociology of Economic Life*, Boulder: West View Press.

Grönroos, C. (1995) 'Relationship Marketing: The Strategy Continuum', *Journal of the Academy of Marketing Science*, vol. 234, pp. 252-4.

Grönroos, C. (2000) 'Relationship Marketing. The Nordic School Perspective', in J.N. Sheth and A. Parvatiyar (eds), *Handbook of Relationship Marketing*, Thousand Oaks: Sage, pp. 95-117.

Gulati, R., Nohria, N. and Zaheer, A. (2000) 'Strategic Networks', *Strategic Managment Journal*, vol. 21, pp. 203-15.

Gummesson, E. (1995) *Relationship Marketing: From 4Ps to 30Rs*, Malmö: Liber-Hermods.

Gurkov, I. (1996) 'Changes of Control and Business Reengineering in Russian Privatized Companies', *The International Executive*, vol. 38, no. 3, pp. 359-88.

Håkansson, H. (1982) *International Marketing and Purchasing of Industrial Goods – An Interaction Approach*, Chichester: Wiley.

Håkansson H. and Johanson, J. (1992) 'A Model of Industrial Networks', in Axelsson, B. and Easton, G. (eds) *Industrial Networks. A New Reality*, London: Routledge.

Håkansson, H. and Johanson, J. (1993) 'The Network as a Governance Structure: Interfirm Cooperation Beyond Markets and Hierarchies', in G. Grabner (ed.), *The Embedded Firm*, London: Routledge.

Håkansson, H. and Östberg, C. (1975) 'Industrial Marketing – An Organizational Problem?' *Industrial Marketing Management*, vol. 4, no. 1/2, pp. 113-23.

Håkansson, H. and Snehota, I. (1995) *Developing Relationships in Business Networks*, Routledge, London.

Håkansson, H. and Snehota, I. (2000) 'The IMP Perspective. Assets and Liabilities of Business Relationships', in J.N. Sheth and A. Parvatiyar (eds), *Handbook of Relationship Marketing*, Thousand Oaks: Sage, pp. 69-93.

Håkansson, H. and Wootz, B. (1975) *Företags inköpsbeteende*, Lund: Studentlitteratur.

Hägg, I. and Johanson, J. (1982) *Företag i Nätverk – En Ny Syn på Konkurrenskraft*, Stockholm: SNS.

Haley, G.T. (1997) 'A Strategic Perspective on Overseas Chinese Networks' Decision Making', *Management Decision*, vol. 35, no. 8, pp. 587-94.

Haley, G.T., Tan, C.T. and Haley, U. (1999) *New Asian Emperors: The Overseas Chinese, their Strategies and Competitive Advantages*, Oxford and Boston, MA: Butterworth Heinemann.

Hallén, L. (1982) *International Industrial Purchasing*, Uppsala: Acta Upsaliensis, Studia Oeconomiae Negotiorum 13 (dissertation).

Hallén, L. and Johanson, J. (1989) *Advances in International Marketing*, Greenwich, CT: JAI Press.

Hallén, L. and Johanson, M. (2004a) 'Sudden Death: Dissolution of Relationships in the Russian Transition Market', *Journal of Marketing Management*, vol. 20, no. 9-10, pp. 941-57.

Hallén, L. and Johanson, M. (2004b) 'Integration of Relationships and Business Network Development in the Russian Transition Economy', *International Marketing Review*, vol. 21, no. 2, pp. 158-71.

Halman, L. (1994) 'Scandinavian Values: How Special are They?', in T. Petterson and O. Riis (eds), *Scandinavian Values: Religion and Morality in the Nordic Countries*, Uppsala: Acta Universitatis Upsaliensis.

Hamilton, G.G. (1996) 'Asian Business Networks', *De Gruyter Studies in Organization*, vol. 64, April.

Hammarkvist, K.O., Håkansson, H. and Mattsson, L.G. *(1982) Marknadsföring för konkurrenskraft*, Stockholm: Liber.

Hampden-Turner, C. and Trompenaars, F. (2000) *Building Cross-cultural Competence: How to Create Wealth from Conflicting Values*, Chichester: Wiley.

Hardin, R. (2002) *Trust and Trustworthiness*, New York: Russell Sage Foundation.

Heenan, D. and Perlmutter, H.V. (1979) *Multinational Organization Development*, Reading, MA: Addison-Wesley.

Heide, J.B. and John, G. (1992) 'Do Norms Matter in Marketing Relationships?', *Journal of Marketing*, vol. 56, April.

Heiskanen K. (2006) *Internationalization of Finnish Small and Medium-sized Companies Towards the New EU Member States in the Baltic Sea Region*, PEI 4.

Hendley, K. (1997) 'Legal Development in Post-Soviet Russia', *Post-Soviet Affairs*, vol. 13, no. 3, pp. 228-51.

Hill, R.M., Alexander, R.S. and Cross, J. (1975) *Industrial Marketing*, Homewood, IL: Irwin.

Hodgson, G.M. (1988) *Economics and Institutions. A Manifesto for a Modern Institutional Economics*, Cambridge: Polity Press.

Hofstede, G. (1980) *Culture's Consequences: International Differences in Work-Related Values*, California: Sage Publications.

Hofstede, G. (1983) 'National Cultures in Four Dimensions: A Research-Based Theory of Cultural Differences among Nations', *International Studies of Management and Organization*, vol. XIII, no. 1/2.

Hofstede, G. (1994) *Cultures and Organizations: Software of the Mind: Intercultural Cooperation and its Importance for Survival*, London: HarperCollins.

Hofstede, G. (2001) *Culture's Consequences: Comparing Values, Behaviours, Institutions, and Organizations Across Nations* (2nd edn), Thousand Oaks, CA: Sage.

Hofstede, G. and Bond, M.H. (1988) 'The Confucian Connection: from Cultural Roots to Economic Growth', *Organizational Dynamics*, vol. 16, no. 4, pp. 4-21.

Hohenthal, J. (2001) *The Creation of International Business Relationships. Experience and Performance in the Internationalization Process of SMEs*, Department of Business Studies, Uppsala University.

Hunt, S.D. (2000) *A General Theory of Competition: Resources, Competences, Productivity, Economic Growth*, Thousand Oaks, CA: Sage.

Hunt, S.D. and Morgan, R.M. (1995) 'The Comparative Advantage Theory of Competition', *Journal of Marketing*, April, vol. 59, pp. 1-15.

Ionascu, D., Meyer, K.E. and Estrin, S. (2004) *The Concept of 'Distance' in International Business – Culture, Regulation and Cognition – and its Relevance to Multinationals' Entry Mode Decision*, Centre for New and Emerging Markets Discussion Paper Series.

Jackson, B. (1985) *Winning and Keeping Industrial Customers*, Boston, MA: D.C. Heath and Company.

Jansson, H. (1982) *Interfirm Linkages in a Developing Economy – The Case of Swedish Firms in India*, Acta Universitatis Upsaliensies, Studia Oeconomiae Negotiorum 14, Uppsala University (dissertation).

Jansson, H. (1987) *Affärskulturer och Relationer i Sydöstasien*, Stockholm: MTC.

Jansson, H. (1988) *Strategier och Organisation på Avlägsna Marknader – Svenska Industriföretag i Sydöstasien*, Lund: Studentlitteratur.

Jansson, H. (1989a) 'Internationalization Processes in South-East Asia: An Extension or another Process?' in E. Kaynak and K.H. Lee (eds), *Global Business: Asia-Pacific Dimensions*, London: Routledge, Chapter, 4.

Jansson, H. (1989b) 'Marketing to Projects in South East Asia', in L. Hallén and J. Johanson (eds), *Advances in International Marketing*, vol. 3. Greenwich, CT: JAI Press.

Jansson, H. (1991) 'Organization of Transactions in Distant Markets: The Case of Swedish TNCs in Southeast Asia', in C.H. Wee and T.K. Hui (eds), Proceedings of the Academy of International Business Southeast Asia Conference, 20-22 June, National University of Singapore, pp. 47-55.

Jansson, H. (1994a) *Industrial Products. A Guide to the International Marketing Economics Model*, New York: International Business Press (Haworth Press).

Jansson, H. (1994b) *Transnational Corporations in Southeast Asia. An Institutional Approach to Industrial Organization*, Aldershot, UK and Brookfield, USA: Edward Elgar Publishing.

Jansson, H. (2002) 'Changing Government Strategy of Multinational Corporations in Transition Countries: The Case of Volvo Truck Corporation in India', in V. Havila, M., Forsgren and H. Håkansson (eds), *Critical Perspectives on Internationalization*, Amsterdam: Pergamon.

Jansson, H. (2006a) 'Gaining Societal Advantages in Emerging Markets: International Stakeholder Management in Malaysia', in S. Söderman (ed.), *Emerging Multiplicity – Integration and Responsiveness in Asian Business Development*, Palgrave-Macmillan.

Jansson, H. (2006b) 'From Industrial Marketing to Business-to-Business Marketing and Relationship Marketing', in S. Lagrosen and G. Svensson (eds), *Marketing: Broadening the Horizons*, Lund: Studentlitteratur, pp. 115-36.

Jansson, H. (2007) *International Business Strategy in Emerging Country Markets. The Institutional Network Approach.* Cheltenham, UK and Northampton, MA, USA: Edward Elgar Publishing.

Jansson H., Hilmersson M. and Sandberg S. (2006) *EU-Enlargement Effects on International Trade in the Baltic Sea Region – The Case of Exporting/Importing SMEs from Southern Sweden*, Paper presented at SNEE Conference, Mölle, Sweden, May 2006.

Jansson, H. and Ramström, J. (2005) *Facing the Chinese Business Network in Southeast Asian Markets – Overcoming the Duality between Nordic and Chinese Business Networks*, 21st Annual IMP Conference, Rotterdam.

Jansson, H. and Sandberg, S. (2008) 'Internationalization of Small and Medium-sized Enterprises in the Baltic Sea Region', *Journal of International Management*, vol. 14, no. 1, (forthcoming).

Jansson, H., Johansson, M. and Ramström, J. (2007) 'Institutions and Business Networks in the Chinese, Russian and West European Markets', *Industrial Marketing Management*. (forthcoming).

Jansson, H., Saqib, M. and Sharma, D.D. (1995) *The State and Transnational Corporations. A Network Approach to Industrial Policy in India*, Aldershot, UK and Brookfield, US: Edward Elgar.

Jepperson, R.L. (1991) 'Institutions, Institutional Effects and Institutionalism', in W. Powell and P. DiMaggio (eds), *The New Institutionalism in Organizational Analysis*, Chicago: University of Chicago Press.

Johanson, J. and Mattsson, L.G. (1987a) 'Interorganizational Relations in Industrial Systems – A Network Approach', in N. Hood and J.E. Vahlne, *Strategies in Global Competition*, New York: Croom Helm, pp. 287-314.

Johanson, J. and Mattsson, L.G. (1987b) 'Interorganizational Relations in Industrial Systems – a Network Approach Compared with the Transaction-cost Approach', *International Studies of Management and Organization*, vol. XVII, no. 1, pp. 33-48.

Johanson, J. and Mattsson, L.G. (1991) 'Strategic Adaptation of Firms to the European Single Market – A Network Approach', in L.G. Mattsson and B. Stymne (eds), *Corporate and Industry Strategies for Europe*, Amsterdam: Elsevier, pp. 263-81.

Johanson, J. and Mattsson, L.G. (2005) 'Discovering Market Networks', Forthcoming in *European Journal of Marketing*.

Johanson, J. and Vahlne, J.E. (1977) 'The Internationalization Process of the Firm – A Model of Knowledge Development and Increasing Foreign Market Commitments', *Journal of International Business Studies*, vol. 8, no. 1, pp. 23-32.

Johanson, J. and Vahlne, J.E. (1990) 'The Mechanism of Internationalization', *International Marketing Review*, vol. 7, no. 4, pp. 11-25.

Johanson, J. and Vahlne, J.E. (2003) 'Business Relationship Learning and Commitment in the Internationalization Process', *Journal of International Entrepreneurship*, vol. 1, pp. 83-101.

Johanson, J. and Wiedersheim-Paul, F. (1975) 'The Internationalization of the Firm – Four Swedish Cases', *Journal of Management Studies*, vol. 12, no. 3, pp. 305-22.

Johanson, M. (2001) *Searching the Known, Discovering the Unknown. The Russian Transition from Plan to Market as Network Change Processes*, Uppsala: Department of Business Studies, Uppsala University (unpublished dissertation).

Johanson, M. (2004a) 'Chains, Holes, and Links: Organisation of Activities in Supplier Relationships in the Russian Transition Economy', *Journal of Purchasing and Supply Management*, vol. 10, pp. 233-45.

Johanson, M. (2004b) *Managing Networks in Transition Economies*, Amsterdam, London, Oxford: Elsevier Science Ltd. Pergamon.

Johanson, M., Polsa, P. and Törnroos, J.Å. (2002) *Business Networks in Different Cultural Contexts: Western-Russian-Chinese*, Work in progress.

Kakar, S. (1971) 'Authority Patterns and Subordinate Behaviour in Indian Organisations', *Administrative Science Quarterly*, vol. 16, pp. 298-307.

Kao, C.S. (1996) 'Personal Trust in the Large Businesses in Taiwan: A Traditional Foundation for Contemporary Economic Activities', in G. Hamilton (ed.), *Asian Business Networks*, New York: De Gruyter Studies in Organization.

Knight, G.A. and Cavusgil, S.T. (1996) 'The Born Global Firm: A Challenge to Traditional Internationalization Theory', *Advances in International Marketing*, vol. 8, pp. 11-26.

Koopman, A. (1991) *Transcultural Management: How to Unlock Global Resources,* Oxford: Blackwell.

Kostova, T. (1997) 'Country Institutional Profiles: Concept and Measurement', *Academy of Management Proceedings*, vol. 97, pp. 180-84.

Kostova, T. and Roth, K. (2002) 'Adoption of an Organizational Practice by Subsidiaries of Multinational Corporations: Institutional and Relational Effects', *Academy of Management Journal*, vol. 45, no. 1, pp. 215-33.

Kotabe, M, (2001) 'Contemporary Research Trends in International Marketing: The 1990s', in A.M. Rugman and T.L. Brewer (eds), *The Oxford Handbook of International Business*, Oxford: Oxford University Press, pp. 457-502.

Kraar, L. and Shapiro, D. (1994) *The Overseas Chinese: Lessons from the World's Most Dynamic Capitalists*, Fortune, October 31.

Kroeber, A.L. and Kluckholm, C. (1952) 'Culture: a Critical Review of the Concepts and Definitions', *Papers of the Peabody Museum of American Archaeology and Ethnology*, vol. 47, pp. 1-223.

Lasserre, P. and Schutte, H. (1995/1999) *Strategies for Asia Pacific*, London: Macmillan Press.

Ledeneva, A. (1998) *Russia's Economy of Favours: Blat, Networking and Informal Exchange*, Cambridge: Cambridge University Press.

Leonidou, L.C. Katsikeas, C.S. (1996) 'The Export Development Process: An Integrative Review of Empirical Models', *Journal of International Business Studies*, 3rd Quarter, pp. 517-51.

Lindell, M. and Arvonen, J. (1996) 'The Nordic Management Style in a European Context', *International Studies of Management and Organization*, vol. 26.

Lu, J. and Beamish, P. (2001) 'The Internationalization and Performance of SMEs', *Strategic Management Journal*, vol. 22, pp. 565-86.

Madsen, T. and Servais, P. (1997) 'The Internationalization of Born Globals – An Evolutionary Process', *International Business Review*, vol. 6, no. 6, pp. 1-14.

Majkgård, A. (1998) *Experimental Knowledge in the Internationalization Process of Service Firms*. Uppsala University, Department of Business Studies, (Dissertation).

Majkgård, A. and Sharma, D.D. (1998) 'Client-following and Market-seeking Strategies in the Internationalization of Service Firms', *Journal of Business-to-Business Marketing*, vol. 4, no. 3, pp. 1-41.

Mattsson, L.G. (1973) 'Systems Selling as a Strategy on Industrial Markets', *Industrial Marketing Management*, vol. 3, pp. 107-19.

Mattsson, L.G. (1993) 'The Role of Marketing for the Transformation of a Centrally Planned Economy to a Market Economy', in H.C. Blomqvist, C. Grönroos and L. Lindqvist (eds), *Economics and Marketing Essays in Honour of Gösta Mickwitz*, Helsinki: Svenska Handelshögskolan, pp. 181-96.

Mattsson, L.G. (1997) 'Relationship Marketing and the Markets-as-Networks Approach – A Comparative Analysis of Two Evolving Streams of Research', *Journal of Marketing Management*, vol. 13, pp. 447-61.

McDougall, P.P. and Oviatt, B.M. (1996) 'New Venture Internationalization, Strategy Change and Performance: A Follow-up Study', *Journal of Business Venturing*, vol. 11, pp. 23-40.

McDougall, P.P. and Oviatt, B. M. (2000) 'International Entrepreneurship – The Intersection of Two Research Paths', *Academy of Management Journal*, vol. 43. no. 5, pp. 902-6.

Meyer, K. (2001) 'Institutions, Transaction Costs, and Entry Mode Choice in Eastern Europe', *Journal of International Business Studies*, vol. 32, pp. 357-67.

Meyer, K. and Gelbuda, M. (2006) 'Process Perspectives in International Business Research in CEE', *Management International Review*, vol. 46, no. 2, pp. 143-64.

Meyer, K. and Skak, A. (2002) 'Networks, Serendipity and SME Entry into Eastern Europe', *European Management Journal*, vol. 20, no. 2, pp. 179-88.

Meyer, J.W. and Scott, W.R. (1983) *Organizational Environments. Ritual and Rationality*, Beverly Hills, CA: Sage.

Michailova, S. and Worm, V. (2003) 'Personal Networking in Russia and China: Blat and Guanxi', *European Management Journal*, vol. 21, nr. 4, pp. 509-19.

Michel, D., Naudé, P., Salle, R. and Valla, J.P. (2003) *Business-to-Business Marketing*, Palgrave.

Mineikytë, A. and Steponavièiûtë, R. (2005) 'Bridging the Gap between Plan and Reality. Relocation of Production – A Case of Emerson Energy Systems', Masters Thesis, Baltic Business School at the University of Kalmar.

Monroe, K.B. (1991) *Pricing – Making Profitable Decisions*, New York, NY: McGraw-Hill.

Morgan, R.M. and Hunt, S.D. (1994) 'The Commitment – Trust Theory of Relationship Marketing', *Journal of Marketing*, vol. 58, no. 3, pp. 20-38.

Morgan, R.M. (2000) 'Relationship Marketing and Marketing Strategy: The Evolution of Relationship Marketing Strategy', in J. Sheth and A. Parvatiyar (eds), *Handbook of Relationship Marketing*, London: Sage.

Naisbit, J. (1996) *Megatrends Asia: Eight Asian Megatrends that are Reshaping our World*, New York: Simon & Schuster.

Nakos, G. and Brouthers, K.D. (2002) 'Entry Mode Choice of SMEs in Central and Eastern Europe', *Entrepreneurship Theory and Practice*, vol. 27, no. 1, pp. 47-63.

Normann, R. (2001) *Reframing Business. When the Map Changes the Landscape*, Chichester: John Wiley and Sons.

Normann, R. and Ramirez, R. (1993) 'From Value Chain to Value Constellation: Designing Interactive Strategy', *Harvard Business Review*, vol. 72, July-August, pp. 66-77.

North, D. (1990) *Institutions, Institutional Change and Economic Performance*, Cambridge: Cambridge University Press.

North, D. (2005) *Understanding the Process of Economic Change*, Princeton: Princeton University Press.

Orru, M., Bighart, N. and Hamilton, G. (1991) 'Organizational Isomorphism in East Asia', in W.W. Powell and P.J. DiMaggio (eds), *The New Iinstitutionalism in Organizational Analysis*, Chicago: University of Chicago Press, pp. 361-89

Oviatt, B.M. and McDougal, P.P. (1994/2005), 'Toward a Theory of International New Ventures', *Journal of International Business Studies*, vol. 25, no. 1, pp. 45-64/vol. 36, no. 1, pp. 29-41.

Parsons, T. and Shils, E. (1951) 'Values, Motives, and Systems of Actions', in T. Parsons and E. Shils (eds), *Toward a General Theory of Action*, Harvard University Press, pp. 53-79.

Parvatiyar, A. and Sheth, J. (2000) 'The Domain and Conceptual Foundations of Relationship Marketing', in J.N. Sheth, and A. Parvatiyar (eds), *Handbook of Relationship Marketing*, Thousand Oaks: Sage.

Payne, A. (2000) 'Relationship Marketing. The U.K. Perspective', in J.N. Sheth and A. Parvatiyar (eds), *Handbook of Relationship Marketing*, Thousand Oaks: Sage, pp. 39-67.

Peck, H., Payne, A., Christopher, M.G. and Clark, M. (1997) *Relationship Marketing: Strategy and Implementation*, Oxford: Butterworth-Heinemann.

Peck, H., Payne, A., Martin, C. and Clark, M. (1999) *Relationship Marketing. Strategy and Implementation*, Oxford: Butterworth-Heineman.

Peng, M.W. (2000) *Business Strategies in Transition Economies*, London: Sage.

Peng, M.W. and Heath, P.S. (1996) 'The Growth of the Firm in Planned Economies in Transition: Institutions, Organizations, and Strategic Choice', *Academy of Management Review*, vol. 21, no. 2, pp. 492-528.

Peng, W. and Luo, Y. (2000) 'Managerial Ties and Firm Performance in a Transition Economy. The Nature of Micro-macro Link', *Academy of Management Journal*, vol. 43, no. 3, pp. 486-501.

Pfeffer, J. and Salancik, G.R. (1978) *The External Control of Organizations*, New York: Harper and Row.

Prahalad, C.K. and Doz, Y.L. (1987) *The Multinational Mission. Balancing Local Demands and Global Vision*, New York: Free Press.

Ramström, J. (2005) *West Meets East. Managing Cross-institutional Business Relationships with Overseas Chinese*, Finland: Åbo Akademi.

Rauch, J.E. and Trindade, V. (2002) 'Ethnic Chinese Networks in International Trade', *The Review of Economics and Statistics*, February.

Redding, G. (1980) 'Cognition as an Aspect of Culture and its Relation to Management Processes: An Exploratory View of the Chinese Case'. *Journal of Management Studies*, vol. 17, pp. 127-48.

Redding, G. (1985) *Networks and Molecular Organizations: An Exploratory View of Chinese Firms*, Department of Management Studies, University of Hong Kong, Departmental Discussion Paper.

Redding, G. (1990) *The Spirit of Chinese Capitalism*, New York: De Gruyter Studies in Organization.

Redding, G. (1991) 'Weak Organizations and Strong Linkages: Managerial Ideology and Chinese Family Business Networks' in G. Hamilton (ed.), *Business Networks and Economic Development in East and Southeast Asia*, Hong Kong: Centre of Asian Studies.

Redding, G. (1995a) *International Cultural Differences*, Aldershot: Dartmouth Publishing.

Redding, G. (1995b) 'Overseas Chinese Networks: Understanding the Enigma', *Long Range Planning*, vol. 28, pp. 61-9.

Redding, G. and Richardson, S. (1986) 'Participative Management and its Varying Relevance in Hong Kong and Singapore', *Asia Pacific Journal of Management*, vol. 3, no. 2, pp. 76-98.

Reid, S.D. (1981) 'The Decision-Maker and Export Entry and Expansion', *Journal of International Business Studies*, vol. 12, pp. 101-12.

Ring, P.S and Van de Ven, A.H. (1994) 'Development Processes of Cooperative Interorganizational Relationships', *Journal of Management Review*, vol. 19, no. 1, pp. 90-118.

Rosen, D., Bonsu, S., Curran, J.M. and Purinton, E.F. (1998) 'Exploring the Dynamic Nature of Relationship Marketing through Key Constructs', *Center for Relationship Marketing*, University of Rhode Island.

Rosenzweig, P. and Singh, H. (1991) 'Organizational Environments and the Multinational Enterprise', *Academy of Management Review*, vol. 16, pp. 340-61.

Roth, K. and Kostova, T. (2003) 'Organizational Coping with Institutional Upheaval in Transition Economies', *Journal of World Business*, vol. 38, pp. 314-30.

Rugman, A. (1981) *Inside the Multinationals: The Economics of Internal Markets*, New York: Columbia University Press.

Rugman, A. (1986) 'New Theories of the Multinational Enterprise: An Assessment of Internalization Theory', *Bulletin of Economic Research*, vol. 38, no. 2, pp. 101-18.

Salmi, A. (1995) *Institutionally Changing Business Networks: An Analysis of a Finnish Company's Operations in Exporting to the Soviet Union, Russia and the Baltic States*, Helsinki School of Economics and Business Administration: Acta Universitatis Oeconomicae Helsingiensis.

Salmi, A. (1996) 'Russian Networks in Transitions – Implications for Managers', Industrial Marketing Management, vol. 25, pp. 37-45.

Salmi, A. (2000) 'Entry into Turbulent Business Network – The case of a Western Company on the Estonian Market', *European Journal of Marketing*, vol. 34, no. 11/12, pp. 1374-90.

Salmi, A. (2004) *Institutional Change of Business Networks: Russian Transition Revisited*, 20th IMP Conference, Copenhagen, 2-4 September.

Scott, R.W. (1995/2001) *Institutions and Organisations*, London: Sage.

Seligman, S.D. (1999) *Chinese Business Etiquette – a Guide to Protocol, Manners, and Culture in the People's Republic of China*, New York: Warner Business Books.

Sharma, D.D. and Blomstermo, A. (2003a) 'A Critical Review of Time in the Internationalization Process of Firms', *Journal of Global Marketing*, vol. 16, no. 4, pp. 53-71.

Sharma, D.D. and Blomstermo, A. (2003b) 'The Internationalization Process of Born Globals: A Network View', *International Business Review*, vol. 12, pp. 739-53.

Shenkar, O. (2001) 'Cultural Distance Revisited: Towards a More Rigorous Conceptualization and Measurement of Cultural Differences', *Journal of International Business Research*, vol. 32, no. 3, pp. 519-35.

Sheth, J.N., Gardner, D.M. and Garrett, D.E. (1988) *Marketing Theory: Evolution and Evaluation*, New York: John Wiley.

Sheth, J.N. and Parvatiyar, A. (1995) 'The Evolution of Relationship Marketing', *International Business Review*, vol. 4, pp. 397-418.

Sheth, J.N. and Parvatiyar, A. (2000) *Handbook of Relationship Marketing*, Thousand Oaks: Sage.

SIF (2004) *Jobben flyttar?* SIF: Stockholm.

Simon, F. (1998) 'Network Theory's New Math', *Journal of Contemporary China*.

Snehota, I. (1990) *Notes on a Theory of Business Enterprise*, Department of Business Administration, Uppsala University (Unpublished dissertation).

Stopford, J.M. and Wells Jr, L.T. (1972) *Managing the Multinational Enterprise*, New York: Basic Books.

Tallman, S.B. and Yip, G.S. (2001) 'Strategy and the Multinational Enterprise', in A.M. Rugman and T.L. Brewer (eds), *The Oxford Handbook of International Business*, Oxford: Oxford University Press, pp. 317-48.

Timlon, J. (2005) *Realizing a New Marketing Strategy through Organizational Learning in Industrial Networks*, Göteborg: School of Economics and Commercial Law, Göteborg University.

Tixier, M. (1996) 'Cross-Cultural Study of Managerial Recruitment Tools in Nordic Countries', *The International Journal of Human Resource Management*, vol. 7, no. 3. pp. 753-74.

Tong, C.K. and Bun, C.K. (1999) *Networks and Brokers: Singaporeans Doing Business in China*, National University of Singapore.

Trompenaars, F. (1993) *Riding the Waves of Culture: Understanding Cultural Diversity in Business* (First Edition), London: Nicholas Brealey.

Tsui-Auch, L.S. and Lee, Y.J. (2003) 'The State Matters: Management Models of Singaporean Chinese and Korean Business Groups', *Organization Studies*, vol. 24, no. 4.

Tung, R. and Worm, V. (1996) *East Meets West: North European Expatriates in China*, Copenhagen: Copenhagen Business School.

Turnbull, P.W. and Valla, J.P. (1986). *Strategies for International Industrial Marketing: The Management of Customer Relationships in European Industrial Markets*, London: Croom Helm.

UNCTAD (2005) *Trade and Development*, New York: United Nations.

Vargo, S.L. and Lusch, R.F. (2004) 'Evolving to a New Dominant Logic for Marketing', *Journal of Marketing*, vol. 68, January, pp. 1-17.

Webster, F. (1979) *Industrial Marketing Strategy*, New York: Wiley and Sons.

Whitley, R.D. (1991) 'The Social Construction of Business Systems in Asia', *Organization Studies*, vol. 12, no. 1, pp. 1-28.

Whitley, R.D. (1992a) *Business Systems in East Asia: Firms, Markets and Societies*, London: Sage Publications.

Whitley, R.D. (1992b) *European Business Systems: Firms and Markets in their National Contexts*, London: Sage Publications.

Whitley, R.D. (1999) 'Competing Logics and Units of Analysis in the Comparative Study of Economic Organization', *International Studies of Management and Organization*, no. 2. pp. 113-26.

Williamson, O.E. (1975) *Markets and Hierarchies: Analysis and Antitrust Implications*, New York: The Free Press.

Williamson, O.E. (1979) 'Transaction-Cost Economics: The Governance of Contractual Relations', *Journal of Law and Economics*, vol. 22 (October), pp. 3-61.

Wilkinson, I. and Young, L.C. (1996) 'Business Dancing. The Nature and Role of Interfirm Relations in Business Strategy', *Asia-Australia Marketing Journal*, no. 1, pp. 67-79.

Woetzel. J.R (2004), 'A Guide to Doing Business in China', *McKinsey Quarterly*, Special Edition: *What Global Executives Think*, pp. 37-45.

Xu, D. and Shenkar, O. (2002) 'Institutional Distance and the Multinational Enterprise', *Academy of Management Review*, vol. 27, pp. 608-18.

Yau, O.H.M., Lee, J.S.Y., Chow, R.P.M., Sin, L.Y.M and Tse, A.C.B. (1994) 'Relationship Marketing the Chinese Way', Business Horizons, vol. 43, no. 1, pp. 16-24.

Yin, R.K. (1989) Case *Study Research – Designs and Methods*. Sage Publications Inc.

Yip, G.S. (2000) *Asian Advantage: Key Strategies for Winning in the Asia Pacific Region*, New York: Perseus Publishing.

Yip, G.S. (2000). *Asian Advantage: Key Strategies for Winning in the Asia Pacific Region*, New York: Perseus Publishing.

Zahra, S.A. (2005) 'A Theory of International New Ventures: a Decade of Research', Journal of International Business Studies, vol. 36, no. 1, pp. 20-28.

Zainulbhai, A.S. (2005) 'What Executives are Asking about India', *McKinsey Quarterly*, Special Edition: Fulfilling India's Promise.

Zou, S. and Cavusgil, S.T. (1996) 'Global Strategy: A Review and an Integrated Conceptual Framework', *European Journal of Marketing*, vol. 30, no. 1, pp. 52-69.

Zou, S. and Cavusgil, S.T. (2002) 'The GMS – A Broad Conceptualization of Global Marketing Strategy and its Effect on Firm Performance', *Journal of Marketing*, October, vol. 66, pp. 40-56.

Name index

Agapitova, N. 117, 119
Agarwal, M.R. 14, 136
Aldrich, H. 51
Anderson, J.C. 17, 31, 35
Andersson, S. 137
Arvonen, J. 129
Axelsson, B. 19, 37, 137

Backman, M. 121, 124
Bansard, D. 85
Barstad, A. 118
Bartlett, C. A. 19, 50-51, 166-7,
    174-5, 181-2, 185
Beamish, P. 152
Bernard, C. 85
Bell, J. 137
Bharadway, V.T. 9
Bilkey, W.J. 136
Birkinshaw, J. 21-2, 190
Bjerke, B. 121
Björkman, I. 121, 137
Blankenburg, D. 34
Blau, P. 36
Blohm, K. 153
Blomstermo, A. 136-7, 149-50
Bonsu, S. 85
Brouthers, K.D. 152
Bun, C.K. 121

Cavusgil, S.T. 14, 20, 136-7, 141,
    150
Chen, M. 121
Christopher, M.G. 40, 85
Chu, C. 121
Clark, M. 40, 85
Cook, K.S. 37
Cova, B. 85

Coviello, N. 137
Crick, D. 137
Curran, J.M. 85
Czinkota, M.R. 136

Day, G. 39
Doz, Y.L. 51
Dunning, J.H. 22, 166
Dwyer, F.R. 85

Easton, G. 19, 34, 37
Emerson, R.M. 37
El-Ansary, A. 30, 38-9, 40
Engström, J. 195
Eriksson, K. 149
Estrin, S. 151

Farrell, D. 8, 165
Ford, D. 18-19, 32-3, 35, 37, 85,
    86, 144, 146
Forsgren, M. 22, 50, 137, 149,
    168

Gadde, L.E. 18-19, 32, 35, 37,
    144
Gankema, H.G. 141, 148
Gardner, D.M. 30-2, 40
Garrett, D.E. 30-2, 40
Gelbuda, M. 137
Ghauri, P. 14, 85, 136
Ghoshal, S. 19, 50-51, 167, 166,
    174-5, 181-2, 185
Gordon, I.H. 85
Granovetter, M. 40
Grönroos, C. 32, 37
Gulati, R. 37
Gummesson, E. 41

Haley, G.T. 121
Haley, U. 121
Hallén, L. 18, 33, 121
Halman, L. 124
Hamilton, G. 121, 124
Hammarkvist, K.O. 137
Hampden-Turner, C. 121, 128
Hardin, R. 50
Håkansson, H. 17-19, 31, 32-3,
    35, 37, 41, 55, 84, 137, 144
Heenan, D. 167
Heide, J.B. 44
Hendley, K. 131
Hilmersson M. 140
Hofstede, G. 121, 124
Hohenthal, J. 136
Holm, U. 22, 50
Hood, N. 22, 190
Hoskins, S. 85
Hunt, S.D. 37, 39

Ionascu, D. 151

Jackson, B. 31
Jansson, H. 5, 11, 13-15, 18-22,
    30, 32, 34, 41, 43-6, 49-51,
    56, 64, 67-9, 85, 87, 111-12,
    120-21, 125-6, 136-8, 140,
    148-50, 167-8, 176, 178, 180,
    183-4, 199-200, 202-3, 205-6
Johanson, J. 17, 19, 22, 32-7, 50,
    121, 136-7, 140, 149-50
Johanson, M. 35, 121, 126, 131
Johansson, A. 121, 195
John, G. 44
Jonsson, S. 22, 190

Kakar, S. 130
Knight, G.A. 137
Koopman, A. 129, 131
Kostova, T. 18, 151
Kotabe, M. 21
Kraar, L. 131

Lasserre, P. 121, 129, 207, 209
Ledeneva, A. 117, 121

Lee, Y.J. 121
Lindell, M. 129
Lindstrand, A. 149
Lu, J. 152
Lusch, R.F. 38-40, 49

Madsen, T. 137
Majkgård, A. 137, 149, 151
Martin, C. 40
Mattsson, L.G. 30, 32-6, 40, 85,
    131, 137, 140
McAuley, A. 137
McDougall, P.P. 136
McKinsey Quarterly 9
McNaughton, R. 137
Meyer, K. 136-37, 151
Meyer, J.W. 45, 50
Michailova, S. 117, 121, 126
Mineikytë, A. 171
Monroe, K.B. 57-8
Morgan, R.M. 37, 39, 84
Munro, H. 137

Naisbit, J. 121
Nakos, G. 152
Naurus, J.A. 31, 37
Normann, R. 39, 138

Oviatt, B.M. 136

Pahlberg, C. 50
Parvatiyar, A. 32, 37-8, 40
Payne, A. 40, 85
Peck, H. 40, 85
Peng, M.W. 19
Perlmutter, H.V. 167
Pfeffer, J. 37
Polsa, P. 121
Prahalad, C.K. 51
Purinton, E.F. 85

Ramirez, R. 39, 138
Ramström, J. 68, 112, 120-21,
    124
Redding, G. 121, 124
Reid, S.D. 136

Richardson, S. 121
Ring, P.S. 85
Rosen, D. 85
Rugman, A. 22

Salancik, G.R. 37
Salle, R. 85
Salmi, A. 121, 138, 153
Sandberg, S. 20, 136, 138, 140, 148
Saqib, M. 34, 50-51, 64, 68, 176, 183, 202-203
Schurr, P.H. 85
Schutte, H. 121, 129, 207, 209
Scott, W.R. 45, 50, 130
Seligman, S.D. 121
Servais, P. 137
Sharma, D.D. 34, 50-51, 64, 68, 136-7, 149-50, 176, 183, 202-3
Shapiro, D. 131
Shenkar, O. 151
Sheth, J. 30-32, 37-8, 40
SIF. 140
Skak, A. 136-7
Snehota, I. 17-19, 31, 32-3, 35, 37, 41, 55, 84, 137, 144
Snuif, H.R. 141, 148
Steponavièiûtë, R. 172
Stojanovski, S. 153
Stopford, J.M. 166
Swaroop, G.M. 9

Tallman, S.B. 19-20
Tan, C.T. 121
Timlon, J. 149

Tong, C.K. 121
Törnroos, J.Å. 121
Trompenaars, F. 121, 126, 128-9
Tsui-Auch, L.S. 121

UNCTAD, 1-2

Vahlne, J.E. 136-137, 149
Van de Ven, A.H. 85
Vargo, S.L. 38-40, 49
Vittal, I. 9

Webster, F. 31
Wells Jr, L.T. 166
Whetten, D.A. 51
Whitley, R.D. 124-5, 129, 131-2
Wiedersheim-Paul, F. 136, 150
Wiktor, I. 137
Wilkinson, I. 85
Williamson, O.E. 34
Woetzel. J.R. 3, 7, 10
Worm, V. 117, 121, 126

Xu, D. 151

Yip, G.S. 19-20, 121
Young, L.C. 85
Young, S. 137

Zaheer, A. 37
Zahra, S.A. 137
Zainulbhai, A.S. 13
Zwart, P.S. 141, 148
Zou, S. 20

Östberg, C. 33

Subject index

action network 51, 88, 178, 186
  capture team 88, 97-8, 100, 103, 105-6
  project management team 88, 100, 103, 106
  screening team, 88, 97, 103-5
  tracking team 88, 96, 103-4
administrative regional hub 206-7, 209
after sales 75, 94, 98, 102
agent 48, 75-6, 136, 138, 140, 143, 152-3, 155-6, 169
aid organizations 63, 65, 90, 96
ARA model 35, 37

Baltic Sea Region 138-40, 169-70
Baltic states 138-40
basic networks model 41, 120-21
basic rules 44-5, 120-32, 168, 180
basic strategic dilemma 20, 174-5, 204
bid 61, 89, 91-4, 99
'blat' 16, 111, 113, 117-19, 126-7
'Born global' 136-7
'brain' 126, 132
Brazil 2, 170
business environment 41-2
  complex 12, 17, 194
  turbulent 12, 17
business marketing process 16, 46-7, 83-107
business marketing strategy 15, 41, 46-8
  segmentation 8-9, 13
business marketing view

business-to-business 31-32, 37, 39
  marketing-mix 30, 33
business mores 44, 196
business network
  Chinese 16, 68, 111-17, 120-32, 151
  European 111, 120-32, 151
  Russian 16, 111, 117-19, 120-32, 151

capability 19, 46-7, 49, 164
  manufacturing 73-4
  organizational 49, 136, 198
  problem solving 72, 74-5
central and eastern Europe (CEE) 1, 3, 5
China 1-3, 5-11, 111, 134, 140, 170, 172-3, 205
clustered group network, 164, 174, 182-6, 190, 198-201, 209
competitive advantage 16, 39, 46, 56, 62, 65, 71, 84, 138, 164, 167, 180
  sustainable 46, 71, 174, 198, 203
competitive strategy 15, 46-7, 55-7, 83
  delivery 70, 101
  finance 63-4, 83, 86-7, 99
  price 67, 69-70, 76, 99, 138, 193, 201
  quality 8, 13, 38, 70, 138, 157
  service 62, 70, 87, 94, 102, 193
completion cycle 86-8, 93, 101-2

consultant 60, 62, 65, 86, 89-90,
   92, 95-6, 98
corruption 8, 116-17, 119, 139
culture 13, 43-4, 196
   Chinese 111-17
   country culture 43-4, 111-32
   shame 127-8, 130-31
customer
   established 61, 99
   new 61, 99
   private 61, 98, 117
   public 61, 98, 117
   value 39, 57-8, 137-8

dealer, 153, 192-7
degree of international outlook
   163, 167-9, 173, 180
differentiated group network 185-
   6
diffuse regional hub 206-7, 209
distributor 48, 76, 138, 140, 143,
   152-3, 169
   service 76, 193
Domestic firm 16, 51, 167-8

educational system 10, 13, 43
efficiency rationale 45-6, 180
embeddedness 12, 17, 40, 44, 126
enforcement mechanism 44, 121,
   130-32, 180
   sanctions 45, 130-32, 178-9
   surveillance system 45, 178-9
entry mode 20, 48-9, 135, 139-40,
   151-2, 158, 189, 201
entry node 20, 48-9, 135, 151-6,
   157-8, 189
   dyad 135, 138, 140, 143-4, 151,
      155, 157-8, 189, 191, 197-8
   triad 135, 138-40, 143-4, 151,
      153-8, 169, 190, 191-8
   triad balance 153-6, 191, 196
entry process 48, 135, 140, 151-2,
   156-7
entry role 48, 135, 152, 157-9
entry strategy 20, 46, 48-9, 135,
   151-9, 168, 189

Ethnocentric MNC 16, 51, 163,
   167-70
European Union (EU) 5, 170,
   173, 200

face 115-16, 128, 130-31
family/clan 42, 44, 121, 129-30
feasibility study 62, 92, 96
first-mover advantage 15, 55-7,
   67, 70-72, 83, 90, 92, 94
follow-up cycle 86-8, 93, 102
foreign direct investment (FDI) 4,
   138-9, 152-3
friendship 61, 68, 101, 114, 117-
   18, 121

General Motors 170, 173
Geocentric MNC 16, 51, 163,
   167-9, 171-3
'genqing' 115-16, 126, 127-9
gifts 100, 116-18
global integration 19-21, 174-5,
   180, 183, 189, 197-8, 201, 204,
   207, 209
global product set 175, 198-9,
   208-9
government 18, 42, 95
'guanxi' 16, 68, 111, 115, 126-7

harmony 116, 128-9
'heart' 115, 126, 128

IMP perspective 14, 41
incorporated regional hub 196-7,
   206-9
   multi-country regional network
      206-8
   multi-set regional network 206-
      8
   one-set regional network 206-8
India 1-3, 5, 8-11, 13, 56, 60-65,
   79-82, 95-107, 170, 201-5
industrial marketing 15, 29-32,
   34, 39, 84
institution 12-13, 16, 18, 41-5

institutional distance 45, 136,
139-41, 150-51
institutional network approach 1,
12-14, 22, 44-6, 111, 149, 151,
164
international business marketing
model 15-16, 41-51
international organization 166,
170, 174, 182, 184
internationalization of firms 16,
46
degree 18, 20, 136, 139, 142,
163, 168
first wave 2, 4, 166
second wave 2, 4, 166
third wave 1-5, 18, 20, 111,
163, 165, 167
internationalization of
organization 163-7, 174
Internationalized firm 5, 16, 51,
163, 165, 167-70, 173-4, 182
Internationalizing firm 16, 51,
163-4, 167-9
internationalization process 4, 16,
18, 48, 86, 135-41, 163-73,
189-90
active involvement stage 49,
141-3, 149-50
committed involvement stage
49, 141-3, 149-50
domestic market focus stage 49,
141-2, 148, 150
experimental export stage 49,
141-3, 147-50
five/five stages 140-41, 147-9
global 3, 139
pre-export stage 49, 141, 148,
150
regional 139
theory 18, 137, 150, 165, 171
inter-organizational approach 15,
17, 19, 29-30, 32-41, 85, 111-
12, 121
interaction aspect 33-4
network aspect 34-5

Japan 2, 166, 170

knowledge 39, 43
experiential 48, 140, 154-7, 197
institutional 143, 149, 154
internationalization 143, 149
network experiential 143, 149,
154

language 139, 155-7, 196
legal system 12-13, 42-3, 93, 129-
32, 151
legitimacy 44-6, 128, 132, 180
liberalization 8, 10, 56, 61
linkage specificity 66-7, 94
linkage strategy 15, 46-7, 55-7,
66-8, 83, 92, 153, 154-5, 202
financial linkage 66, 71, 90
information linkage 66, 71, 84,
90, 92, 154-7
knowledge linkage 66-7, 71,
90, 157
product linkage 66, 71, 90
social linkage 66-8, 71, 84, 90,
92, 113-15, 154-5
local adaptation 8, 16, 19-21, 67,
164, 174-5, 180-81, 183-4, 189,
192, 196-9, 201, 203-5, 207,
209
local hub 189-91, 197-204, 207-9
local market cluster 198-200, 207
local network organization 16, 21,
46, 164, 174, 189-204

main contractor 60-61, 90
main interest 176, 180-82
global 167, 176, 180-82, 184,
198-9, 202, 204, 207-8
group 176, 181, 204
local 167, 176, 181-2, 184, 202,
204, 208
managerial school 30, 40
marketing process 46, 48, 85-6,
103
marketing theory 29-41
macro marketing 30, 40

services 32, 37-40
matrix organization 182, 185, 208
MENA 2, 191-7
micro-marketing approach 29-31,
    40-41
MNC-government network
    (MGN) 190, 202-3
multinational organization 166,
    182
multi-set organization 183-4, 199-
    200, 208-9

negotiation 61, 76, 79, 93, 100,
    113-14, 192, 206
net
    authority 103, 175-9, 182-6,
        198-200, 207-9
    lateral 103, 154, 175-9, 185-6,
        200-201, 208-10
    social 79, 175-9, 185-6, 208-10
network
    action 48, 50-51
    financial market 10, 18, 41-2,
        46, 58, 60, 63-4, 138, 167
    government, 41-2, 59-60, 64,
        119
    hierarchical 47, 50-51, 58, 163-
        5, 174-86
    intelligence 65, 79-80, 90-91,
        95-7, 100, 106, 119, 192-3, 206
    labour market 41-2, 48, 64
    linking grid 197-8
    loosely coupled 58, 124, 153,
        174, 183-4, 199-203, 209
    MNC 41-2, 64
    organizational 51, 79-81, 103,
        185
    perspective 21, 174
    social 119, 121, 124, 126-7
    supplier 60, 62
    vertical market 56, 138
    tightly coupled 58, 153, 174,
        183-4, 199-201, 203, 209
network capability profile 47, 49,
    56, 72-7

customer specialist 49, 72-5,
    206
distribution specialist 49, 73, 75
distributor network specialist
    49, 73, 75-7, 153, 191-7
product specialist 49, 72-5
network cluster
    buyer 60-62, 64, 89-90, 92, 100
    competitor 89-90
    government 89-90
    seller 89-90, 92, 94, 99-100
    macro 60-62, 98
    micro 60-62, 64, 90, 92, 99
network controls 164, 175-6, 178,
    182, 201
    direct 203-4
    indirect 203-4
    input 176, 178-80
    output 176, 178, 180
    process 176, 178-9
network map 55, 58-64, 89-91,
    145, 153, 175
    diagonal dimension 55, 59, 63-
        4, 175, 178, 185
    horizontal dimension 55, 63,
        175, 178, 184-5
    methodology 55
    vertical dimension 55, 60-63,
        175, 178, 184
network organization
    external 16, 50-51, 163, 175,
        189, 198, 204
    global/group 21, 46
    internal 16, 50-51, 164, 175,
        189, 198
network position 36, 47, 63, 67
    internal 190, 201-4
network strategy 15, 46-7, 55-7,
    64-5, 83, 87, 92, 153, 154, 202
'nomenklatura' 117, 119, 126
norms 44-5, 49-50, 121, 126-7,
    179-81

offshoring 4, 142, 158
one-set organization 183-4, 199-
    200, 209

organization cluster 175, 184
organizational field 42-4, 55, 141, 151
organizational learning 140, 144-5, 148-50
   conceptual 141, 149-50
   operational 141, 149
   process 136, 156
   style, 141, 149-50
organizational routine 150, 156
outsourcing 4, 8, 139, 157-8, 163

package deal 69, 74, 83-4
Poland 2-3, 10, 117, 138-40, 153-9
political system 10, 13, 42, 119,139,151
Polycentric MNC 16, 51, 163, 167-9, 174, 180
price 8, 13, 61-3, 113
   norm 69-70
product/service process 16, 46, 48, 85-7, 103
   bidding period 48, 86-7
   execution period 48, 86-7
   formation period 48, 86-7, 94
   termination period 48, 86-7
production 86-7, 91, 93, 101, 136, 139, 158
   internationalization 5, 18, 158, 163-5, 172-3
   relocation 171-3
projects
   committee 61, 98-9
   financing 65, 96-8, 101, 104
   government 63, 97
   internationalization 4, 158
   large 4, 62, 80-82, 83-107, 185
   marketing 48, 60, 62, 64-5, 81, 83-107
   organization 48, 64, 85, 103-7
   purchasing 15, 41, 62, 65, 89, 112-14, 155, 157-8
   small 103-4

regional hub 190-97, 204-10

regional network organization 16, 21, 51, 79-82, 164, 174, 189-97, 204-10
   headquarters 189, 195, 207, 209
relationship
   adaptation 35-6, 74, 144-7, 156-7
   complexity 35-6
   conflict solution 35-6
   formal 7, 61, 116, 128-9
   informal 7, 61, 63, 114-16, 128-9
   interests 35-6
   investments 35-6
   social 63, 113-14, 129
relationship marketing approach 29, 37-41, 85
relationship process 12, 16, 33, 46, 84, 85-6, 103, 136, 141
   development stage 86, 94, 141, 144-6, 148, 156
   early stage 86-8, 94-5, 141, 144-6, 148, 156-7
   final stage 33, 86, 141, 144-7
   long-term stage 86, 88, 102, 141, 144-7, 149, 157
   pre-relationship stage 48, 86-7, 141, 144-8
religion 42, 44, 196
'renqing' 115-16, 129
resourced-based view (RBV) 37, 39
   macro rules 41-2, 44, 120-32, 151
resources 19, 35-9, 46-7, 49, 56, 74, 182, 198
Russia 1-2, 10, 111, 117-19, 124, 138-40, 205

scanning cycle 86-92, 94-7, 104
   scouting phase 86, 88, 96
   screening phase 86, 88-9, 94, 96-7, 99
   tracking phase 86, 88-9, 94, 96
Slovakia 172-3
SMEs 4-5, 20, 136-41, 152, 169

social capital 49-50
social exchange 35-37
societal sector 42-3, 55, 141, 151
Southeast Asia (SEA) 2, 67-8,
    112-17, 120-32, 199-202, 205-6
South Korea 2, 166, 170
subcontractor 60-61, 65, 90, 95,
    100, 157
subsidiary 21-22, 48, 50-51, 75-6,
    136, 139, 152, 166, 169, 174-5,
    178, 181, 184, 189-210
Sweden 3, 153, 172-3, 196

tendering 61, 85, 94
    single 97-8
    two-step 97-8
tendering cycle 86-88, 91-3, 97-
    101, 106
    pre-tendering phase 65, 86, 91-
    2, 98, 100,
    tendering phase 86, 91-2, 100-
    101
    post-tendering phase 86, 91-3
tender specification 62, 65, 85,
    87, 91-2, 95, 98-103, 117
tightly coupled group network
    185
theory-in-use 149-50
thought style 44, 120-26, 132,
    149-50, 167, 169-70, 179-
    81

causality 125-6, 132
    perception of time 125
    self 121-25
transition economy 11, 35, 60
transition point 88-9, 93-4, 97,
    102
transnational organization 167,
    170, 174, 185
transparency 117, 129
trust 50, 99, 115, 117, 131-2, 145,
    148, 155, 192
trustworthiness 47, 49, 67-8, 126-
    7
    individual 50, 68, 126
    organizational 50, 68, 126
    professional 68, 119, 126
    social 68, 119, 126-7

uncertainty 12, 34, 36, 43, 70, 84-
    5, 91, 96, 119, 125, 132, 136-7,
    144-7, 154, 156-7, 191, 194

values 12, 44, 121, 179-81
    achieved vs ascribed status 127
    inner vs outer direction 127-8
    universalism vs particularism
    127-9
Volvo construction equipment
    (VCE) 170, 191-7
World Bank 63, 65, 90, 95-7,
    104